AMERICAN SHOTGUN DESIGN AND PERFORMANCE

L. R. Wallack

WINCHESTER PRESS

Library of Congress Cataloging in Publication Data

Wallack, Louis Robert, 1919–
    American shotgun design and performance.
    Includes index.
    1. Shot-guns. I. Title.
TS536.8.W34   683'.42   77-21886
ISBN 0-87691-236-6

WINCHESTER is a Trademark of Olin Corporation
used by Winchester Press, Inc. under authority
and control of the Trademark Proprietor.

Winchester Press
205 East 42nd Street
New York, N.Y. 10017

Printed in the United States of America

DEDICATION

To the Bill of Rights

The first ten amendments to the Constitution, known as "A Bill of Rights," were adopted by the first Congress, called to meet in New York City, March 4, 1789. They were later ratified by the various States, and on December 15, 1791, were made a part of the Constitution.

Amendment I

Freedom of Religion, Speech, and the Press;
Right of Assembly and Petition

CONGRESS shall make no law respecting an establishment of religion, or prohibiting the free exercise thereof; or abridging the freedom of speech, or of the press, or the right of the people peaceably to assemble, and to petition the government for a redress of grievances.

Amendment II

Right to Keep and Bear Arms

A well regulated militia, being necessary to the security of a free state, the right of the people to keep and bear arms shall not be infringed.

Amendment III

Quartering of Soldiers

No soldier shall in time of peace be quartered in any house without the consent of the owner, nor in time of war, but in a manner to be prescribed by law.

Amendment IV

Regulation of Right of Search and Seizure

The right of the people to be secure in their persons, houses, papers, and effects, against unreasonable searches and seizures, shall not be violated, and no warrants shall issue but upon probable cause, supported by oath or affirmation, and particularly describing the place to be searched and the persons or things to be seized.

Amendment V

Protection for Persons and Their Property

No person shall be held to answer for a capital or otherwise infamous crime, unless on a presentment or indictment of a grand jury, except in cases arising in the land or naval forces, or in the militia, when in actual service in time of war or public danger; nor shall any person be subject for the same offense to be twice put in jeopardy of life or limb; nor shall be compelled in any criminal case to be a witness against himself, nor be deprived of life, liberty, or property, without due process of law; nor shall private property be taken for public use, without just compensation.

Amendment VI

Rights of Persons Accused of Crime

In all criminal prosecutions, the accused shall enjoy the right to a speedy and public trial by an impartial jury of the State and district wherein the crime shall have been committed, which district shall have been previously ascertained by law, and to be informed of the nature and cause of the accusation; to be confronted with the witnesses against him; to have compulsory process for obtaining witnesses in his favor, and to have the assistance of counsel for his defense.

Amendment VII

Right of Trial by Jury in Suits at Common Law

In suits at common law, where the value in controversy shall exceed twenty dollars, the right of trial by jury shall be preserved, and no fact tried by a jury shall be otherwise re-examined in any court of the United States, than according to the rules of the common law.

Amendment VIII

Protection Against Excessive Bail and Punishments

Excessive bail shall not be required, nor excessive fines imposed, nor cruel and unusual punishments inflicted.

Amendment IX

Constitution Does Not List All Individual Rights

The enumeration in the Constitution of certain rights shall not be construed to deny or disparage others retained by the people.

Amendment X

Powers Reserved to the States and the People

The powers not delegated to the United States by the Constitution, nor prohibited by it to the States, are reserved to the States respectively, or to the people.

CONTENTS

INTRODUCTION

A shotgun should weigh between 6 and 8 pounds; its barrel or barrels should be between 25 and 30 inches long; and it should fire a charge of shot weighing 1 to 1¼ ounces at a velocity obtained by a charge of 3 to 3½ drams of powder. If a gun is made lighter than 6 pounds (in 12 gauge) it will produce too severe a recoil; if heavier than 8 pounds it will be too awkward to swing easily. The barrel lengths given produce a satisfactory combination of sighting plane, ample length, and sufficient shortness to swing easily and quickly. The shot-charge-and-powder combination produces the most desirable ballistics for virtually all shotgun uses.

Those specifications should sound pretty familiar, because most shotguns on the market today fall within them, although there are a few exceptions for special purposes. But for a hunting gun, those guidelines are pretty reliable. It is interesting that these "rules" were established before 1800. The two persons most responsible for the rules were a celebrated London gunsmith, Joe Manton, whose productive period was approximately 1780 to 1825, and a famous authority and writer, Colonel Peter Hawker, who was Manton's biggest booster.

As a sporting firearm, the shotgun has been in use since the late sixteenth century. Many of the early guns were very long barreled (guns with a total length of 6 feet were not uncommon) and of surprisingly small bore diameter. But these guns were not used to shoot at birds on the wing. It remained for Joe Manton to develop and design the shotgun into its present form and to formulate the specifications just given.

While the modern shotgun was sired by Manton, recent improvements in ammunition, propellants, steels, action systems, and the like have brought the shotgun a long way in the ensuing years. Still, today's most modern gun fires a cluster of shot pellets from a gun much within the confines of the dictates set down by that pioneering English gunmaker.

While the ballistics of a shotgun are no different than they have been for more than 200 years, we are still experimenting and still finding out how little we really know. Choke boring, for example, was invented and perfected about a hundred years ago and was claimed to have advanced the shotgun and its performance significantly. Today, we are again wondering about that, and there is a prevalent notion now that no choke at all is a better bet than the choked barrel for many kinds of shooting.

Why are these things not better understood today after all this experience in hurling clusters of lead shot pellets at birds and considering that some of the best brains in the world's ballistic laboratories have been working on the problems for years using the most modern techniques, including computers? One reason is that there are so many variables. Among these are gauge size, shot-size variations, magnum and standard loads, hard and soft shot, and differences in loads among the different manufacturers. There also are some variations in the guns themselves in choke, forcing cone, length of chamber, and inside diameter of barrels. Rifles (and handguns) are more predictable. They deliver a single projectile, which we can isolate and photograph, and the velocity and flight of which we can read and measure. These things cannot be accomplished accurately with a shotgun charge.

This book will not give answers to these problems because there are no answers yet and may never be. Nonetheless we are learning, and a great deal of what we are learning is that habits and theories dropped long ago may have been more accurate than those that replaced them. The study of shotguns and the behavior of a cluster of shot is quite fascinating; we may not have many answers, but if we can open the door to all the questions, we will have a better chance of someday getting those answers. Moreover, we'll have a larger group of people with more knowledge of, and appreciation for, what goes on when the trigger of a shotgun is pressed. It's some complicated affair indeed.

Ammunition used to test the various guns in this book was supplied by the principal makers of ammunition in this country: Federal, Remington, and Winchester; Navy Arms supplied a few boxes of its imported black powder loads. In the world of reloading tools and components, I'd like to acknowledge CCI/Omark, DuPont, Federal, Hodgdon, Lee, Lyman, Pacific, Remington, and Winchester. Additionally, manufacturers and importers were helpful in supplying sample products for photography and testing.

You will note that the name of the publisher of this book is Winchester Press. That's a division of the Winchester that makes guns and ammunition. I want to make it clear that the publisher has put no pressure on me to push his products against those of any of his competitors. And by the same token, most of the major competitors have been among the leaders in offering me all the help possible in the preparation of this book. That's the way it ought to be and I'm glad to say that's the way it is.

L. R. Wallack
February, 1977

PART ONE

THE SHOTGUN

CHAPTER ONE

BASIC SMALL ARMS

Ever since man invented guns several hundred years ago he has consistently tried to improve upon them by increasing accuracy or velocity, rapidity of fire, size of projectile or charge of shot, and the effect of that projectile or shot charge upon its arrival at the target. There have been dramatic developments in some of these areas; in others there has been no significant advance in hundreds of years, largely because the laws of physics cannot be repealed.

Wars have always stimulated small-arms development, often to a degree that resulted in advantages to the civilian rifleman but rarely to the advantage of the shotgunner. Of course, some of the action systems that have been perfected for military use have found some applications to shotguns, but these are much more rare than is true of riflery. And at least one form of shotgun, the double barrel, owes none of its origin to warfare. The double is the only firearm entirely sporting in both design and development.

World War I, for example, was fought with manually operated firearms (except for machine guns) while World War II was fought on both sides with semiautomatic rifles. The sporting use of semiautomatic rifles and shotguns has increased greatly since then. The rifle is a shoulder arm with spiral grooves in its bore to spin a single projectile (the bullet) and force it to rotate in flight. Pistols, revolvers, machine guns, and submachine guns also have rifled barrels, as do artillery pieces. The shotgun, on the other hand, has a smooth bore. It fires a charge of shot that varies in weight depending upon a number of factors. A musket, like a shotgun, is smooth bored; but it is not a shotgun. Muskets were in wide use by most European armies until the 1800s because they were easier to load than rifles. These were muzzle-loading days, and black powder was the propellant. Black powder leaves a heavy, dirty, gritty, and grimy residue after each shot. To force a tight-fitting bullet down a dirty bore after fouling had accumulated was difficult. It was much simpler to ram a ball down a smooth musket barrel. Muskets have poor accuracy, because the projectile is usually a round ball (which is the worst shape possible for accurate flight) and because that ball was undersized and rattled down the barrel like a dry pea in a garbage can. But accuracy was not important in the warfare of the period as all firing was done at very short range.

Machine guns and submachine guns are firearms that continue to fire until their ammunition is exhausted or the trigger is released. They are therefore truly automatic firearms because the energy developed by the gun does all the work. The words automatic and semiautomatic are often confused and misused. An automatic gun is a machine gun. Semiautomatic guns, also correctly called autoloading, require a separate pull of the trigger for each shot. Otherwise the energy of the gun does everything else. Most semiautomatic guns are simply called autos or automatics. This is not only true among sportsmen, but also by the industry in catalog copy and so forth. An excellent example is the Browning Auto-5, Browning's famed semiautomatic repeating shotgun.

I suspect people will go on calling these guns by the wrong name forever, but it's no big deal. I will make every attempt in this book to call things by their proper names, but you can run upstream just so long and just so hard. Browning can call its gun by the wrong name since 1900, I'm not about to try to change that usage.

USE DICTATES DESIGN AND DEVELOPMENT

Over a period of time the German and Palatine Swiss gunsmiths in Pennsylvania and New York State changed the heavy Jaeger rifle they had brought with them from Europe into the slim, elegant, and small-bored Kentucky rifle. The changes were made because the Jaeger was too heavy, too awkward, and needlessly powerful. Similarly, when the frontier moved west of the Mississippi, the Kentucky rifle proved too light and too fragile for Western frontiersmen who had to contend with buffalo, grizzly bears, and elk. So the Kentucky evolved into the Plains rifle — shorter, and with a heavier stock for horseback use and a larger bore to handle the tougher game.

To a degree the same things happened with shotguns over the years, although the results were by no means as dramatic. The major reason why the changes were lesser is that a shotgun fires a cluster of round pellets. You can drive round projectiles just so fast and no faster — due to the laws of physics; you can drive just so many pellets — otherwise the recoil is too severe. Consequently a shotgun delivers essentially the same load at the same velocity today that it did 200 years ago and these aspects cannot be changed. Improvements in shotgun design and performance have been dictated by use, but they apply to methods of operation and ease and quickness of handling rather than to ballistics. While there have been many improvements in shotgun ammunition over the years, none have been nearly so significant as those involving firearms with rifled bores.

THE SEVEN STEPS OF OPERATION

Every gun, no matter what its type or method of operation, goes through seven steps of operation every time it is fired. This is true with everything from a single-shot firearm to the most modern machine gun. And a thorough understanding of these basics is essential to an understanding of how and why any gun works — or doesn't work. The steps do not necessarily work in the same order; sometimes two or more occur at the same time. But in every gun, they must all be performed.

In a single-shot shotgun, for example, these steps work in the exact order listed below and each step is performed by hand. In a lever- or pump-action repeater, some of the steps occur simultaneously and don't always correspond with the order given here. In an autoloading system, every one of the steps is performed by the gun's energy except pulling the trigger. Again, the important thing to remember is that every single one of the following steps *must* be performed for every shot fired with any firearm using self-contained cartridges.

1. Firing. Pulling the trigger releases a mechanism, either a hammer or firing pin under spring tension, that strikes the primer of the cartridge in the barrel's chamber. The primer is activated by the blow and ignites the powder charge which, in turn, generates propellant gas to drive the shot charge down the barrel.

2. Unlocking. The breech pressure required to drive the shot charge must be contained until that charge has left the bore. It is obvious that the magnitude of gas pressure we're talking about must only move the shot charge and it should be equally obvious that to open the breech prematurely would allow gas under enormous pressure to flow into the action with disastrous results. Consequently, the breech must be locked securely against this presssure. Before any of the following steps can take place, the action must be unlocked. Unlocking is always performed by the very first part of the movement of operating lever, pump handle, bolt, or operating rod.

During unlocking, another completely automatic event occurs called "primary extraction." In firing, the pressure that is developed forces the cartridge case tightly against the chamber walls. The precise amount of loosening required depends upon several factors, including the amount of pressure, smoothness of chamber walls, and condition of the case. Before this empty case can be withdrawn, it must be loosened from the chamber. This is always accomplished by mechanical leverage during the very first part of unlocking. Primary extraction is extremely vital in a Magnum cartridge, while it is far less important in guns developing lower chamber pressures.

3. Extraction. The withdrawal of the fired, or empty, cartridge from the chamber. Extraction is usually performed by a hook on the breechbolt that pulls the empty out as the bolt is withdrawn from the barrel.

4. Ejection. The removal of the empty case from the gun. Note the difference between extraction and ejection; the words are often confused, but the distinction is important to an understanding of operating systems. Ejection is generally performed at the end of the rearward stroke of the breechbolt when the empty is flipped out of the gun.

5. Cocking. Storage of energy in the firing mechanism spring by drawing and holding back either hammer or firing pin by a small part connected with the trigger or by the trigger itself.

6. Feeding. Moving the fresh, unfired cartridge from the magazine into the chamber of the barrel ready for firing. In a single-shot firearm, feeding is manually performed by simply placing the new cartridge directly into the chamber with the fingers.

7. Locking. The reverse of unlocking, locking holds the breechblock securely against the gas pressure generated during firing. Firearms are locked in many ways, as we shall see. As a safety feature, most guns will not fire until they are fully and securely locked.

That's what every firearm must do to shoot, and shoot again. A successful gun must perform every one of these steps logically, simply, and with as few parts as possible, and it must have the capability to perform them thousands of times without failure.

We can now break down the guns we're going to talk about into two groups: those that are manually operated and those of semiautomatic (or autoloading) type.

The principal manually operated shotguns in common use today are bolt, pump, single shot, and double barrel. Semiautomatic types of actions are operated either by gas, short recoil, long recoil, or blowback.

CHAPTER TWO

MANUALLY OPERATED BREECH ACTIONS

THE BOLT ACTION

The bolt action has been popular in America only since the end of World War I. Despite that, it is one of our oldest systems inasmuch as the first bolt action is credited to a Prussian named Johann Nicholaus von Dreyse, who patented what is known as the Prussian Needle Gun in the early 1800s. Long before the days of metallic cartridges, the needle gun used a paper-wrapped load with the primer buried in the powder charge. The term "needle" came from its abnormally long firing pin, which had to penetrate the powder charge to reach the primer.

Popular as the bolt action is in the rifle, it is of almost no importance whatever in shotgunnery. However, a couple of bolt shotgun actions are worth mentioning: First, in the years just following World War I, many German gunsmiths followed a practice of altering Mauser rifles, many of which had been picked up off the battlefields, to shotguns. The majority of these were 12-gauge guns and it's necessary to know just a little bit about the Mauser action to understand just how these guns were made. A Mauser Model 1898 bolt action, which is what was used in World War I (and which remains the single most outstanding bolt-action development of all time), has two stout locking lugs at the front end of the bolt. When locked, the bolt handle turns down and these lugs engage recesses in the receiver to support the cartridge during firing. The action

7

also has a safety lug, located at the bottom of the bolt in closed position and almost at the rear end of the bolt. The function of this safety lug is to operate only if the front locking lugs fail. That means the safety lug does not engage, but turns into a recess with some clearance (otherwise it would tend to force the bolt forward and disengage the actual locking lugs).

An additional feature of the 98 Mauser that contributed greatly to its strength was an inner collar against which the barrel was screwed. (As a matter of interest, most modern sporting bolt-action rifles employ a similar inner collar.) When these Mauser actions were converted to shotgun use, it was necessary to rework the actions drastically. For example, the bolt face had to be machined off flat and then counterbored so that a new bolt head could be inserted. Of course, considerable work also had to be done to the magazine, extractor, and follower so the action would feed a shot cartridge (these were two-shot guns). But the most important modification required the original rifle barrel to be thrown away and the front end of the receiver bored out to a large enough diameter to handle the bigger shot cartridges. This removed the inner collar and the locking lug recesses, which meant that the stout locking lugs were not working. The only lock these altered actions had was the safety lug! For this reason these guns were widely condemned by most authorities who wrote for the magazines in those days.

There is no question these were cobbled-up guns of little value and questionable reliability. There was ample justification for the condemnation, and yet I have never heard of any of these guns failing. Most of them were in 12 gauge with a smattering of 16s and a very few in 20. I saw my last one, a 12 gauge, back in the 1930s and, along with the fellow who owned it, fired it a few times. We were aware of the criticism, but shot it anyway. While there must be some of these guns still around, I haven't seen one since then. Should you run across one, you are advised that although I've never heard of any actual trouble with one, the lockup is suspect and it might best be kept as a curio. (It cannot be altered back to a rifle should that be a consideration.)

But there are other bolt-action shotguns on today's market, all low priced and reliable, although they are not the sort of guns in which one can take pride. Quite likely the best-known bolt-action shotgun on the market today is Marlin's Goose Gun. This is a 36-inch barreled job in 12-gauge Magnum with full choke. With the long action necessary to stroke those big cartridges combined with the 36-inch barrel, it's a rather enormous gun. The long barrel makes it sell like mad and Marlin is quite proud of the sales record this gun is setting.

One of the smartest uses for a bolt-action shotgun is by deer hunters in slug country, who buy one of these guns, mount a scope, and use the gun for this purpose exclusively. That makes sense. It is also just about the only practical use for a bolt-action shotgun. There are a few bolt-action guns in .410 gauge available, usually touted as the "ideal beginner's gun." That's as far from the truth as you can get. The .410 is an expert's gun, because it throws such a small shot charge; it has some limited use for potting grouse on a hunting trip where you're after big game but don't want to make too much noise when shooting a few birds for the pot. Aside from that, the .410 hasn't much use regardless of the type of action.

Even though there are few bolt-action shotguns, it will be worthwhile to take a few moments to follow a typical bolt action through the "seven steps of operation." Using the Model 1898 Mauser as an example (bolt-action shotguns are similar), here's how a bolt action operates:

1. Firing. Pulling the trigger releases the firing pin which has been under tension of the mainspring. This pin drives ahead smartly and its point crushes the primer of the chambered cartridge, causing it to fire.

2. Unlocking. Simply raising the bolt handle 90° turns the locking lugs out of engagement with their recesses in the front ring of the receiver. (Some bolt systems today have a much shorter lift, some as small as 55°.) This initial movement also drives the bolt backwards a fraction of an inch, with the powerful mechanical advantage employed by an extracting cam, and the cartridge is broken loose from its seal in the chamber.

3. Extraction. Withdrawing the bolt extracts

Few lever-action shotguns have ever been made; this Winchester Model 1887 was the most famous and stayed in the line until 1920. While never a runaway success—because it was big and bulky—it did achieve significant sales.

the fired cartridge from the chamber by holding it against the bolt face with the extractor hook.

4. Ejection. When the bolt reaches its rearmost point and just before it is stopped by the bolt stop, the left side of the cartridge is contacted by the ejector. With the extractor hook on the right side pulling, and the ejector on the left side stopping further rearward movement, the cartridge is simply flipped clear of the action.

5. Cocking. This was accomplished during the initial lift of the bolt handle by means of the cocking cam forcing the firing pin back.

6. Feeding. The bolt is now thrust forward and the bottom edge of its face will engage the next cartridge lying in the magazine. The fresh cartridge is forced ahead, its nose is raised by the feeding ramp and is guided into the chamber. Meanwhile, the base of this new cartridge is forced upward against the bolt face and its extracting groove engages the extractor hook.

7. Locking. Turning the handle back down causes the locking lugs to engage their recesses in the receiver ring, the cartridge to become fully seated in the chamber and ready to fire, and the final cocking is accomplished. During the final closing in the locking step, a notch in the firing pin contacts the sear (which, in turn, is connected to the trigger); at this point, the sear holds the firing pin in cocked position while the bolt rotates closed and locked. The firearm is now ready to fire.

LEVER ACTION

The lever-action shotgun is of interest only in that one once existed. There is little likelihood of your ever seeing one, and if you do it will be a collector's item. A patent was awarded to John Browning in 1885 for the lever shotgun that became the Winchester Model 1887. It was the first lever shotgun made in the U.S. For that matter, it was virtually the only one. According to Browning sources, some 78,000 were manufactured before the model was finally abandoned in 1920.

Like all of Browning's designs, this gun worked and worked well, but a lever-action shotgun was pretty awkward and its action had to be rather massive. It was no beauty and set no sales records, but it was one of the first successful repeating shotguns ever marketed. Another, and perhaps more important, reason the lever-action Winchester never really achieved great popularity was that Browning followed it very quickly with his pump designs, which met with much more market acceptance.

It must be kept in mind that, prior to the Browning inventions of repeating-action shotguns, most shotguns were double barreled. The abundance of game in this period of the late 1800s and early 1900s led to the development of repeating guns offering greater fire power. These repeating guns were almost a 100 percent American proposition, and they are still primarily American. The British, who established game gunning in the first place, have always looked down their noses at such "shooting machines," and there are some countries that will not allow entry of any gun but a double.

PUMP ACTION

This action system is probably the most popular in the U.S. today. While there was some disagreement years ago about who had invented the first pump gun, the credit for the first *successful* gun goes again to John Browning for the one

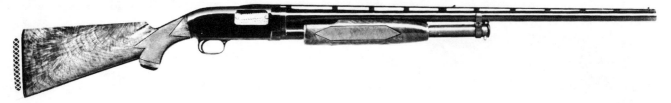

The Winchester Model 12 was probably the most famous and popular pump gun of all time. Dropped from the line a few years ago, it has been returned, due to demand, in the higher grades. Shown is the Pigeon Grade, a high-priced trap gun.

Winchester's Model 1200 is a competitively priced pump-action gun meeting all the needs of the upland gunner or waterfowler. It features Winchoke, a screw-in optional choke method of changing from full to modified to improved cylinder in the same barrel.

that became the Winchester Model 1893. This was a solid-frame gun—meaning non-take down; that feature was added later, and the gun reissued as Model 1897. The old 97 was one of the biggest sellers of all time and stayed in the Winchester product line until 1958. More than a million and a quarter of the combined 1893 and 1897 were made.

A pump gun is stroked by moving the pump handle back and forth to work the action and perform all the steps of operation except firing. Pump actions are fast. It is generally acknowledged that the smoothest of all was the great Winchester Model 12, and a good hand with a Model 12 could empty its magazine faster than an equally good hand with an autoloader. The reason is that the hand really can operate an action faster than the power generated by the gun! A Model 12 is usually used for this example primarily because if you keep the trigger pressed, the gun will fire as the pump handle is slammed forward (it's the only gun like that; you must release and re-press triggers on all other pump guns).

Winchester's Model 12 was one of the very few pump guns that was not of John Browning's design. Among his pump actions were the Stevens and Savage models (still being manufac-

tured, although they have been revised since their inception in 1903). The Remington Model 1917 was another Browning pump design, and when its patent expired the basic design was adopted by others, including Ithaca in their Model 37, which is still in production.

Every pump-action firearm contains some method of releasing the action slide lock so that you may stroke the pump handle and empty the chamber. This is usually in the form of a button that, when pushed, disengages the lock. There isn't much uniformity among the various brands in the location; the new Marlin tucks it into the loading port on the underside of the receiver, for example, while others are usually in more obvious places.

While nearly all pump shotguns eject from the side, there is one major exception today and years ago there was another. The Ithaca Model 37, which is still being manufactured today, was based on patents issued to John Browning for the Remington Model 1917, a popular gun some years ago. An earlier Remington, Model 10, which was made from 1907 until 1929, also was a bottom-ejecting gun and was quite popular.

Pump shotguns were extensively used during wartime. During World War II they were chiefly used for guard duty, but in World War I many

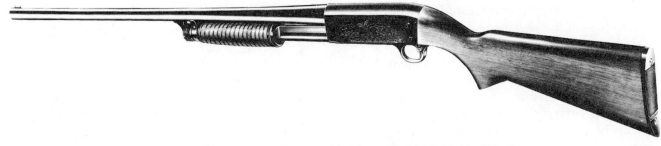

Another famous pump gun that has stood the test of time is this Ithaca Model 37 "featherlight."

thousands of them, especially the old Winchester Model 97 equipped with a 20-inch riot-gun barrel and bayonet, saw service in France. They were especially useful in that war when a noise was heard in no-man's land at night. A "sound shot" with buckshot charge was usually enough to end the disturbance. These guns were also frequently employed to deflect incoming enemy grenades.

Pump actions work relatively simply and it will be interesting to follow them through the seven steps of operation:

1. Firing. Pulling the trigger releases the hammer, which is urged forward under spring tension to fire the gun. Firing also releases the action slide lock enabling you to open the action. When the gun is fired there is no delay in moving the pump handle, but if it is dry-fired (snapped without a loaded cartridge) you will have to push forward slightly on the pump handle until you will hear a little click. At this point you can stroke the handle; this occurs in most pump guns but not all of them; some disengage the slide lock instantly upon the fall of the hammer.

The pump handle, which is actually the forearm on a pump gun, is connected to the action by either one or two action bars. When a single bar is employed it is usually on the left side. There is sometimes considerable advertising copy written about guns with twin action bars. It is claimed that these cause less binding, which implies that they are less likely to hang up. As a point of fact there are some guns that require twin bars—an example is the Remington pump-action high-power rifle Model 760, which has an action system and lockup totally different from those used in shotguns. But a couple of the most famous pump guns of all

time used a single action bar and if there was any disadvantage to it, these guns could not have been so successful for so many years. These were the Winchester Models 97 and 12.

2. Unlocking. The initial movement of the pump handle, transmitted through the action bar or bars, unlocks the breechblock.

3. Extraction and *4. Ejection.* Further backward movement of the pump handle pulls the fired cartridge out of the chamber; moving the handle all the way to the rear causes the empty to be ejected from the gun when the front of the cartridge case has cleared the barrel.

5. Cocking. Cocking is accomplished during the rearward stroke by the simple act of allowing the breechbolt to push the hammer down until it's caught by the sear. At the same time, the hammer spring is being compressed to store energy for firing.

6. Feeding. As the pump handle moves backward it activates the "shell stop' which has been holding cartridges in the magazine. This action allows one cartridge to move back onto the carrier (sometimes called the lifter) and then shuts off the magazine supply again. In the forward stroke of the pump handle the breechbolt picks up the cartridge which has been raised by the carrier and pushes it forward into the chamber.

7. Locking. Final closure of the breechbolt by pushing the pump handle all the way forward relocks the action and secures the pump handle in its forward position. The gun is now ready to be fired again.

With the immense number of pump shotguns on the market today, plus all those old guns still in service, there are some variations on the above procedures. It is important to realize that all these events must occur and a study of your own gun will disclose what happens when and precisely how each step is accomplished.

A pump shotgun is meant to be manhandled. This is not always understood by shooters, and working the action too slowly can cause it to jam. A shotgun cartridge is a difficult form to feed reliably because it is flat at the front end. A comparison of any shotgun cartridge with a round-nosed metallic cartridge, such as the .45 Auto pistol, will make it easy to understand that the .45 is readily guided into the chamber from virtually any angle. On the other hand the flat-nosed shotgun load must be raised promptly at exactly the right time to be led into the chamber. So you work a pump handle hard and fast, as though you were mad at the gun. Slam it.

Pump guns are fast because you don't have to move the hand to operate them. With a bolt action you have to release your grip and work the bolt. The same with a lever. But with a pump, your hand is on the operating slide and you simply slam it back and forth without changing your grip. Moreover, the action works the same for a left-handed person (and left-hand safeties are available for nearly all pumps; in fact some may be turned around if you're a lefty).

There are a number of very popular pump guns on the market. I think it quite safe to say that the most popular one of all time was Winchester's Model 12, a gun that was introduced in 1912 and dropped from the line in the late 1960s. It was dropped because manufacturing techniques have changed so much that the old gun was unprofitable to make any longer. But it wouldn't stay dead. The Model 12 is back again, but at a much higher price and only in a couple of grades. Meanwhile, Winchester has added a lower-priced pump gun capable of being made competitively in terms of price. But by far the most popular pump gun available is Remington's Model 870, very likely the largest volume seller in the world. Another popular old model that has continued for many years is Ithaca's Model 37. This was based on Pedersen and Browning designs that were employed in the Remington Models 10, 17, and 29—all of which were dropped by 1933. Ithaca slightly modified the design and introduced the gun in 1937, from which point it has been a continual best seller.

Another famous oldie is the Savage Model 30, which began as the Stevens 520, another Browning design. While the gun today is changed somewhat from the original, it's still the basic Stevens action patented in 1903.

It's hard to see how there can be very much new in pump-gun design. And it's hard to justify anything new. One of the most recent pump actions to be placed on the market is the Marlin Model 120. It is a blend of several famous old designs, borrowing various features from each. This is not criticism; in fact, it's the smart way to design a new gun. A parallel can be seen in modern bolt-action rifle design, where almost every modern bolt is a derivation of the Mauser 1898 system. There's nothing whatever wrong with utilizing features that have been so good they have withstood the test of time. Like all modern guns, the Marlin pump gun has a few exclusive features as well as many that it shares with other good guns on the market.

SINGLE-SHOT SHOTGUNS

There are two basic types of single-shot shotguns on today's market, and they're as far apart as you can get in shotgunnery. There are, for example, single-barrel trap guns that are among the finest of all shotguns for their purpose. These range from such purely competitive models as the Perazzi and Ljutic to the famous Ithaca "$5,000 Grade." This Ithaca is one fine old gun, which was once known as the "Sousa Grade," after John Philip Sousa, the great band leader and composer who was also an avid trap shooter. Ithaca figured that hardly anybody knew about Sousa anymore, so they changed the name to the dollar designation some years ago.

Single-shot trap guns are generally made to superb quality standards, and they are usually choked to a degree of full choke often known as "super pucker." Sometimes expressed as "really full," these barrels deliver a tight cluster of shot for handicap shooters when the targets are often 50 to 60 yards out. Such manufacturing excellence runs costs up, as you might well imagine; the fiddling around with chokes necessary to produce such patterns is very costly. I've been shooting a Perazzi Comp I (about a $1,500 gun in 1976) and it simply powders a clay target when I

Harrington & Richardson's famous Topper—a single-shot, break-open gun that the company has made in high volume for many years. It's available in many gauges (and a number of rifle calibers as well). This is one of those famous "hen house" guns that are the tool of a farmer, and a popular choice for a boy's first gun.

do my part, even at 50 to 60 yards. And it does so even with the very light 1-ounce reloads I've been shooting.

There are other single-shot shotguns, such as the Model 37 Winchester, Harrington & Richardson's famous Topper, and the Stevens Model 94, which are the old farmer's henhouse guns. The H&R and Stevens cost little more than $50, while the Winchester takes about $20 more, so you can see that these guns are far from the quality of a trap gun. But they do the job and are what are usually described as "safe, dependable" firearms. Both these types of gun are of the break-open, down-swinging barrel type, much like a double gun. Some have top levers, some side levers, and a few are operated by a bottom lever. Some of the trap models have an automatic ejector, as do nearly all the "farm and ranch" specials. Ithaca has a switch on this type of gun in that the opening lever is fashioned like a lever-action rifle. Otherwise, it's similar to the rest of these guns. So, as you see, single-shot shotguns run all the way in price and quality.

Operation of any of these guns is quite simple and almost entirely manual. Loading is by hand, simply by placing the cartridge directly into the chamber. Cocking is sometimes by hand with the visible-hammer models, although others—including the costly trap guns—are cocked automatically when the barrel is lowered. Extraction is usually automatic, although many competitive shooters prefer guns without this feature so they can pick out the fired cases for reloading. Either way, *extraction* is performed by the enormous mechanical advantage such guns possess because the long barrel acts as a lever. It forces the extractor back slightly to allow you to pick out the cartridge whether fired or unfired, or to loosen

the cartridge by backing it out slightly, at which point the ejector can kick it out of the gun.

PRIMARY EXTRACTION

When a shotgun is discharged, the gas pressure exerts great forces in equal directions. Since the shot charge is the only movable object, it is what begins to move. However, the gas pressure also stretches paper or plastic shotgun cartridge to the limits of the gun barrel's chamber. The net effect is to render the fired case harder to extract from the chamber than one that has not been fired. And the degree of tightness is usually proportionate to the amount of pressure generated. (Other factors may also be involved, such as old, dirty ammunition, scratched chamber walls, or the like, which can make extraction difficult as well.) Moreover, the cartridge case seals the rear end of the barrel during firing so that the gas pressure will propel the projectile and not escape into the action, which would ruin the gun and could injure the shooter.

It follows that fired cartridges must be broken loose; that is, they must be moved slightly by great mechanical advantage to break the seal caused by the pressure of firing. This is primary extraction, and it is always performed by the very first movement of the breechblock—or whatever means of operation a particular gun has. With a single-barrel shotgun, or a double, it is easy slowly to open the action and watch the extractor back out a distance of about ⅛ inch. If the gun is a nonejector model, that ends the phase; but if it has automatic ejection, the ejector will now be released and will sharply kick the front end of the extractor and the empty will be thrown clear of the gun. This also cannot occur

A fine Merkel side-by-side 12-gauge double. This one is a sidelock, meaning that the lock work is in the side plates where you see the fancy engraving. The double gun is probably the most complicated of all mechanisms. Its development, over several centuries, has been entirely for sporting use.

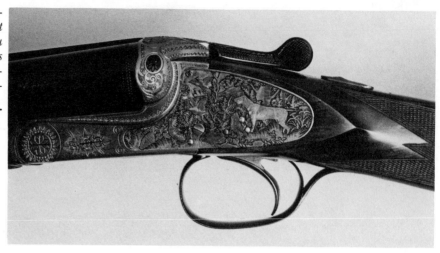

until the barrel is dropped far enough to allow the empty cartridge to clear the breech face.

Primary extraction is of most importance with high-power rifle cartridges such as the .300 Winchester Magnum and the various Weatherbys. Shotguns operate at much lower pressure levels and, in most cases, do not require the same degree of primary extraction to loosen the case. But in a gun like an autoloader, where the parts move very fast, the bolt must be gradually brought up to the speed of the operating rod or it will tear out the rim of the case. In such circumstances you might say that primary extraction is a by-product of the necessity of gradual acceleration of the action parts.

THE DOUBLE BARREL

I suspect most people think a double gun is one of the simpler types, possibly rivaling the single shot in this respect. If you are among those who think a double is pure simplicity, accept it as a tribute to the design geniuses, who have packed so many intricacies and subtleties into what appears so simple a gun. In all truth, more time, thought, and ingenuity have gone into double-gun design than any other type. And, significantly, all double-gun inventiveness and evolvement has been directed toward the sporting market. That can be said about no other action system. It's doubtful that any gun evolved more slowly than the double.

The double gun is virtually entirely British in

origin and nearly every improvement in them has come from one or another of the great makers in London, Birmingham, or Edinburgh. Even today, "best" English guns are to the firearms world what Rolls-Royce is to automobiles. There is no competition.

Some years back, in the late 1940s I believe, I had a chance to buy a pair of cased double-barreled rifles made in 1921 by Holland & Holland of London. They were Holland's Royal Grade (the finest) and had never been fired. The story was that they had been ordered by a gentleman from Philadelphia who had passed away before delivery and now were being offered for sale by his estate. The price tab was $2,100. I was short by about $2,095. Today, I wish I'd gone into hock to buy that matched pair; it would have been an excellent investment.

Sometime during the 1960s I had another chance. This was a fine Woodward 20-gauge over/under gun that had been used a bit but had been well tended. The price was a rather heavy $3,200 (I was just as short as before). Today that gun is probably worth an easy $8,000 to $10,000. Why so much money? Workmanship, pure and simple. Nobody, not even Holland & Holland, makes a gun today as they made that pair in 1921. And the Woodward plant was destroyed by German bombs in World War II; even though Messrs. James Purdey now make the Woodward over/under, it's not the same as a pre-War "genuine" Woodward. Still, the double guns made today by such firms as Holland & Holland, Boss, Purdey, and a very few others

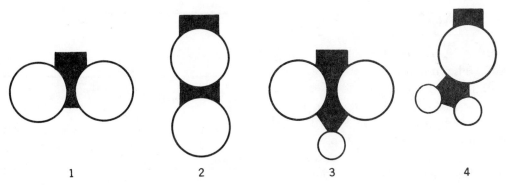

1   2   3   4

Various combination guns are fairly popular in Europe. Shown here are typical side-by-side and over/under shotguns (Figures 1 and 2). Sometimes these are made as double rifles. Figure 3 is a pair of shotgun barrels with a rifle barrel underneath and Figure 4 is a single shotgun barrel with rifle barrel below and another on the side. There is almost no limit to what styles you can find even including 4-barrel shotguns. Aside from Savage's popular rifle/shotgun combination, there is not much interest in this country in these combinations.

are the finest guns being made in the world today—just as they've always been.

Both shotguns and rifles are made as doubles, but there are very few of the latter and they are made mostly because they are so traditional. By this I mean that a double rifle usually is still preferred by many who tackle the big, dangerous game of Africa. That's partly tradition, partly sentiment, partly good sense, and partly just plain stubbornness. These heavy double rifles are made for enormous cartridges, the sort that can knock an elephant silly with a head shot even if the brain is missed. And a double provides the fastest two shots in all gundom, which can be a blessing. Since the British have used doubles in Africa since before they can remember, tradition and sentiment play a large part in the choice, too. Englishmen just don't consider magazine rifles very sporting, possibly being somewhat conditioned by the general unreliability of the rifles exported to Africa from Germany during the 1920s and 30s. This has all been changed since the advent of the .458 Winchester Magnum in 1956 and, to a large extent, to the popularity given Magnum cartridges in bolt-action rifles by Roy Weatherby. Worldwide distribution of that mighty Winchester and worldwide publicity and distribution of Weatherby products has changed all that.

Double guns come in both side-by-side and over/under versions. Those terms are quite simple; the barrels are either mounted side by side, or stacked one on top of the other. Either is also available as a boxlock action or a sidelock. In the boxlock action, all the firing mechanism parts are contained within the frame (the word frame in double guns is used in place of receiver). In a sidelock gun, these firing mechanisms are located on sideplates that are fitted into both metal and wood. There is still another lock system usually called the Blitz, or trigger-plate, action. This is closer to a form of boxlock than anything else, the firing mechanisms being fastened to the trigger plate or to the bottom plate of the frame.

To further complicate this picture a little, there are many combination guns made in Europe. Some of these consist of a double-barreled shotgun with a single rifle barrel underneath it. Called a drilling, these actions are a bit more complicated than ordinary double guns. Another variation is the four-barrel gun: double shotgun plus two rifle barrels, usually in different calibers. Sometimes the two shotgun barrels are in over/under fashion, rifle barrel or barrels on either side.

The purpose of such exotic combinations, and of the other forms (because there are more variations than I've listed here), is to furnish the hunter with a suitable answer to whatever game may be flushed. Such guns have more purpose in Europe than in America, because a bird hunter may well be charged by a boar when in heavy cover. A few combination guns are imported into the United States each year and a few were brought back after World War II; otherwise you won't find many in the U.S. and we won't spend any more time on them in this book.

DOUBLE-GUN ORIGIN

Lost in antiquity. A reasonable assumption is that doubles have been made since the 15th century—remember that some early doubles were handguns. As we know the double gun, it has been in development for a couple of hundred years or more. Both side-by-side and over/under double guns were made as far back as in flintlock days. In fact, there are those who claim the shotgun has not advanced in 200 years. They have a point because we still use the same load—a charge of shot—and we still drive the same amount of the same kind of shot at the same velocity!

Double guns have remained popular, and have been regaining popularity in America over the past few years, for some very good reasons. After two centuries of development by some of the world's finest gunmakers, the double is a marvel of efficiency, combining superb design and workmanship in a lightweight, well-balanced, smoothly functioning gun.

A well-made double gun of good or high quality is the fastest shoulder gun to get into operation. It is also the safest and provides the quickest second shot. It has been claimed that a double is also the most dependable of all actions, the reason for advancing that claim being that a double contains two separate locks, one for each barrel. Should one of the locks fail for any reason, the other one will be operable since it is entirely independent.

One of the leading advantages of a double gun above all others in terms of speed in getting it into action is that its action is shorter than any other. No space must be taken up with moving breechbolts and other parts of a repeating-action gun mechanism. The double gun can be as much as 5 inches shorter than a repeater with the same barrel length. Moreover, most of the weight in the gun is centrally located between your hands. That's why you can get a double into action faster than any other shoulder gun.

DEFINITIONS

Before we begin to study how and why double guns work, we should review some of the terms used because the double is of English origin and

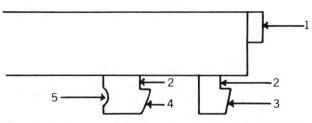

The principal parts of the breech end of a pair of barrels from a side-by-side gun: 1, top extension; 2, bites; 3, rear lump; 4, front lump; 5, hook.

A Merkel side-by-side double showing the action bar (serially numbered section at right) with its "flats" (where the numbers are stamped), also sometimes called the "water table." The corresponding flats of the barrels are shown at left. The two small projections extending from the knuckle of the action bar are the cocking rods, which are pushed down when the barrels are opened to cock the locks.

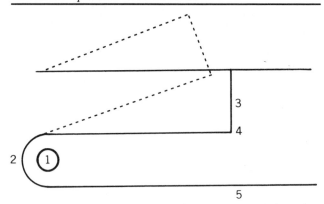

A side-by-side double shotgun is represented: 1, indicates the hinge pin; 2, the knuckle; 3, the action face; 4, the junction of face and bar (the weakest part of a double gun), 5, the point at which the action tends to rotate in recoil. Recoil is a force extending straight rearward in a continuation of the bore line. This tends to make the action rotate around 5. In opening the gun, however, the barrels rotate around the hinge pin, 1.

these terms are strange. In fact, there is a separate set of names we'll be using for the barrels and another for the actions. First the barrels.

Lumps: the projections that protrude below the breech end of a set of barrels; they are used to fasten the barrels to the action.

Bites: slots cut into the lumps; they are lock recesses into which the locking bolt (contained in the action body) engages to lock the gun closed.

Hook: the recess cut into the front of the lump; it hooks over the hinge pin in the action body and forms the pivot over which the barrels swing in opening.

Flats: the flat surfaces on the bottom of the set of barrels, on either side of the lumps, that fit against the flats of the action body when the gun is closed. The flats have also been called the "water table"; the origin of this term is obscure to me, except that I have rarely heard it applied to any gun except the American Parker.

Top extension: a projection at the breech end of the barrels acting as an additional connection between barrel and action in some guns and used for locking in some gun systems. Top extensions do not exist in all guns and they appear in a wide variety of shapes, types, and uses when they are employed.

Those are the major barrel terms we'll be using. Now let's look at some action-part names. Most confusing at first will be the word "lock." In a double gun, a lock is a complete firing mechanism. It has nothing to do with locking the gun. That's done with a bolt, which (in most conventional guns) slides back and forth to engage the bites in the lumps.

Action body: the housing for the action.

Bar: a forward extension at the bottom of the action.

Bolt: (usually) a part moving back and forth that engages the bites in the lumps to lock action and barrels together. In some systems using a top extension for locking, the bolt moves laterally and engages the top extension.

Flats: the flat upper surface of the bar that fits against the barrel flats when the gun is closed and locked.

Face: the vertical face of the action body against which the cartridge rests when the gun is closed. The face is often called the standing breech.

Knuckle: the rounded front of the bar, around which the barrels pivot in conjunction with the hinge pin.

Hinge pin: a device into which the hook on the barrel lumps fastens. In operation, the barrels rotate around both knuckle and hinge pin.

Top lever: the opening lever located on top of the action body that unlocks the gun for opening and snaps shut automatically when the barrels are closed.

Locks: the firing mechanisms. In a boxlock action they are contained within the action body. In a sidelock gun they are attached to side plates that fit into both action body and stock.

Side clips: small projections on each side of the action face of a side-by-side double gun to prevent any chance of the barrels moving sideways. These are generally regarded as unnecessary in ordinary guns, but quite useful in guns frequently employed with heavy loads. The reason is that the right barrel exerts a thrust to the right of center, and the left barrel to the left of center, so there is a tendency to shove the barrels from side to side. Side clips are an advantage to a gun in which high-pressure loads are used and they may be regarded as a reinforcement of any action.

Tumbler: British parlance for hammer.

Strap or tang: the rearward extension of the action body, which is used to help fasten action and stock together.

There are some variations in the nomenclature between side-by-side and over/under guns; that given above is primarily for the side-by-side, but many of the words are just as applicable to over/under guns.

BARRELS

Double-gun barrels are made as separate tubes, then joined together into a unit. The barrels must be set at a slight angle in order for the shot charge from each to hit the same point (because the breech end of any barrel—where the pressure is highest—must be larger in diameter than the muzzle); it's also true that the right barrel will shoot a little to the right, the left to the left. That's because each barrel is set slightly to the side of the center line, and a gun tends to recoil in a straight line, which is an extension of the bore axis. By the same token, the top barrel of an over/under tends to rise a little more than the lower in recoil. Inasmuch as recoil starts to move the gun before the charge leaves the muzzle, these points must all be factored into exact positioning of the barrels.

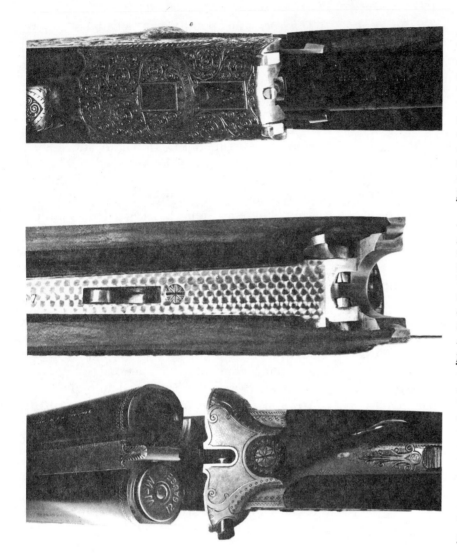

Bottom of the frame of a Merkel over/under sidelock gun with forearm removed but barrels in place. The two cocking rods are visible at either side of the knuckle, while the small projection in the center works the extractors when the gun is opened. The two longer pieces located on either side of the barrel are the legs of the ejectors, which are activated by that mechanism located in the forearm. Note the high quality of the engraving of this superbly made gun from East Germany.

Inside the forearm of a Merkel over/under gun, the forearm catch is visible to the left of the screw. At the right of the picture note the ejector hammers located on either side. They are shown in cocked position. When the gun is opened, these hammers will be activated to fly back and kick the ejectors, tossing the fired empties out of the gun. Note the fine workmanship including the perfect alignment of the screw slot.

A side-by-side gun opened after firing the right barrel. Note that the right ejector has snapped out the empty from that barrel while the cartridge in the left barrel has merely been raised. This is a Merkel gun; note the top extension between the barrels and the slot in the frame for it with locking bolt partly opened. Note, too, the side clips on the frame and corresponding surfaces on the sides of each barrel, which helps strengthen the action.

Following a double gun through the seven steps of operation is quite simple. Firing is accomplished in standard manner by pulling the trigger which releases a small hammer (tumbler) to strike the firing pin. Unlocking occurs when the top lever is pushed aside and the lock or locks are withdrawn. Moving the barrels down accomplishes extraction, ejection, and cocking all during the same motion. As the barrels begin their downward movement, the extractors are moved back slightly in the motion we have already explained as primary extraction. Very powerful mechanical advantage can be employed with the barrels. During the same movement, cocking is handled by a small lever (that you can't see) between the barrels and the action knuckle. It just shoves the hammers back into cocked position.

On guns with automatic ejectors (known as ejector guns), the empty cartridges are ejected from the gun automatically. In a nonejector gun you withdraw the fired cartridges by hand.

Reloading is accomplished by placing new cartridges into the chambers by hand; closing the barrels causes the top lever to snap shut and the gun is locked.

EJECTORS

Properly the mechanism of an ejector gun is called selective ejection, because only the fired empties are ejected. That is, if you fire just the right barrel and open the gun, only the right ejector will operate. The left extractor will only move the cartridge out slightly, about 1/8 inch. But the right one will sharply snap the empty clear of the gun. This is accomplished by a separate extractor for each barrel, instead of the single, common extractor that works both barrels at once in a nonejector gun. In the "best" ejector guns, there are two very small locks built into the forearm. These are smaller, but similar to, the locks that fire each barrel. When either (or both) barrel is fired, a small projection moves out of the knuckle of the frame and, as the barrels are lowered, causes the ejector lock to cock and then to "fire" as soon as the barrels have opened far enough for the empty to clear the action face. The "firing" of the ejector is really a sharp kick that is given the front end of the extractor. Incidentally, in a "best" gun, the makers take great pride in adjusting the ejectors so that not only do both barrels eject at the same precise moment, but the two spent cartridges will land at the same spot and at the same time! That may not mean a damned thing to anyone, but it is one of the niceties of a "best" gun.

At one time, I think there must have been as many ejector systems as there were gunmakers in England. One of the most common, and still popular today, is called the Southgate. Located in the forearm, consisting of two separate ejector locks, the Southgate works on the over-center principle. The best way to understand this is to compare its action with that of a pocketknife blade. You know that as you close a blade it reaches the point where it simply snaps shut. That happens after it has gone over center, and the spring lying along the knife's back snaps it shut.

The Southgate works similarly. Fire a barrel and the firing mechanism forces the small projection out of the knuckle. Here the projection engages the ejector and, as the barrels are pushed down, the ejector tumbler is slowly brought into cocked position against the tension of the ejector spring. Once the barrels are down far enough for the cartridge to clear the action face, the ejector tumbler goes over center and flies rearward, giving the extractor a good swift kick, and the empty flies out. If you don't shoot, the projection stays inside the knuckle and the ejector is inoperative. It's really pretty simple and quite ingenious.

Most of the double guns now on the market have a far less sophisticated, but just as efficient, ejector system. Many of these are installed on the barrels rather than the forearm and are coil-spring operated. The British will tell you, correctly, that the leaf spring, such as they use for lock and ejector tumblers, is faster than coil springs. As a matter of fact, there was a time, not long ago, when it was claimed that the lock of a "best" quality sidelock double gun was the fastest of all systems in terms of lock time. Nonetheless, the coil-spring operated ejectors are just as functional as the best Southgate. Their added redeeming feature is that they are far less costly to make, less complicated to service, and the net result is that you can buy a good, reliable ejector gun for much less money than one with Southgate ejectors.

TOP EXTENSIONS

Top extensions are used for a variety of reasons, some valid and some that are a little hard to justify. They are rarely used on a "best" quality English gun and to realize why you have to understand the way the English gentlefolk do their shooting. Typical British wing shooting consists of shooting driven birds from blinds. In this form of shooting, say grouse in Scotland, the "guns" (i.e. shooters) are in blinds accompanied by a loader (a man to load the extra gun, which is why many British doubles come in matched pairs). Birds are driven by drivers—men who line up far away and slowly walk toward the shooters. Flushed birds fly past or over the pits and furnish some of the finest wing shooting known to man.

This shooting is often fast and furious, for the birds are in full flight and going like merry hell. And there may be very large flocks. This is the reason for the two guns and the loader. Your loader, if he's really good, can load the spare and hand it to you (while you never take your eyes from the birds) without your missing a stroke. But this rapid loading can't take place with a gun using a top extension; it gets in the way. So the English like their breeches clean and easy to load.

In any side-by-side double gun, the weakest point of the action is in the right angle formed by the face and the bar. I doubt there is a gun being made today in which this juncture is not cut in the form of a small radius, which adds greatly to the strength (as opposed to a square

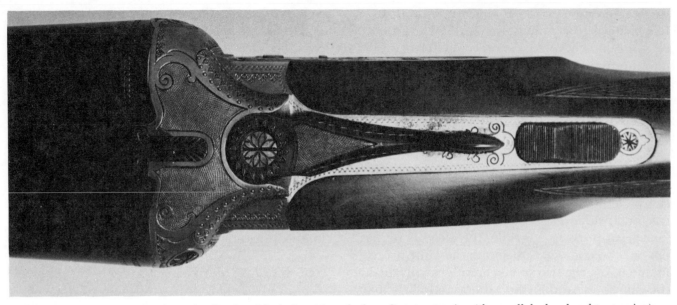

In this top-extension gun, shown in closed and locked position, the barrel's top extension (the small dark-colored protrusion) extends into the center of the frame. It's also bolted and you can see the round bolt at the left side of the action.

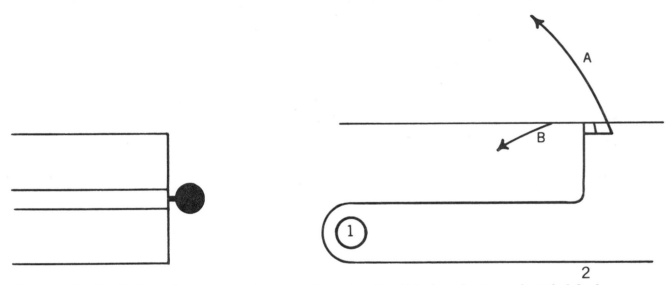

The principle of the "doll's head" top extension is rarely understood and is widely claimed not to work. At the left, above, you see the doll's head as viewed from the top. Referring to the diagram at right, when the gun is opened the barrels rotate around the hinge pin, 1, and the doll's head describes the arc labeled A. During recoil, however, the action wants to rotate around 2, and to describe the arc marked B. The barrels are prevented from taking this direction by the shape of the doll's head. Years ago the British proved the merits of a correctly fitted doll's head although the device is seldom used today.

corner) and resists bending of the action at this point. In the double gun, when fired, there is a tendency for the action to bend at this point. And where there is no top extension, there is a certain amount of bending. In a "best" gun, it is inconsequential and the gun has been designed around the anticipated bending. But a much simpler way to secure the barrels to the action at the top was evolved by Westley Richards in the late 1880s. One of the earliest top extensions, Richards' answer was called the "doll's head"; it works simply and easily, even though it's difficult to *see* how it works.

As the diagram shows, the doll's head top extension fits into a corresponding recess in the top of the frame. Since the knob of the doll's head slips in and out with ease as the gun is opened and closed, you wonder how this can help hold things together. The answer is that while the barrels revolve around the hinge pin in opening, that's not the point where they want to bend down when the gun is fired. Since the barrel flats are secured to the action bar at its flats, the tendency is for the action bar to bend at the junction of the face. Thus the fulcrum is several inches to the rear of the hinge pin which produces an entirely different arc and the doll's head will help prevent a bend in the action during firing.

Doll's heads are often reinforced by a bolt, the most famous of which is the Greener cross bolt, which fits into a very solid top extension. As Mr. Greener commented, before 1900, the cross bolt must be round, for the cutting of a square hole with corresponding square bolt (as was used by some makers), actually weakens the system. This is true of course; it's always better in such an application to use a round bolt in a round hole that leaves no weak corners. And that doesn't even include the very difficult job of fitting a square bolt so it bears on all four sides.

Some guns use a combination of under locks, called the Purdey double lock, with a top extension of some sort. And top extensions come in all sizes and shapes. The American L. C. Smith, for example, used no bottom lock at all—just the top extension held down by a cross bolt. The same system has been in wide use for many years.

There are, as a matter of fact, so many different and varied systems and variations of systems that enumerating all of them would be simply consuming vast quantities of paper for no useful purpose. The main purpose in this book is to explain what must be done, and how it's done in some of the more popular actions. With the knowledge of what must be done, you can figure out by yourself some of the oddities you're sure to run across.

An interesting feature found on a very few "best" guns is a self-opening device. This shows to what length top English makers can go to make a "best" gun the superb work of art it is. By employing a rather long coil spring located under and between the barrels, the self-opening action virtually opens by itself when you push the top lever aside. I say "virtually" because you do have to exert some light pressure, particularly if the gun has been fired. Closing the gun is slightly more difficult because you have to get

that spring back under tension. But there's nothing else for the barrels to do on the upstroke so that isn't a factor. Self openers are quite rare, quite unique, and just about as ritzy as you can get.

OVER/UNDER GUNS

There has been a revival in over/under gun interest over the past few years that is rather astounding. In the 1950s, or thereabouts, American gunmakers virtually dropped *all* double-gun manufacture. The great old Parker was gone; it has been bought by Remington, made by that firm for a while and then dropped. The L. C. Smith was bought by Marlin and also made for a while and then dropped. Marlin's Model 90 over/under was gone as was Remington's Model 32 over/under. The only major American double gun of any sort to survive was the Winchester Model 21, but that gun was so escalated in price that it was far removed from consideration of all but the most wealthy. Now Ruger has come out with a long-heralded O/U, presently only in 20 gauge, but with a 12-gauge model planned.

As nearly as I can learn the first double guns were over/under types, although nobody is willing to offer a reason for that at this time. That was changed in the 1780s, when Henry Nock's patent breech significantly improved the ignition of flintlock mechanisms. The over/under slipped out of sight and out of mind for more than a hundred years in favor of the side-by-side. Again, there are no reasons advanced for this and I suspect the major reason is that both types are superb and that the advantages for one over the other are probably more imagined than real anyway.

In any event, the over/under staged a revival in the first quarter of this century, for no apparent reason except the one advanced by Burrard in *The Modern Shotgun*. I suspect Burrard is correct. He said the primary object "was for something new." The side by side had been advanced to its ultimate high level and there really was nothing left to advance. Then the development of the modern over/under gave shooters something to talk about and gunmakers something to get their teeth into and develop.

The modern over/under probably reached its

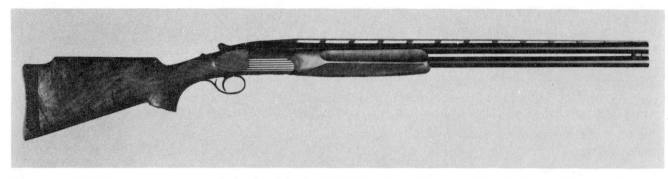

The Perazzi MT-6 trap gun was especially developed for the 1976 Olympics in Montreal. This sort of competition is so demanding, however, that next time around a new design will be necessary. The MT-6 was developed by a previous Olympic winner in conjunction with Perazzi.

peak in elegance with the superb James Woodward gun which is generally acknowledged to have been the finest. (Woodward's plant was bombed out of existence in World War II; what was left, including the name, was taken over by James Purdey after the war and the Woodward over/under gun is now made by that firm.) The lines of this gun are sheer perfection, largely due to the low silhouette because the locks lie along the sides rather than underneath. Many others have copied the system right up to the newest gun of all, the Ruger over/under. Bill Ruger makes no bones about copying the Woodward, because it's the best. Among the others using a similar system are Perazzi and Beretta.

Various reasons are given for the popularity of the over/under, the chief one being that the bottom barrel provides less recoil than the right barrel of a side by side. Therefore you get back on target quicker with the second shot. The single sighting plane is offered as another advantage. Over/unders are very popular in this country and several authorities have advanced the theory that this is because we are a "rifle-minded" people, thus more used to a single barrel. I don't believe that reason is valid, because, while we might be rifle minded to a degree, we also have been shooting single-barrel shotguns primarily since the early 1900s when John Browning's pumps and autoloaders began to hit the market in numbers never before imagined. I rather think the "single-barrel-mindedness," which would include rifles and shotguns, might well be a more valid reason.

The usual disadvantages of an over/under are

its cost, compared to a side by side, and that it has a greater resistance to a side wind. The latter point can be eliminated. In a game gun the side wind is not a factor. Over/unders do cost more because they require more work, but the advances in machine-tool and manufacturing technology are sharply cutting those costs.

Aside from personal preferences, there is no reason to choose an over/under over a side by side, or the other way around. The man who feels more comfortable with one or the other should go in that direction. Of course, there are specialized trap guns available in over/under models—the famed Perazzi is a good example—that are not available in side by side. But for the average game gun, the choice is up to the user and, after having cast the die, he should not look back.

Most of what we've discussed has been the side-by-side, though much of it applies equally to the over/under gun. But there also are many differences. What's been said about locks (that is, the firing mechanisms) and ejectors remains basically the same. Over/unders are made in boxlock and sidelock, ejector and nonejector, and they all work very much the same as a side by side.

The action body of an over/under is a good deal stronger than that of a side by side due to its very deep U construction with the barrels contained almost entirely within the frame. There is, however, a real difference in the locking method, because the conventional underlock system used with bottom lumps is a long way from the top barrel. It is, in fact, a full barrel-

This is a boxlock gun, the Winchester Model 101 in Pigeon Grade, single trigger, 12 gauge.

width farther away than in a side by side. This has led to a good deal more top locking systems on over/unders than side by sides. One of the more popular is called the Kersten lock and is used extensively on such fine guns as the Merkel. The modern O/U gun most often employs a pair of small, round locking lugs that project forward from the action face and into recesses in the barrels' monoblock when the gun is closed. There is a wide range of adaptations of that principle in use today and often a combination of top locks with under-bolting.

LOCKS

As said earlier, double guns are made in two basic systems: boxlock and sidelock. Boxlock guns are more common; they are easier to manufacture. Most of those who appreciate a fine double think the sidelock is a prettier gun; in fact, there are a number of boxlock guns on the market that use fake side plates to give the appearance of a sidelock simply because of the attractive lines that result. This is strictly for the

A finish machined Winchester Model 21 frame. In this boxlock gun, the action parts will be fitted within the frame. In 1940 the Model 21 listed at $77.45 in 12, 16, or 20 gauge with two triggers and non-selective ejectors. Today it's made only in Custom, Pigeon, and Grand American grades, all on special order only. Prices in the spring of 1977 begin at $3500.00 and go from there.

sake of appearance, not an attempt to upgrade the boxlock by a phony device. The fact is, there is nothing significantly superior enough about either system to choose one over the other.

Sidelock boosters claim their system is stronger, because it removes less metal from the action bar. The point is true, but only becomes significant in those very few super-light English guns that make every attempt to reduce weight. Most American doubles, including the Parker, Winchester 21, Ithaca, Fox, and today's Remington 3200, have been boxlock guns. Famous "imports" such as the Browning, which is really almost as American as apple pie, and the Winchester 101 are also boxlock guns. At one time, there were two famous sidelock guns made here: the original Dan Lefever and the L. C. Smith.

Among "best" guns, Woodward, Purdey, Boss, Holland & Holland, and a few others were virtually all sidelock guns. Westley Richards on the other hand, even though he made some sidelocks, specialized in the boxlock. Webley & Scott, which at one time made many sidelocks, now concentrates on the boxlock which was recently imported by Harrington & Richardson.

The major differences in these systems are that the boxlock is constructed so that all the parts of both locks (i.e. the firing mechanisms) are located within the action body. This system, as we know it today, was invented in 1875 by two employees of Westley Richards whose names were Anson and Deeley. In general, the system is still used just about as originally designed and the Anson & Deeley system was the first efficient hammerless double-gun design. It is simple and reliable. In addition to the one "weakness" (in comparison with a sidelock) already mentioned,

These two views of the Savage Model 33 show the gun open and closed. Note the unique lock on this gun. It appears to be a dust cover on top of the action but this part really slides forward and holds the barrels closed. (So far as I know this lock was pioneered on the Remington Model 32—it's also used in the Remington 3200.) Note too that the buttstock is held securely by a "through bolt" reached through the stock by a long screwdriver.

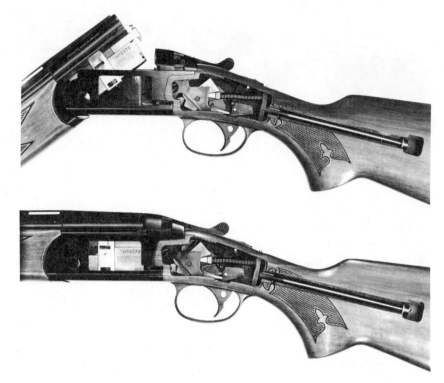

a boxlock gun requires that its tumbler (hammer) pin extend clear through the action body from side to side almost directly under the junction of face and bar, the weakest point of the action. I can see where this could be claimed a weakness, but the action has been around so long in so many successful guns that surely any merit the argument might once have had should have been forgotten long ago.

As a matter of fact, one of the most famous boxlock actions, made by Westley Richards, is made with detachable locks that can be easily removed from the gun for cleaning, inspection, or replacement. It also does away with the pin all the way through the action body. Those order-

Left and right locks from an over/under sidelock. This is a "back action" sidelock; in the other type, the "bar action," the main spring lies to the front, that part of the lock plate extending into the bar. This high-grade gun also has intercepting sears designed to catch the hammer should it jar off the sear.

ing Westley Richards' guns with detachable locks (an expensive extra) often ordered a duplicate pair of locks for emergency use. So far as I know, Richards alone made this feature and he introduced it in 1899.

The basic difference between a boxlock and sidelock is that in the latter, the locks are mounted on plates, called side plates. These plates, in turn, are fitted partly into the action, extending forward into the action bar and extending rearward into the stock. The result is a pleasing appearance and considerable extra space for engraving. Some side plates may be removed by the simple turning of a screw, which can be hand removed; these are called hand-detachable locks. They were first made by Holland & Holland. All side plates are easily removable, however, since a single screw holds them in position at the back by extending through the stock at this point; another screw at the front secures the front end to the action body.

Other things being equal, there is little to choose from between a boxlock and sidelock gun. However, most English "best" guns are sidelocks. I'm not sure the reason for this can be pinpointed except that the appearance of a sidelock is generally considered superior chiefly because there is more room for engraving. An added reason may well be that sidelocks cost more, and, presumably, many buyers of "best" guns are wealthy shooters who don't know or care that much about the workings of a gun.

When the dollars are equal, your choice should be a boxlock gun because it will be a better gun. (Assuming other factors are also equal, but you can sometimes find a real bargain due to currency fluctuations, so it's difficult to make positive statements.) The reason is that a sidelock requires more time to manufacture, hence costs more, and, if you're considering two guns each with a price of say $300 and one's a box and the other a sidelock, you should choose the boxlock.

SINGLE TRIGGERS

The single-trigger system in double guns is most complicated. Complicated because each time you pull the trigger of any firearm you actually pull it twice. You don't know you do it, but it happens due to the recoil that pulls the trigger away from your finger so fast that you take up the slack involuntarily. This second pull is known as the involuntary pull. The single-trigger mechanism of every double gun must contain a method of wasting the involuntary pull or blocking it so it won't function. Unless this is done, your double would simply fire both barrels; this is called "doubling" and is most unpleasant. At one time, there were nearly as many ways of making single triggers as there were gunmakers. And some of them were marvels of complicated ingenuity.

At one time, the double gun fancier was at a distinct disadvantage. He could haunt the few gun stores that specialized in good doubles; and they were very few, as were the guns. Or he could settle for one of the mass-produced lesser guns, or often one of the cheaper imports, many of which were inferior in both design and workmanship.

Today however, the double gunner has plenty of choice. He can order a Holland & Holland or Purdey or Boss or Webley & Scott and he'll wait perhaps as long as eight to ten years and pay as much as he'd pay for a Rolls-Royce. Or he can get a very similar gun, not quite as good but damned near, from Spain, Italy, or one like the Merkel out of Suhl in East Germany. Most of

these sell for from a quarter to half the British cost. The guns are not quite so good, but that's a big cost break. Or he can settle for one of the excellent over/under guns made in Japan and currently imported by a number of firms under some well-known brand names. Some of those brands are Winchester, Charles Daly, and so on. Now, too, there are fully American O/U guns—including the Remington 3200 and the—at this writing—brand-new Ruger, which will be made entirely in the U.S. and will certainly become a factor in the market.

REMINGTON 3200

This story really started in 1932, when Remington introduced the Model 32 over/under gun, which was quite a departure from the norm. Model 32 was abandoned in 1942 and never came back after World War II was over. The 32 was not all that popular and never sold in really good volume, so there was no economic reason to bring it back into the line, especially when there were so many other models crying for redevelopment and the company was pouring millions into new models, new tooling, and new machinery. Besides, the only shooters who really took to the 32 were skeet shooters. And you could count the numbers of them pretty quickly. So the 32 was dropped.

But the clamor among skeet folks kept on going and by and by the old West German firm of Krieghoff made a copy of the 32 that began to sell in respectable volume. Enough interest developed to make the gun attractive again to Remington. Their new Model 3200 was introduced in the early 1970s. Model 3200 bears a lot of outward resemblance to the older 32, but it's an entirely new gun designed to be made efficiently on modern machinery. One of the most noticeable departures in either model from any other shotgun is that there are no ribs to tie the barrels together. There is nothing but a bracket at the muzzle, which is fastened to the upper barrel and allows the bottom barrel to slip back and forth as it heats during shooting.

Remington's 3200 also has a unique lockup consisting of a back-and-forth sliding block on top of the frame. When locked, this slide is forward and holds the barrels down. At the same

If more evidence is needed that a double shotgun is not a simple mechanism, here is the inside of a Savage Model 333 over/under gun in fired position; the gun has single trigger and ejectors. There is an incredible amount of engineering, experience, knowhow, and time in the development of this or any double gun.

time a pair of large lugs on either side of the barrels mate with corresponding lugs in the frame. These lugs are designed to withstand the thrust load during firing. (The Swedish Valmet, whose products are imported by Savage, uses a similar sliding top lock.)

LOOK EAST YOUNG MAN

Shortly after World War II, a gun buff friend of mine who had seen service in Japan showed me a floorplate he'd had engraved by a Japanese engraver. The animal shown was a moose—or so he said. It looked more like a mouse with horns. But that was in the late 40s; the Japanese have come a long way since then. Everybody knows what they've done in such industries as optical, electronics, and so forth. Now they're in the gun business in a big way. One of the leading Japanese gun manufacturers is Kodensha, who make the Winchester Model 101 and who were shown how by Winchester. The same firm also made the Miida for a brief time until it was taken off the market. (It has since been re-distributed here as the Nikko.) Other famous all-American names marketing Japanese-made guns include Ithaca, Weatherby, and others.

Such guns as the Kodensha-made Winchester, Miida, and Nikko are basically a copy of the Browning Superposed with enough cosmetic differences to make it seem legitimate. The main point is that the Japanese can do what we can't do here—make a good-looking, fairly richly decorated gun that sells at a decent price. These Japanese-made guns are very good in quality, not excellent, far from superb. But they are available, they are priced within reason, and they perform well and look good.

In my opinion you're going to see more of this happening. At least for a while. By this I mean that costs in Japan are already skyrocketing by the standards of the 50s and 60s so the time will probably come soon when the cost of labor in Japan is as high as it is here. As "second-world" countries move into the "first world" and "third worlders" move to "second-world" status, these gaps are going to narrow. It's also a reminder of the days when the American textile industry moved from New England to the Southeast where labor was cheap. They were followed by dozens of other industries. But that's pretty well leveled off now and the same thing will be repeated across the globe if present events continue.

The wise gun buyer will continue to shop around. Right now, in 1977, you can get some good buys in high-quality guns being made in parts of Europe and Asia, not to mention an occasional American product. Prudent buying, provided you know your merchandise, can get you some fine investments that will appreciate as time goes along.

This situation is about the same as it was 30 years ago when the smart guys with some money were buying English shotguns. Try to find one today.

CHAPTER THREE

SEMI-AUTOMATIC BREECH ACTIONS

A ll you have to do to shoot a semiautomatic gun is pull the trigger each time you want the gun to fire. That means the gun does all the rest of the work. To put it another way, the energy developed by firing the gun performs six of the seven steps of operation (all except firing).

In an automatic gun (machine or submachine gun), all seven steps are performed automatically. There are a number of words used interchangeably here, and one term used improperly. A semiautomatic is often referred to as "autoloader," "autoloading," or "self-loading." All these terms are used; they all mean the same thing; and all are correct. The word automatic is often incorrectly used for the semiauto and this is a mistake. It is in such common use, as automatic pistol or automatic shotgun, however, that some acceptance of the term is obvious. The important thing to remember is that it's in error and that only a machine gun—that is a *fully automatic mechanism*—should be called automatic.

Two basic methods of utilizing the firing energy to work the action are employed. These are recoil, meaning the kick of the gun; and gas, meaning that the same gas that drives the shot charge is used to work the action. There are numerous variations, but those are the two basic forces employed.

While there are many ways to use the gas supply, all modern gas guns operate by bleeding off a little gas to drive a piston which, in turn, works the action. Recoil operation, on the other hand, breaks down into two basic types—short

27

The world's first recoil-operated shotgun was the Browning, patented in 1900. This is a photo of the first "Browning Auto-5," a model that is still in the Browning line and has been one of the most popular guns ever made. Guns on the same patent have been made by Remington, Savage, Franchi, and many others around the world.

For a brief period Browning manufactured a short-recoil shotgun known as the "Double Automatic." Browning went from a steel receiver to an alloy one, with some versions in color, and the market apparently wasn't ready for such a departure. The gun is now obsolete.

The Winchester Model 50 was in the Winchester line during the 1950s but has been dropped. It was an unusual gun in that it used a recoiling chamber *and was thus a recoil-operated gun even though the barrel did not move. A variation of this gun was the Model 59, with a barrel made of glass fibers wrapped around a thin steel tube.*

recoil and long. Then there's still another semi-automatic system, very similar to recoil in most respects but a bit different, called blowback.

The study of how and why various action systems work is fascinating. Keep in mind those seven steps of operation and you won't have any trouble understanding the hows and whys.

RECOIL OPERATION

You know that each time you fire a gun it kicks. That is, it develops recoil which you feel against your shoulder. This is the force that is used to operate a recoil-operated gun. To understand this, visualize a lever-action rifle, like the Model 94 Winchester .30/30. Now visualize this rifle mounted so that the end of its finger lever is secured to something solid, as if you clamped the lever in a vise. Now fire the rifle. You know it will kick, that is recoil, backwards and accomplish the steps of unlocking, extraction, cocking, and ejection.

Take your imagination one step further. Place a heavy spring against the buttstock and fire the rifle again. This time, after the gun has fully recoiled, it also has stored energy in the heavy spring that will now drive the rifle forward again. As it does, it will complete the steps of feeding and locking. It's ready to shoot again. (And if we add something to trip the trigger after the gun is relocked, it will be a fully automatic machine gun.)

In very basic terms, these forces are what operate a recoil-actuated semiautomatic or fully automatic firearm. Naturally, you can't fasten a lever in the vise each time you want to shoot a semiauto gun, so gun designers figured out how to make the mechanism recoil *within* the outside framework of the firearm. Now we have arrived at the real actuation of a recoil-operated gun—the barrel moves. Fixed barrel, no recoil. Moving barrel, recoil.

Sir Hiram Maxim is generally credited with inventing the first recoil-operated gun with the Maxim machine gun. If Maxim found it first, John Browning put it on the map. Maxim's invention was perfected in 1884; during the next 20 years, Browning discovered and perfected gas and blowback operation and designed dozens of recoil-operated mechanisms, many of which are still being used.

Recoil operation breaks down into two somewhat different systems, short recoil and long recoil. The definitions simply mean that in short recoil the barrel moves a very short distance—from about ⅛ to ½ inch depending on the type of gun and the power of the cartridge. In long recoil, the barrel moves all the way to the rear—about 3 inches in a shotgun, more than 1 foot in the 37mm aircraft cannon.

A RECOIL EXCEPTION

I said above that, in a recoil-operated firearm, the barrel moved and that you could always identify the system because of that. Now I have an exception. At one time, during the period 1950 to 1960, Winchester manufactured a shotgun known as the Model 50, which was based on an unusual operating principle. It had a fixed barrel, but it was still recoil-operated because the barrel had a recoiling chamber. That is, *part* of the barrel moved (which really means that the definition remains valid), and that part activated the action in the usual manner of a recoil-operated gun. This model did not achieve the desired sales goals and was dropped. It's mentioned here because its action was exceptional.

The Model 50 led a few years later to the Model 59 which had, in addition to that movable chamber, a most unique barrel. It was made of a very thin steel tube reinforced by wrapping in *glass*. Many miles of glass fiber were wrapped around the tube to produce the finished barrel. It made a very muzzle-light gun that swung

Details of the Model 50's unique operation are shown in these diagrams. The recoiling chamber, within the barrel, moved back a short distance to operate the gun.

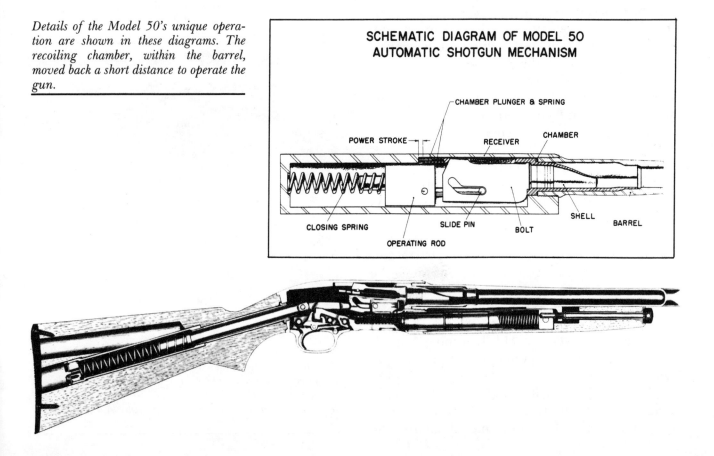

nicely, but it, too, didn't make much of a dent in the market. Sometimes it's hard to know just why guns fail in the market. So far as I know there were no operational problems with this gun; I used one for a while but not enough to spot any problems. The public just didn't get turned on and the model was dropped.

Another gun that saw some activity during the same period was the Browning Double Automatic, an invention of Val Browning, son of the famous John. The double automatic, a two-shot capacity short-recoil operated shotgun, was introduced in 1958 and dropped from the line during the 1960s. While this gun was technically a short-recoil operated gun, it differed from the usual short recoil. Normally, a short-recoil gun lets the barrel recoil a very short distance, at which point the barrel is stopped firmly while the bolt is allowed to proceed all the way to the rear unescorted. But this Browning gun let the barrel recoil about 1½ inches with Magnum loads and about 1 inch with field or target loads before unlocking. There was therefore an automatic adjustment for the different loads. The unlocking phase was performed by an inertia weight running from the bolt down into a tube inside the buttstock, which will explain why unlocking could be achieved in different positions.

When introduced, the Browning double automatic used a steel receiver and optional aluminum receivers. A little later they dropped the steel entirely and concentrated on the aluminum, but neither one survived.

LONG-RECOIL OPERATION

Long-recoil operation differs from short recoil primarily in the distance the barrel moves. As explained earlier, the barrel of a short-recoil gun moves from about ⅛ inch to a maximum of about ½ inch. In a long-recoil system, barrel and breechbolt, locked together tightly, move all the way to the rear as a unit.

Without question the best known long-recoil operated gun is the Browning Auto-5 shotgun. This was the invention Mr. Browning himself called his greatest achievement. The gun was patented in 1900 and guns under this patent were made in the U.S. by Remington and Savage, in Belgium under the Browning brand name, and in countless other makes and models all over the

The Browning Auto-5 in locked position ready to fire. Note that breech bolt is fully forward. (Browning Arms Corp. made its cut-a-way gun available for these photos.)

The same gun in full recoil position. Note that barrel and bolt are both *fully to the rear. The same action has shoved the hammer back down into cocked position; it also has stored energy in the recoil under the barrel and in the bolt spring inside the butt.*

Close-up view of the Auto-5 in full recoil. The pointer shows the part called the "dog," which will hold bolt to the rear. The barrel is now free to fly forward separately and strip itself off the empty cartridge, which will then be ejected. When the barrel moves forward, it will release a new cartridge from the magazine which, in turn, will release the bolt to move forward, chamber the fresh cartridge, and lock itself in the barrel.

world. Browning Arms has no way of determining how many autoloading guns have been made under this patent, except that there are "many millions," nearly 2 million in the Browning brand alone.

Mr. Browning's difficulty in designing the autoloading shotgun was the immense variety of loads on the market which were inconsistent in pressures developed and which, in those days, included black-powder loads. This posed much greater problems than designing an autoloading rifle with one standard load and pressure. Browning solved the problem, and he did so in such a way that it was not till 54 years later that another successful functioning autoloading shotgun of different design was developed.

The definition of a moving barrel still holds, but you can easily tell a long-recoil shotgun because you can push the barrel back about 3 inches. The easiest way to do this is to place the muzzle on the floor and shove down on the gun's butt.

Let's follow the Browning autoloading shotgun through its operational phases and note how it differs from short recoil.

1. Firing is accomplished by pulling the trigger, which releases a hammer that strikes the firing pin in the breechbolt.

2. Unlocking. Before getting into the actual step of unlocking, let's explain that the barrel is permanently fitted into a barrel extension which rides inside the receiver. The breechbolt itself is locked to the barrel extension, so barrel and bolt are firmly fastened when locked. The recoil of the gun forces the barrel, barrel extension, and breechblock to the rear while locked. At the very end of this rearward stroke, the lock is cammed down out of engagement with the barrel extension and at the same time the breechbolt is caught in its rear position. At this point barrel and barrel extension are freed and permitted to return forward under tension of the big recoil spring located under the barrel within the forearm.

3. Extraction and *4. Ejection* occur as the barrel moves forward. Instead of the standard method of using the bolt to withdraw the empty cartridge from the barrel, this gun reverses the procedure and, with the bolt stationary, the barrel strips itself off the empty cartridge case. When the barrel has moved forward far enough, the ejector spins the empty out of the gun.

5. Cocking is also performed during this rearward stroke of recoiling by shoving the hammer down. Browning invented a very neat, safe way to catch the trigger in this gun. There is a u-shaped top to the trigger, with a sear hook on each inside of the top of the u. The hammer is designed with a double sear notch so that in the recoil stroke, while the trigger is still in "pulled" position, the rear sear notch catches in the rear of the u. After the gun is reloaded automatically, the trigger is relaxed and moves forward and up slightly to engage its forward sear with the hammer's front sear notch. The illustration will help explain this novel feature that accomplishes disconnection and prevents a full-automatic operation.

6. Feeding occurs when, still on its forward stroke, the barrel strikes a latch that releases a cartridge from the magazine, permitting it to slide to the rear onto the carrier for feeding. As the cartridge reaches the loaded position on the carrier it hits another latch, which releases the bolt. Now the bolt is free to move ahead, under tension of its spring (in a tube inside the buttstock). As the bolt moves ahead it drives the new cartridge into the chamber.

7. Locking. During the final movement of the bolt, the lock is driven up into its locking position in the barrel extension. The gun is now ready to fire again.

Browning's solution to the thorny problem of the many different cartridges giving varied pressures was neatly solved by a method still employed in the guns using his system. The solution was simply to place a friction ring ahead of the heavy recoil spring in a way that it would grip the magazine tube more tightly when high-velocity cartridges were used. When standard or field loads are used, the friction piece is reversed (sometimes removed, depending on the model) and the barrel is permitted to recoil without further restriction. This has the effect of leveling out the charges and producing more or less the same force of recoil to operate the mechanism without damaging the gun. We do not have the variety of ammunition today that existed in 1900, but there is a wide variation in force between Mag-

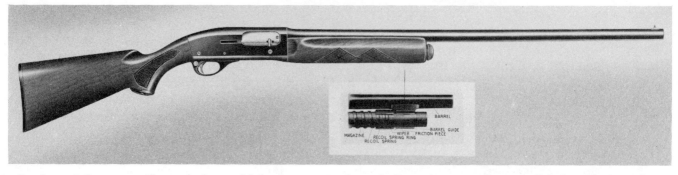

Remington's Sportsman 48 was the last model that company made on the Browning-patent long-recoil design. The inset shows the friction collar that provided adjustment for heavy vs. light loads in all guns made under this Browning patent system.

num and field or target loads today, and the friction ring is still required for the hot ones or the gun will recoil so hard that internal parts can be damaged.

Long-recoil guns have an operating handle which, when pulled to the rear, unlocks the action and allows you to retract the breechbolt without having to pull back the whole barrel against the pressure of the strong recoil spring. This is merely a convenience and it is only when the gun is fired that barrel and bolt remain locked for the entire rearward stroke.

The trend today is away from recoil operation in shotguns; nearly all the new guns are gas operated. The major recoil guns are the Browning Auto-5 and the excellent Franchi, a Stoeger import. I've been shooting a delightful Franchi 20 gauge that is said to be the lightest such gun in the world. And I believe it. It is the slickest autoloading field gun I've seen in a long time — and it, too, operates on the Browning system.

It is claimed by some that the trend to gas is correct; others claim that it ain't necessarily so and that there's nothing wrong with long recoil, that we should not abandon this great old system entirely. I frankly doubt we'll live to see the end of recoil-operated shotguns and I hope we don't. I've a great respect for the gas gun, but something of a sentimental respect for the great recoil guns that have never let us down going back to 1900.

GAS OPERATION

The story goes that when John Browning watched the muzzle gases blowing leaves and grass on the firing range it occurred to him that this force could be applied and harnessed to work the mechanism of an automatic system.

Whether the story is true or not, John Browning did harness the propellant gases and make them work to operate a gun action. He first adapted an old Winchester .44-caliber rifle by placing a small cap over the muzzle with a hole for the bullet to pass through. The cap was connected to a rod that operated the lever just the way a lever-action rifle operated. Next he drilled a small hole near the muzzle underneath the barrel and filed for patent in 1890. The world's first gas-operated gun was an adapted .44/40 Winchester lever action that could fire 16 shots a second (that was the full magazine). Next he refined the design and made a .45/70 machine gun that was demonstrated to Colt and military officials. It fired 1,800 rounds in a little more than 3 minutes without a hitch.

The first practical, operational gas gun design was a Browning pistol that was offered to Colt, accepted, but never put in production because new Browning ideas came so fast that they were considered more marketable. Next, Browning perfected the gas-operated machine gun of 1895, which saw much service in the U.S. armed forces and was known as the "potato digger," because its operation was such that a small amount of gas, bled from the barrel near the muzzle, drove a flapping lever downward which, if too close to the ground, dug into the turf.

Gas-operated shotguns really didn't surface with any degree of popularity until the mid-1950s. The real trend setter was Remington's Model 58, which operated in what had become,

The first of the new breed of gas autos was Remington's Model 1100, a unique operational system that has changed gas-gun design throughout the industry. Remington used an oversize piston, which, when in motion, suspended the felt recoil. The result was a slightly longer time span over which recoil was felt, making the gun seem to have less recoil.

by this time, conventional gas operation (referring to successful gas designs of the past such as the 1918 BAR, the M1 Garand, Hotchkiss, and other machine guns). These guns all utilized a gas cylinder slung underneath the barrel with a small hole to bleed off gas after the propellant passed the bleed hole, allowing that gas to enter the cylinder and push the piston back to operate the action.

Model 58 therefore operated in this conventional way. The cylinder was actually the front of the magazine tube and, aside from limiting magazine capacity to 3 shots, it had few disadvantages. Frankly, I see no disadvantage to a limit of 3 shots for any purpose, but that was considered a drawback to the 58; another problem was that the parts built up a caked fouling which had to be chipped off on occasion. The 58 is now gone. It has been replaced by a superior design, the first of the modern gas guns and the one that truly revolutionized gas shotguns.

The gun is the Remington 1100 and the head

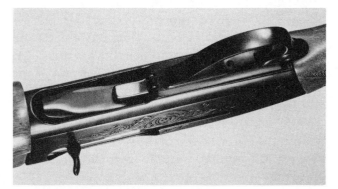

The bottom of Remington's Model 11 shows the small latch (at the rear, center of the lifters) that is pushed in to permit the bolt to close after loading and to permit loading the magazine. Most modern gas shotguns copy this feature in one way or another.

of the design team responsible for it was Wayne Leek. It was long known that gas operation had an interesting side benefit: it reduced apparent recoil sometimes expressed as "felt recoil." This refers to the fact that you cannot actually reduce recoil, because every force must have an equal and opposite reaction and so forth, but you can reduce the *effect* of recoil. And that's what Remington set about to do with the 1100.

You notice at once when you heft an 1100 that it's a pretty heavy gun, and it's obvious that this extra weight helps soak up some recoil. But there's a lot more to it than that. Leek designed the 1100's gas cylinder oversize, so oversize that it surrounds the magazine tube. The piston is a ring sliding back and forth on the tube. This piston unit is quite heavy; here's how it helps reduce recoil effect.

After the shot charge passes the bleed hole,

The Remington 1100 has a large gas cylinder and employs two gas ports to bleed gas from the barrel. The piston itself is also large and is positioned outside the magazine tube.

Winchester's newest gas gun is the Super-X Model I; it operates similarly to the Remington 1100 except that the piston stroke is a short, fast one. A comfortable gun to shoot, the "Super" is available in a number of grades. Shown is the Trap Model.

gas is fed into the big cylinder and sets the heavy piston in motion. It takes time for that big piston to move. You actually feel part of the gun's recoil right away, but not all of it because there are those heavy parts in motion (piston, rods, bolt) as you begin to feel recoil. A fraction of a second after you have felt initial recoil, the moving parts stop their back stroke and you get the rest of the recoil. So it's a matter of timing. The net effect is that recoil is spread over a longer time period. While it's the same amount of total recoil, it doesn't feel as heavy because it's been spread over a longer time period. It's really quite simple, ingenious, and practical. It makes the 1100 very pleasant to shoot at a day-long session at trap or skeet.

Since the 1100, many guns have adopted similar systems. The 1100 is also self-metering; to put it another way, shoot whatever loads you please so long as they are the correct gauge and size for the chamber. You need make no adjustments for light or heavy loads, nor do you have to clean the parts, because the 1100 is self-cleaning. It does achieve some buildup of powder residue but when it reaches a certain point the cak-

ing gets blown off automatically. The self-metering is accomplished by the weight of the piston: Light loads cause the piston to move slower, which allows more pressure buildup; heavy loads move it faster because the gas pressure buildup is quicker.

The Remington 1100 will eventually go down in history as almost as important an invention as the Browning Auto, because it pioneered a gas system that was sufficiently different and that reduced recoil beyond other known limits. Its system has been copied by so many other guns that its position as the trend setter is molded in concrete.

Early in 1977, Remington introduced a new, lightweight 20-gauge version of the Model 1100, which will be a joy to field and skeet shooters, especially the former where toting an 1100 has been somewhat rugged duty. The 1100 soaks up recoil, but it has always been a heavy gun. Remington has lightened this new model by scaling down the basic steel rather than switching to an alloy. The result, in the field model, is a nice-handling 6¼ pounds for 2¾-inch ammo and 6¾ pounds in the skeet model (you want more

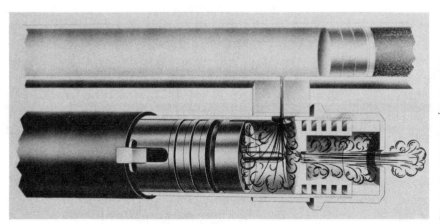

Browning's new Model 2000 uses a more or less conventional system, in that the cylinder and piston are located inside the front of the magazine tube. In this sketch, the shot charge has moved past the gas port and gas is entering the cylinder. Once the piston has moved a certain distance (and achieved a certain velocity), gas is permitted to vent out the front as a sort of exhaust relief. This is a new system and a good one.

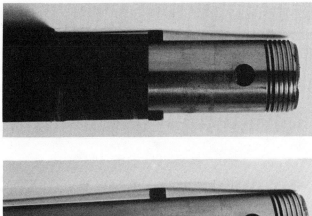

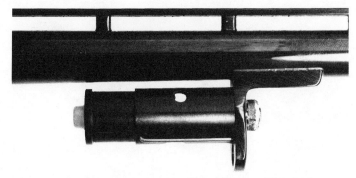

Nearly everyone's gas system is a little different. This is the Ithaca Model 51 shotgun, which bleeds gas from the barrel into the conventional cylinder. The piston, at left, is shown at its rear stroke and the hole you see is a vent to exhaust excess gas. This kind of a system is known as "impinging," which simply means the piston gives the operating parts a swift whack and sets them on their way. The alternate system is known as "expanding" and permits pressure to be gradually increased.

The gas cylinder of the Browning 2000 viewed from the top. In the top picture, note that the bar that is visible sticking out of the magazine tube on either side rests against the operating tube. In the bottom illustration, the bar has driven the operating tube to the rear and the bar has returned forward. In firing, gas enters the big hole and drives the piston and bar back to activate the autoloading system.

weight in a skeet gun, which is fired over long periods and you don't carry the gun very far).

Another point is that Remington has gone to mahogany in field models of this gun while retaining walnut in skeet models "to match the appearance of other 1100 skeet guns." Since walnut has been so traditional and substitute woods have almost always been used on promotional and private branded guns, this departure, while not new, is pretty significant. It may suggest things to come since sycamore, elm, and birch have also been used, among other woods, in the past. That "walnut finished hardwood" copy line might be employed more in the future.

This lightweight 20 appears much like any other 1100 until you place it next to a 12 gauge. Then the scaledown becomes noticeable indeed. About ¼ inch shallower through the receiver and ⅛ inch narrower. This may not sound like much, but it cuts weight noticeably and appears more than those figures might suggest. The receiver is also a bit shorter, but not all that

much, since the 2¾-inch 20 gauge is the same length as the 2¾-inch 12 gauge.

Remington plans to produce these guns with a variety of barrel lengths and chokes, plain or vent rib, and there is a 3-inch Magnum model sporting a recoil pad. The new gun (my sample is a field model with 25-inch ventilated rib Improved Cylinder barrel) shoots well, patterns well, and is a joy to shoot. For those who like an autoloader for upland gunning this ought to be a fine answer.

Despite the many types of autoloading operation available to gun designers, all auto shotguns use either gas or long recoil. So far as I know, no popular shotgun was ever made using short recoil; and blowback operation is impractical for shotgun design and has never been employed.

For any practical purpose, gas shotguns perform the seven steps of operation in the same way as the pump gun described in the last chapter. If you simply substitute the gas piston for the pump handle, your picture of how the gun works will be correct.

To borrow another comparison, the gas system works precisely the same as an internal combustion engine, in which the piston works to help drive the car engine's crankshaft. In the gun, the piston thrust is to the rear and it works the action, storing energy in heavy springs for the return stroke.

CHAPTER FOUR

BREECH-ACTION LOCKING SYSTEMS

It should be clear by now that the breech end of a gun barrel must be securely locked at the moment of firing so that the pressures generated may be contained within the gun. To open the action too soon would allow gas, under dangerously high pressure, to spill into the action. It would also deprive the shot charge of part of its propelling push. Guns are locked in a variety of ways, most of which are ingenious. Many of them are also quite plain, simple, and obvious.

A locking system must not only contain the generated pressure, but must continue to do so for many years and many thousands of shots. That a lockup will safely contain one shot counts for little if it weakens sufficiently to fail in a matter of a few more shots. Similarly, a locking system required to hold only light field loads will not be adequate to retain some of the Magnum loads on the market. Most of today's guns are strong enough to handle nearly any shotgun ammunition being made today, so this is a small problem. Where the problem does exist, though, is in some of the older double guns, which were made for extremely light loads. The only safe rule to follow is to use ammunition for which the gun is made, assuming a gun of current manufacture. If it's an older gun, and an import, you had best consult an expert who will be able to decipher the proof marks and tell what ammunition to use.

The simplest lock found on any shotgun today is probably the bolt action. We call this a turning-

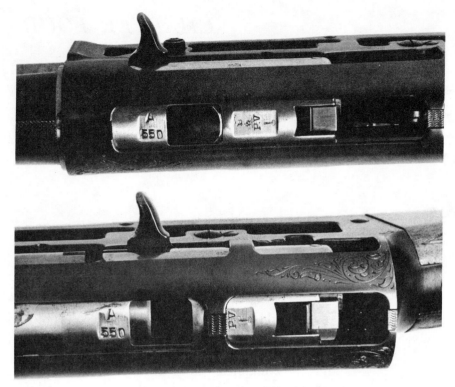

At top, the Browning Auto-5 in locked position, viewed from the top of the cutaway action. The locking block is visible as the dark area to the right of the number "A 550" and the surface against which the lug bears is part of the barrel extension seen just to the left of the proof mark. The gun's parts are in firing position. Below, the same parts unlocked. Note that the locking block has been lowered out of its notch in the barrel extension and that the bolt is now free to move within the barrel extension. In this photo the parts are in nearly full-recoil position.

bolt lock, and it's based on the design of Peter Paul Mauser of Mauser rifle fame.

BOLT ACTION

While the high-power rifle requires a strong system of locking lugs on its bolt, the same is not true of the shotgun. The reason is that a shotgun does not develop anywhere near the chamber pressure that a high-power rifle cartridge, such as the .300 Winchester Magnum, does. As a matter of fact, the shotgun bolt locks like a .22 rifle, by using the shank of the bolt handle itself to turn down into a recess in the receiver. This is adequate locking for the shotgun; it's larger for a 12 gauge than a .410, naturally, but the gun must be larger too, so things are pretty much in scale.

Another turning-bolt lockup system is seen in the Ithaca Model 51, a unique design by Jim Tollinger. This is a gas autoloading shotgun that locks by a slight turning of the bolt so three fairly small lugs on the bolt's side may be turned into their locking recesses in the receiver. You can't call that system a bolt action, but its locking principle is derived from the bolt action just the same. We say that because any rotating bolt

lockup, no matter how it's arranged, is a derivation of the basic rotary bolt. Three small lugs appear on the lower left edge of the Model 51's bolt and engage three corresponding recesses in the barrel extension along the left side of the receiver. These are plainly visible when the bolt is open. To unlock, the bolt rotates very slightly to the left, about 10°-12° and just enough to disengage, whereupon the bolt moves backwards freely.

This is as good a place as any to discuss the difficulty of machining several surfaces of a locking system so they all bear and bear evenly. It is a hard thing to accomplish. If you examine most bolts from standard bolt-action rifles, you will find it a rare case indeed when more than half of the second lug bears. The same thing is true when multiple lug systems are used. It's rare when more than 1½ lugs bear, even if it's a 9-lug system! Consequently, *any* multiple lug system—which means any gun action employing more than two locking surfaces—should be examined with a critical eye to make sure these surfaces are really bearing.

Neither the true bolt action nor the rotary bolt has much application to shotguns, primarily because shotguns do not need the massive locking support required by some high-pressure rifle cartridges.

ROCKING WEDGES

The rocking wedge lock is a locking block that rocks up and down, on the approximate order of a rocking chair, in a manner that it engages the barrel and bolt in locked position. This method is used in the Browning patent auto-loading shotguns (which includes the long-recoil guns once made in this country by Remington as Model 11 and Savage as Model 720 plus the Auto-5 Browning and a number of other imports made under these patents) as well as the earlier Stevens Models 520 and 620, also Browning patents.

In these guns the barrel is fitted into a barrel extension which extends into the receiver and into which the bolt moves. The barrel extension has a square notch in its upper surface which is a locking notch. When moved forward to firing position, the breechbolt contains the rocking wedge lock which is shoved up into the recess to lock the breech. In the auto guns, the rear end of this rocking wedge is connected to the breechbolt spring and the bolt itself is driven forward by this spring, through the connecting rod and lock. Once the bolt reaches lock position the rocking wedge slips up into the locking recess and securely fastens bolt and barrel together. The locked position also provides a clear opening for the firing pin (which isn't permitted to fire the gun unless the lock is fully engaged).

A locking arrangement that is quite similar is seen in those actions with a slide and sliding

These locking parts from an Ithaca Model 37 show an old and excellent locking system in which a slide is used under the breech bolt. At top, the bolt is pulled down out of locking engagement, and the raised rear hump of the bolt is the locking surface that engages either receiver top or a barrel extension. The slide is connected to the operating pump handle and pulls the bolt's rear end up and down, as a study of the bottom photo will show; in this photo the bolt is in locked position, solidly supported by the slide.

breech. The slide is defined as a part that is connected to the operating rod (all present applications to my knowledge are pump guns) and the sliding breech is the breech bolt that rests on top of the slide.

In the Stevens and Savage guns, the slide moves forward after the bolt (sliding breech) has come to rest, and in this last movement of approximately 1/4 inch the slide pushes the rear end of the bolt up into locking engagement with a notch in the barrel extension at the top of the action. A variation in the system may be seen in the Marlin Model 120 pump shotgun, in which the lock is at the front end of the bolt and is raised into locked position similarly, except that the bolt doesn't rock *up*, as in the older Browning designs, but remains stationery. Only the lock itself moves into engagement and this is positioned at the forward end of the bolt.

There is no particular advantage to one system over the other; both work well.

The barrel extension of a typical pump or autoloading shotgun, showing the barrel itself at the left, permanently fastened to the extension. The open area near the right hand of the extension is the locking surface. This system permits interchangeable barrels without factory fitting and it permits the use of alloy (aluminum) receivers, since the bolt locks to the steel barrel extension.

HUMP LOCK

This is a locking system in which the rear edge of the breechbolt top has a hump that is moved up into a recess or against a shoulder to lock the action. Common examples are the Winchester Model 12 and Ithaca Model 37 shotguns.

Winchester's famous Model 12 pump gun is one of the more famous guns employing this hump lock. So was the now-obsolete Model 42 Winchester .410 pump gun. These guns have set endurance records that are hard to equal. The locking is accomplished simply by shoving the rear end of the bolt up into a notch in the receiver as the bolt is fully closed. The system is adaptable to pump and lever actions and doubtless could be employed by other systems as well. Unlocking is just the reverse; the rear of the breech bolt is lowered by the first movement of the opening stroke.

PURDEY UNDERLOCKS

Most side-by-side double-barreled shotguns are locked underneath the barrels by a sliding bar that moves back, to unlock, and forward to slide into engagement with the barrel lumps and hold

Most double guns are locked by an underbolt that slips into the two surfaces, called bites, that you see in the rear surface of the underlugs, called lumps, under the barrels. This particular gun, a Victor Sarasqeta high-grade 12 bore, also has a top extension, which you see protruding between the barrels. The top lever activates a locking block in the frame that moves across the top of this extension to help hold the barrels down.

the barrels down onto the action bar. Invented by the famous London gunmaker James Purdey, the system is still referred to as "Purdey locks." In many ways this has always disturbed me, since the reference to Purdey locks (Holland & Holland side locks, Anson & Deeley system, etc.) seems a direct attempt to ride on the coattails of these famous names in London gunmaking. Often, the quality of guns that claim to have "Purdey locks" or "Holland & Holland side-locks" needs every bit of help it can get. But I think it's a cheap way to exploit a famous name rather than to offer an accurate description of the type of locking employed (which wouldn't mean much to the prospective buyer anyway).

Be that as it may, the locking system worked out by James Purdey is simple, foolproof, and has lasted for years. Purdey, by the way, is still in business in London and still making fine double guns.

Although it includes a top extension, the illustration of my Victor Sarasqueta shows how simple the Purdey locking bolt is and how it works. The English, however, like a "clean" breech with nothing protruding if possible. Remember also that the British sportsman rarely uses anything like a Magnum, or even a heavy load. He knows he doesn't need it (and he's right!) so it's possible to build a light gun without locking gadgets that aren't necessary. When you're shooting small birds, such as grouse or pheasant, at relatively close distances you don't need heavy loads. Consequently, English makers often made 12-gauge guns chambered for the 2-inch cartridge firing a light load with a light shot charge. Its chief advantage was that you could build a very light gun, and therefore one that could be handled very quickly. According to Holland & Holland, such a gun, in 12 gauge with 28-inch barrels, would weigh approximately 5½ pounds.

The Purdey locking-bolt system is perfectly adequate in any well-made English gun for the ammunition for which the gun was made. Added locking is used in most English guns chambered for heavier cartridges such as pigeon guns. A pigeon gun (or pigeon-grade gun) is designed for live-pigeon shooting, a very expensive sport in which the bird, thrown by hand by a skilled thrower who can make the flight of the bird uncertain and erratic, must be killed before

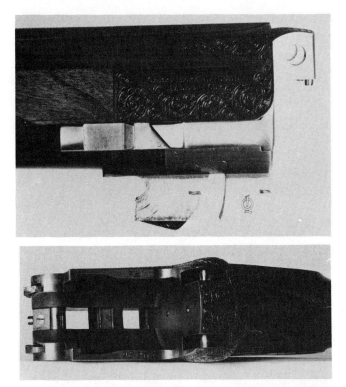

An over/under gun with underlug bolting and a top extension. Top, the underlugs and the top extension with a round hole. Below, the frame of this gun (with top lever in closed position). A careful look will disclose the locking surfaces in the bottom of the frame as well as the round locking bolt near the top of the frame. This gun is a Merkel, imported by Champlin Firearms, Enid, Oklahoma.

it flies over a circular fence. The pigeon gun is full-choked and carries a heavy shot charge. There is often a large amount of money riding on each bird, and with only two shots available to the shooter, he wants to drop that bird in the area that counts.

Holland & Holland also offer a treble-grip gun, a form of barrel extension located between the extractors (which keeps it out of the way of loading), fitting into the action face where it is held in place. Westley Richards offered a similar extension locking. W. W. Greener, however, probably produced the strongest locking system in a double gun, which he called the "patent treble wedge fast," a fancy name for an extension made as part of the barrels which fitted into a slot in the action face where a round cross bolt fitted into the extension. When correctly fitted, it is a very strong system. As Greener was careful to point out, since his system was copied by dozens of less capable workmen, unless properly

The Italian-made Beretta over/under is one of those shallow-frame guns with locking lugs between the barrels that extend forward out of the frame when the action is closed. The massive lugs seen here on the barrels, with corresponding recesses in the frame, also assist in holding the force of firing. In opening the gun, the barrels, of course, pivot around the hinge pin, but the tendency during recoil is for the gun to bend at the bottom of the action face. Since this force describes a different arc, the lugs shown help hold the barrels in a locked position.

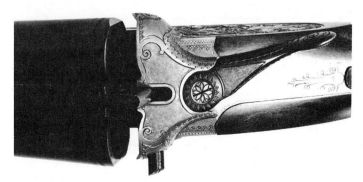

The Merkel side-by-side sidelock shotgun has a top extension and crossbolt locking in addition to the underbolting. Provided all lugs bear evenly (which is difficult to achieve), this is a very strong system. Note that this action has "side clips," the small, angled projections at either side of the action face that help hold the barrels securely from side-to-side movement.

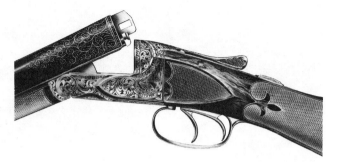

An original Ansley H. Fox high-grade double that uses only a top extension lock. When closed, the locking surfaces in the frame move through the slot seen in the top extension. The L.C. Smith also employed only a top extension for its locking with no under bolting. Both guns were American.

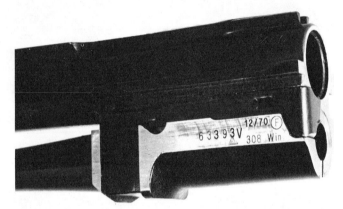

A rather unusual system of joining barrels to frame is seen in this Savage combination gun with 12-gauge barrel on top, .308-Winchester barrel on the bottom. The barrels tip in conventional fashion, but are dismounted by lifting straight up and off a square lug in the frame. Locking is via a sliding breech cap that moves forward over the rear end of the barrels similar to the Remington 3200. This gun is made in Finland by Valmet.

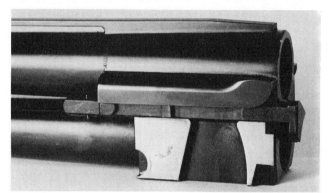

fitted any system of multiple locks is useless. Moreover, some of the Greener adaptations utilized square bolts instead of round. And, as Greener also correctly stated, the use of a square hole in a given surface is much weaker than a round hole. Not to mention the added difficulty of fitting four sides correctly.

A somewhat similar bolting system is used on the Continent and has been well popularized by such fine guns as the Merkel. Known as the Kersten lock, the system employs an extension on each side of the top barrel (over/under guns) with corresponding round-bolt fastening within the action frame.

Remington's 3200 is locked by a slide over the top of the frame that slides forward to lock the barrels down in place when the action is closed. Most of the strain of firing is absorbed by a large lug on either side of the frame, which fits into the gap formed by the two lugs you see on the lower barrel just below the ejector rod. One of the newest designs in an over/under gun, this is a very strong lockup.

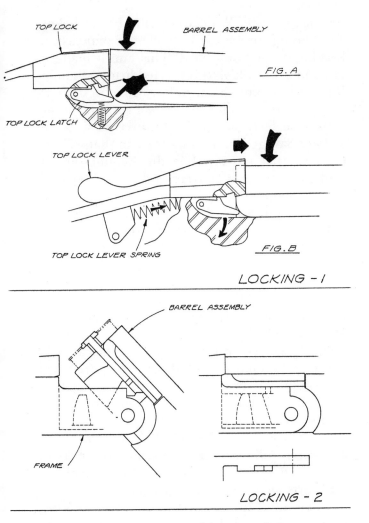

LOCKING - 1

LOCKING - 2

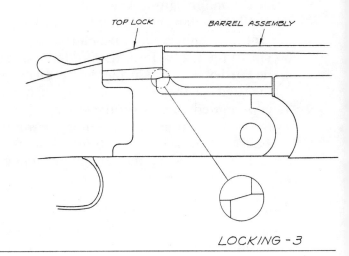

LOCKING - 3

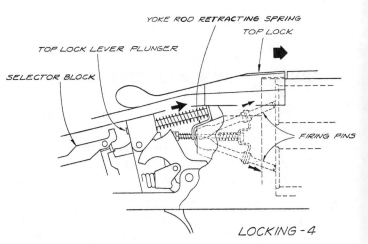

LOCKING - 4

The Remington 3200 is one of the newest designs, and contains considerable modern engineering. The sketches and following descriptions of its lockup are directly from Remington engineering.

1. Just prior to complete closing of the action, but after the top of the barrel assembly clears the top lock, a radius located on the right rear section of the barrel assembly cams the top lock latch downward (Fig. A), releasing the top lock and under action of its spring forces the top lock forward and over the top section of the barrel assembly, securely locking the system. (Fig. B).

2. As closing of the action takes place a large locking lug located on each side of the barrel assembly engages a mating set of lugs in the frame. These lugs are so designed to withstand the thrust load during firing.

3. The lower front section of the top lock contains a cam which in turn engages a mating cam on the barrel assembly. These two cams effectively wedge the locking system of the top lock and barrel assembly into a tight unit and through their action tend to keep the system tight regardless of wear in this area through continued use.

4. As the top lock is released to a normal position during the locking cycle the top lock lever plunger moves forward, eliminating the blocking action of the selector block. The yoke rod retracting spring is also released to a forward position, allowing the two firing pins to move forward so that the nose of each pin is resting on the primer of each shell with a spring force of 4 oz. This feature nullifies marked primers and a jar-off condition in case the gun is accidently dropped.

The gun is now ready for firing.

Two London gunmakers, Woodward and Boss, pioneered the bifurcated-lump locking system for over/under, which permitted the reduction in action height. Instead of underlocking, as in the Purdey system, a smaller lock (or half lock) was located on the side of each set of barrels. This permitted just as strong locking and did away with the bottom lumps entirely, permitting a reduction in action depth of close to ½ inch. The result was a thoroughly pleasing gun with slimmer lines than any conventional underbolted O/U gun, at least to my eyes.

In recent years there have been a number of variations on the Boss or Woodward method; most of them are Italian and use round pegs fitting into mating round holes in the barrels. This is equally excellent in my opinion. One of the leading guns using such a system is the Beretta.

REMINGTON 3200 SLEEVE LOCK

An interesting variation in double-gun locking is seen in the Remington 3200, which employs a sliding top lock that moves the entire top of the frame, or so it appears. Actually this lock extends clear across the frame and is held in place by two lugs that ride back and forth in notches on either side of the frame. When forward in the locked position, this sliding top lock extends to hold the barrels down by a slightly angled surface on either side. The slight angle compensates for wear and the gun can be expected to last for many thousands of shots.

Remington has provided two very stout lugs on either side of the barrels that engage mating lugs on either side of the frame, deep in the U and extending from bottom to top of the lower barrel. These lugs are designed to take the main thrust of firing.

A similar locking system is also seen in the Savage Model 2400. My sample has a 12-gauge barrel on top, .308 Winchester rifle barrel below. The sliding top lock is virtually the same as the Remington just described. This gun is made in Finland by the old and respected firm of Valmet. Valmet has eliminated the lugs Remington employs to take up the thrust of firing, however. This is perfectly acceptable in this case since the Valmet/Savage is a hunting firearm that will not be fired that much, while the Remington will find its major use at skeet and trap, which require much more shooting. Moreover, the added weight is more acceptable in a target gun than a field gun and these lugs do add weight.

It should also be added here that an over/under gun has a much stronger frame than any side-by-side shotgun. The reason being the very deep U-shaped frame, which greatly resists the tendency for the frame to bend during recoil. Moreover, the lower barrel is buried within the U and, particularly in a game gun, the lower barrel is fired much more often (because it's fired first and often only one shot is taken). On the other hand, both barrels on a side-by-side double are positioned above the action bar.

The word lock is often used in shotgunnery in an entirely different context because there are so many takedown shotguns and, when assembled, the parts may be said to be locked together. There is a vast number of different ways this fastening is accomplished. It's not truly locking in the ordinary sense, but it is an important function just the same. I've shown a photo of one of the earlier fastening systems, that of the Winchester Model 12 pump gun. It's a pretty unique system that contains a method of taking up wear by adjusting an inner collar.

A takedown feature in shotguns is handy for storing, shipping, and transporting purposes. The same feature is seldom seen in rifles today because takedown rifles do not usually maintain their accuracy.

CHAPTER FIVE

FEEDING SYSTEMS

Feeding is the act of moving a fresh, unfired cartridge from storage (the magazine) into firing position in the barrel's chamber. In the single-shot or double-barrel firearm, feeding is simply the removal of a new cartridge from your pocket or cartridge box and sticking it into the chamber. But in any repeating mechanism, a different sort of storage must be provided for ammunition; plus a simple, reliable method of moving these stored cartridges into firing position.

There are a number of basic magazine types, all of them invented and in wide use before 1900 and most of them still in use to some degree. These types are tubular (both forward under the barrel and to the rear in the buttstock), box (removable and fixed), rotary, gravity hoppers, belts, and drums. All repeating shotguns use tubular magazines, under the barrel, with the single exception of those few bolt-action guns on the market, so we will not concern ourselves with the other types of feeding systems.

A shotgun cartridge poses unique feeding problems due to its shape. Its front end is as flat as a barn door. When a nicely rounded cartridge is pointed in the general direction of the chamber, it will be fed pretty easily. But a flat-nosed cartridge, like a shotgun shell, must be raised from its magazine in an attitude that will reliably guide it into the chamber.

Also keep in mind that any good feeding system must work whether the gun is held right side up or upside down, or on either side, and you begin to appreciate the designer's dilemma   45

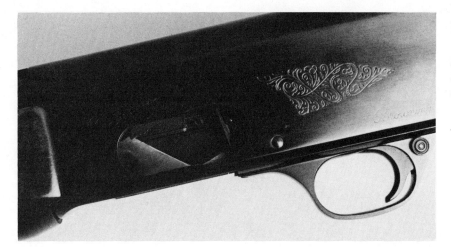

An innovative loading method is seen in the Browning Model 2000 shown here. With the bolt retracted, simply feed a shotgun cartridge into this port on the left side. The feeding causes the bolt to slam shut and the gun is ready to fire. Very handy when you want to keep the gun unloaded until you're ready to shoot.

A Winchester Model 12 with cartridge on the carrier. When the slide handle is fully retracted, it will move the bolt back which will force the rear of the carrier down, raising the front end with the cartridge. Then, the forward movement will chamber the cartridge and force the carrier down again.

when it comes to incorporating a reliable feeding system.

If you own a pump shotgun and work the action very slowly with a live cartridge (which should only be done at the range with the gun safely pointed downrange) you will note that feeding is very precise as to positioning of the cartridge. You will also note there is a tendency for the cartridge to jam when the action is worked slowly but that it won't when you slam the action. You must *always* slam a pump action.

TUBULAR MAGAZINES

This is the type of magazine used on every repeating shotgun except the bolt action. Both pumps and autos use it, and the system has many advantages for these action systems. It is under the barrel and out of the way where it won't interfere with anything and it holds enough supply for any purpose. (Federal regulations for

migratory bird shooting call for a maximum of three shots, meaning two in the magazine and one in the gun, which is surely ample for any purpose.) Most guns are usually made to hold 5 2¾-inch cartridges and are furnished with a plug so you can easily alter the magazine to comply with the federal 3-shot maximum. These plugs are easy to mislay, easy to forget, so you should add "plug" to your check list before you take to the duck and goose marshes. As a matter of fact, I make it a rule to leave the plug in since there's little reason to load more than three shots anyway.

Cartridges in the tubular magazine are under spring pressure urging them rearward. They are held in the tube by a part called the shell stop which, at a precise point in the feeding cycle, allows one cartridge to move rearward onto the carrier and then the shell stop again shuts off the magazine to retain the rest in reserve. This applies whether the gun is a pump or auto, since only one cartridge can be fed at a time or the gun will jam. Some guns, the Browning Auto-5 is an example, have a magazine cutoff, the purpose of which is to allow you to keep the magazine in reserve and use the gun as a single loader. This can be a handy feature in certain situations where you want to fire a single shot with a different shot size than those cartridges in your magazine. The alternative would be to fire the gun as a single shot with no magazine in reserve —or to load the first shot with a shot size you might or might not actually want to use. I've never felt this was any real big deal, but it is there if you want to use it. You could, for example, have your magazine loaded with No. 4 shot while sitting in a duck blind and, should a single come in to your decoys, load a single No. 6 cartridge,

in which event you'd have heavier loads for repeat shots if you missed. Frankly I'd rather use 6's all the way for decoyed birds and hold my fire until they were in range.

In the operation of an autoloader you know that you pull the bolt back and it stays there when the gun is empty. Drop in a cartridge, push the button and the carrier slaps up, the bolt slams forward and the load is chambered. If you do this slowly, without a cartridge, you can hold the bolt back and then push the button while very slowly letting the bolt move forward. The first thing that happens is that the carrier flips sharply up. It does so in a way that the nose of the cartridge hits the receiver or barrel extension top which is even with the top of the chamber. The rear end or base of the cartridge

Browning's Auto-5 cutaway with a cartridge being fed into the chamber. The pointer shows the carrier still guiding the cartridge; the bolt is pushing from the rear, and the chamber has the cartridge well centered.

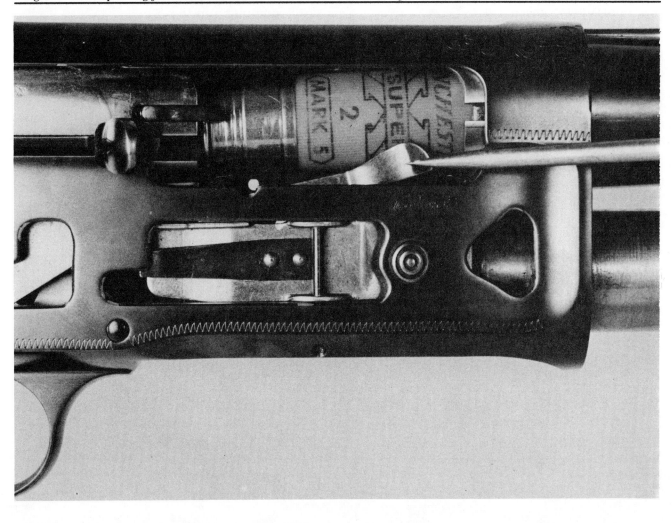

is raised high enough for the bolt to engage it and shove it into the chamber. At the same time most gun mechanisms have a guide to prevent the cartridge from falling out of the ejection port if the gun lies on its right side.

A rather unique loading system is seen in the Browning 2000 gun, which was introduced in 1975 in 12 gauge with a 20 gauge introduced the following year. This gun is a more or less conventional gas autoloader, except that it has a big loading port in the left side of the receiver. With the gun empty you simply slip a cartridge into this opening; there are no buttons to push or anything else. The action closes with a rush and you're ready to go. Just be sure your thumb gets out of the way. You also can unload the gun by picking out the cartridge in this loading port, then allowing the remaining loads in the magazine to slide out into your hand. This is one of the simpler guns to unload; the only criticism of the big loading port is that it's one more place for rain, snow, pine needles, twigs, and other matter to get inside the gun. But anything that allows emptying of a magazine without having to jack the cartridges through the action is not only safer but also preserves the shape of the load. And with a shotgun cartridge that's important.

MAGAZINE CAPACITY

I believe there is an advantage to a large magazine capacity in some rifles. For example, a .30/ 30 carbine that holds seven cartridges in the magazine makes it unnecessary to carry any extra cartridges (in most cases). The full magazine doesn't add enough weight to matter and it's an ideal way to carry your surplus. But the same is not true with a shotgun. First of all you're going to fire more shots with a shotgun — at least you hope you will get more shooting. This means that even if you had a capacity of, say, ten loads, that would not be enough to take afield. So you will have to carry extra ammo anyway, and it's my feeling the fewer cartridges you have in the magazine the better off you are for several reasons. First, there's no need in the world for more than three shots and little need for more than two. Second, the more you stuff the magazine the more weight you add, which makes the gun slower to swing. Balance is what's vital in a shotgun, as opposed to sheer weight. You must keep the bulk of the weight between your hands, and the more shells you stuff in the magazine tube the farther out you're spreading the weight. I suggest the upland gunner will be better off and will have better shooting if he carries those extra loads in his pocket and loads the gun with no more than three shots. He'll have a faster pointing gun that way.

BOX MAGAZINE

The box magazine is widely used in rifles but only in the bolt action among shotguns. These customarily hold just two cartridges because, with one in the chamber, it becomes a three-shot repeater to comply with federal regulations. In the shotgun, a box magazine is clumsy and awkward, because two cartridges plus the necessary follower and spring are deeper than the stock. The result is that the magazine box hangs down roughly ½ inch, which looks atrocious and which comes right at the balance of the gun where you'd want to carry it in one hand.

CHAPTER SIX

EXTRACTION AND EJECTION SYSTEMS

Extraction and ejection are so often confused that the point bears repeating. Extraction is the act of withdrawing the cartridge from the gun barrel. Period. Ejection is the flipping out, or removal, of that cartridge from the gun itself.

Extraction is a good deal more complicated than it appears, and much variation in extraction systems occurs, often beyond the eye. There are four basic requirements for satisfactory extraction: (1) a smooth chamber in the gun barrel, the smoother the better; (2) a cartridge case of correct dimensions and proper construction so the rim won't tear out; (3) an extractor hook, or claw, sufficiently large that it won't tear out part of the rim; and (4) satisfactory primary extraction to break the grip a cartridge has gotten on the chamber walls.

EXTRACTION TIMING

Extraction may take place when there is no pressure remaining in the firearm (as is the case with every manually operated gun) or it can take place when there is still some pressure remaining or when there is enough residual pressure to retract, or help retract, the breechbolt. You must visualize that propellant gas develops very high chamber pressure, which builds progressively. Of course we're speaking relatively; these things happen in fractions of a second. The point to be made is that you don't go from zero pressure to maximum instantly. Nor does pressure drop instantly when the charge leaves the barrel. Let us

49

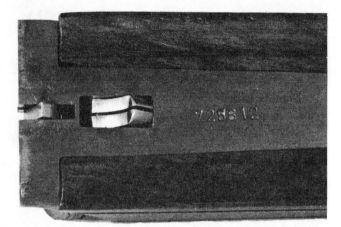

The ejectors on most side-by-side double guns appear like this: a pair of small hammers barely visible in the forearm. When you fire a barrel its ejector hammer is cocked and, when the barrels are lowered enough to clear the action, that ejector hammer "fires" and hits the front end of the extractor, which pops the fired cartridge out of the gun.

compare, just for a moment, the different action of a heavy machine gun and a semiautomatic rifle as regards extraction. In the first place, any automatic or semiautomatic action must provide enough energy to drive the breechblock all the way back, otherwise it will not work. This means that the source of power, and its timing, must be so arranged. The heavy machine gun, with its heavy breechbolt, can be started earlier, because it takes longer for the heavy block to start moving. This results in slower primary extraction and less tendency to allow the extractor to tear through the rim of the cartridge.

On the other hand, a semiautomatic mechanism designed to be fired from the shoulder has a lightweight breechbolt. It must be started fast (the only substitute for weight—inertia—is speed) in order to make the full backward movement. The result is a violent jerking start, usually with the gas still under some residual pressure. In the event of an exceptionally soft case, a sticky chamber, or any one of a dozen other things that might cause the cartridge to stick, this sudden jerk could easily rip the extractor hook right through the case rim.

It is also important to note in this connection that these guns are designed to be fired from the shoulder, meaning that the gun is held securely. If you should fire the gun held loosely in your hands the bolt will usually fail to come back all

the way and a jam will result. This is because the kick of the gun, if allowed to recoil freely, will offset the action of the moving parts and their momentum will never be built up sufficiently to perform all the functions required (i.e. unlocking, extraction, ejection, cocking, and storing energy in the recoil spring).

EXTRACTOR POSITIONING

The position of the extractor, the part of the circle where it should grasp the cartridge, is of primary importance in the direction ejection must take. This is because the next role of the extractor is to help provide the force for ejection.

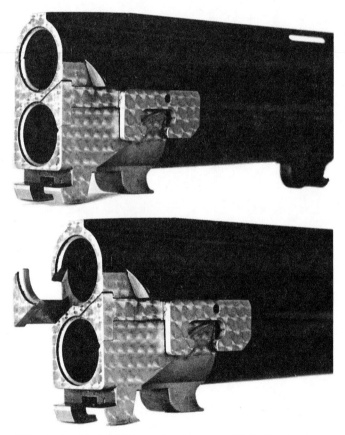

Winchester Model 101 over/under gun with both extractors forward as when the gun is closed (top), and with one extractor fully extended (below). When an "ejector" gun is fired, only the fired cartridge will be ejected from the gun. As the barrels begin to drop, the extractors move the cartridges back slightly; once the barrels have dropped enough to clear the action face, the ejector mechanism kicks the extractor sharply to the rear and the fired cartridge or cartridges are thrown from the gun.

Figure 1

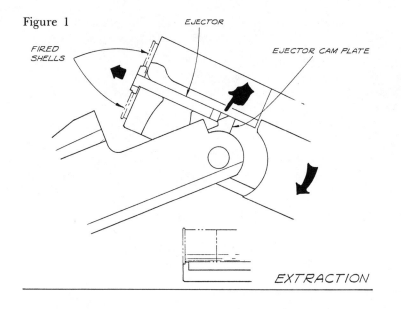

Figure 2

Figure 3

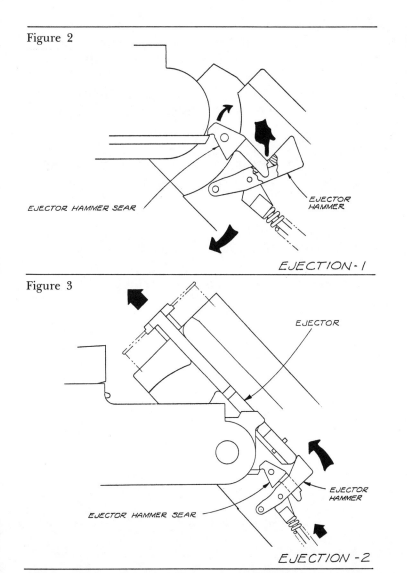

Extraction and ejection in the Remington 3200 are illustrated by these sketches: In Figure 1, the fired cartridges are moved back slightly as the ejector cam plate forces the ejectors to the rear in primary extraction. In Figure 2, as the barrels are dropped farther, actually to 47°, the ejector sears force the ejector hammers into cocked position and, when the barrels have reached the fully open angle, the sears slip off the hammers, which are then permitted to drive forcefully against the ejectors and expel the fired cartridge, or cartridges. Only barrels actually fired perform steps in Figures 2 and 3.

The Merkel Over/Under uses spring-loaded extractors that are released or not released depending on whether or not the gun barrel was fired. Here the lower barrel has been fired and the lower extractor is extended fully. The unfired top barrel does not have its extractor extended.

Most guns eject spent cartridges either directly to the side or up and to the right. There are advantages and disadvantages to all these systems, but few are of major importance unless they interfere with something. There are also several bottom-ejecting guns, like the old Models 10 and 17 Remington pump shotguns and Ithaca's Model 37. These guns position the extractor on the bottom of the bolt.

DOUBLE EXTRACTORS

Many repeating shotguns have double extractors —one on each side of the bolt. Actually, only the right-hand one is a real extractor; the left-hand one is merely a guide that holds the cartridge against the right-hand extractor. You'll note, if you look closely, that the right-hand extractor is sharp with a well-defined undercut on its rear surface. On the other hand, the left-hand extractor is more of a small spring with a little bump. Its sole function is to help hold the case in place.

EJECTION

Ejection is relatively simple compared to extraction, except that you must remember that most guns require full rearward movement of the breechbolt to provide ejection. If the fired cartridge is not flipped out of the mechanism cleanly, and on time, a jam will result.

Ejectors can be categorized easily into three kinds; fixed, movable, and plunger. Even though plungers can accurately be called movable, they are sufficiently different to be classed by themselves. The simplest type, found on most shotguns, is the fixed ejector. They are simply a small post, sometimes just a cut in the frame. The ejector functions when the bolt moves back carrying the fired case on its face held by the extractor. When the bolt is nearly all the way back, the base of the left-hand side of the cartridge strikes the ejector. By shoving forward on the left side, the cartridge is forced to rotate around the extractor hook and is thrown clear of the action.

One of the most useful (and fascinating) tools employed by today's gun designers is the Fastax camera which takes slow-motion pictures. The slam-bang of operating parts can be studied, with the result that engineers can perfect extraction and ejection as desired.

CHAPTER SEVEN

TRIGGERS

Anybody of kindergarten age can tell you that a trigger is the part you pull to make a gun go off. While that may be an accurate dictionary definition, there's quite a bit more to the subject. A trigger does start a motion that results in the gun's firing. But we have triggers in autoloading guns that only allow a single shot for each pull of the trigger. And we have a single trigger in double-barreled guns. Why these work as they do, along with other considerations, are all a part of the broad subject of triggers.

Trigger pulls can be hard or light, smooth or rough, good or bad. The simplest trigger of all is that used on most hammer guns, where the top of the trigger directly engages the hammer. Pull the trigger bottom, its top disengages and allows the hammer to fly forward to fire the gun. But even this simple trigger can be one or more of those things.

It is easy to establish what a trigger pull should be: (1) consistent; (2) crisp; (3) with as little movement as possible; (4) smooth; (5) heavy enough to be safe; (6) light enough to permit an easy letoff. Some of these requirements are more important to the target rifleman than to the shotgunner. But the shotgunner also needs a good trigger pull, and this applies to target shooter and bird hunter alike.

Let's go back to the simple, direct trigger again. It can be controlled by the distance from the finger curve (where you pull it) to the pin on which it pivots and by the distance from that pin to the nose where it engages the hammer. This trigger is a simple lever; the better the mechanical advantage the easier will be the pull. The part of the trigger that engages the hammer is called the sear, a generic word for that part of any firearm that holds back the firing mechanism. Its mating notch in the hammer or firing pin is called the sear notch.

The fit of the sear in the sear notch, which includes the angle of both surfaces, their depth, their hardness, and their smoothness, will dictate the quality of the trigger pull. Some folks are bold enough to stone sears and sear notches with a fine, hard Arkansas stone to make the surfaces smooth. The procedure is all right *provided* you do not change the angle, which is easier said than done.

It's not at all difficult to improve the pull of one of these direct hammer guns we've been talking about. Simply place a wide-bladed screwdriver under the tailpiece of the cocked hammer and twist while applying pressure to the trigger. Twist the screwdriver as though you're trying to force the hammer down. Do this a few times and you'll smooth out some of the roughness and will actually improve the pull. Naturally, you'll do this with no cartridge in the gun and you'll stick a piece of cardboard under the hammer to prevent the screwdriver from marring the gun. I don't necessarily recommend this procedure though I have used it. It's rough and should never be used on a good gun, but it does work.

CREEP

Creep in a trigger is defined as a scratchy movement that hesitates, jumps a bit, and stops again before the pull is resumed. It is often compared to a rusty barn gate. There should be no lost motion in a decent trigger pull and no hesitation. You shouldn't feel anything as you squeeze a trigger. When it goes off it should resemble breaking a glass rod—the gradual increase of pressure eventually breaking the connection cleanly and sharply. Nor should there be any follow-through. Rearward movement of the trigger should cease immediately as the trigger releases the sear. Most triggers are not that good. And some of them cannot be, especially those in pumps and autos where the parts slam back and forth in operation.

While it may be argued that the target rifleman has much more need of a good trigger pull than a shotgunner, you can't tell that to the experienced trap shooter. He wants a trigger just as fine as that of the rifleman. His requirements are a little different, but he won't take a back seat to the rifleman anytime. A good shotgun trigger ought to meet the same specifications a good rifle trigger should.

Probably one of the major differences between rifle and shotgun triggers, speaking now only of the better class of guns, is that most rifle triggers contain adjustments for weight of pull, backlash, and follow-through, while most shotgun triggers are set as you buy them and there is no adjustment.

While many rifle shooters like a very light pull, some use set triggers to help achieve pulls so light they can sometimes be fired by just blowing on the trigger. Most shotgun users do not need so light a pull. Shotguns are fired differently than rifles and there is no need, in fact no use whatever, for a very light trigger on any shotgun. The rifleman learns to "squeeze" the trigger, a practice that has been drummed into anyone who's ever been in the service. You are not supposed to know when the rifle will go off. And, by way of explanation, you should only be squeezing when you're on target.

A shotgun trigger isn't really squeezed, not in the same sense of the word. I would say it's *pressed* rather than squeezed. You want the gun to fire at a certain instant because you're shooting at a moving target and the situation is entirely different than with the rifle. Once you're on target and moving the gun, instinct tells you to press the trigger. What you want is instant reaction from the gun, with no further thought on your part.

RELATIONSHIP BETWEEN TRIGGER AND SAFETY

Most shotgun safeties simply block the trigger. That is, they prevent you from pulling the trigger by blocking its movement. Rarely do they hold back the firing mechanism itself, as they do in a bolt-action rifle, for example (where most safeties restrain the firing pin). Broadly speaking, although perhaps a bit oversimplified, this means the shotgun safety is not quite as safe as that of the bolt-action rifle, which does restrain the firing pin. It may be accepted that any safety that simply blocks the movement of the trigger is not as safe as a safety that grabs and holds back the firing mechanism itself, so long as the latter is in proper working order.

Therefore most shotgun safeties, by blocking the trigger from movement, make the gun subject to being jarred off. I do not mean to imply that these guns are dangerous because their safeties are inadequate, but it is certainly true that they cannot be as safe as a gun designed so its safety holds the firing pin. This should help explain why any experienced shooter will tell you never to trust the safety. And to obey that commandment that says *thou shalt never point a gun at any object at which thou dost not intend to shoot.* The people who wrote that line had safeties in mind, as well as common sense and courtesy.

Most of my big-game hunting has been done with the magazine loaded but the action closed on an empty chamber; except of course when I expect to go into action momentarily. Bird hunting is another matter entirely; the shotgun is usually carried loaded and on safe when afield. This is not only acceptable, it would be stupid to hunt otherwise, but it's still necessary to obey the commandment. Anyone who hunts for any length of time learns when the gun ought to be loaded and when it should not; when the magazine should be loaded and the chamber not; and so forth. When you expect to shoot, or have reasonable expectation that you may have to shoot, then the gun should be loaded. Otherwise it's best not to depend upon a tiny piece of steel that has no brain of its own. It just makes sense, it seems to me, that it's always best to keep in mind that the only thing preventing a gun from firing is a tiny fraction of an inch of engagement between two steel pieces that are incapable of acting on their own.

I've dwelt on safeties even though the subject is triggers, because the two are related and interact. Most people don't realize how a safety works and why it ought not to be depended upon, so some discussion is important.

SHAPE

One rarely hears much about the shape of a trigger—that is, the part you see. It's called the trigger bow; it is the part you press to fire the gun and its shape is important to both function and appearance. Triggers are traditionally curved because the finger is curved and you should be able to get a good grip on the trigger. Another reason for curving is to distribute the pressure over as wide an area as possible, which will make the pull seem lighter than it is. (For the same reason, a large butt plate helps distribute recoil over a wider area and makes it feel less.) By the same token, a wide trigger (or a trigger shoe that can be added to many triggers to make them wider) will distribute the pull over a wider area and make it feel lighter.

Since one spends a great deal more time looking at guns than shooting them, it helps if those guns look good. Other things being equal, there is no reason in the world why a gun can't be shaped so it looks good instead of like an ugly duckling. A pleasing curve on a trigger is attractive and should complement the remaining parts and other lines of the gun. Contrariwise, a handsome, elegantly shaped gun with a trigger dangling like a well-used nail would look like hell.

It should go without saying that a trigger ought to be positioned in the rear part of the guard, with ample clearance so it doesn't contact the guard itself, and so there is room for a fat finger or one with a glove on. And, up above, where it's out of sight, there must be sufficient clearance between metal and wood so no stock swelling or warping can possibly interfere with the trigger's movement.

It will be obvious that the requirements for a trigger will vary among the various gun actions. The difference between a simple trigger on the old single barrel behind the henhouse door is quite different from that of an expensive double gun with single trigger. And from a pump and bolt-action shotgun. And from an autoloader which must not fire more than one shot with

That little button right in front of the firing pin hole in this .45 Auto is the disconnector. Located in the frame, it is moved up by spring pressure, down by the slide. The disconnector must be up for the gun to fire; when the slide is fully closed and the gun locked, the disconnector is permitted to move up into a small recess in the slide and the gun can be fired. When the slide opens, it pushes the disconnector down, breaking the engagement between sear and trigger and the gun cannot be fired again until the trigger is relaxed.

each pull. The most important thing about the autoloading trigger is that it must disconnect, that is, it must not permit more than one shot.

DISCONNECTORS

When you press the trigger on an autoloader, it fires and goes through all the remaining steps of operation automatically, but it doesn't fire again. It won't until you relax the trigger and pull it again. That's because the trigger is disconnected during the operation and isn't connected again until you relax it. This happens in a variety of ways, all of them quite simple and foolproof. Some gun mechanisms would fire and keep on firing so long as the trigger is pressed and there is ammunition in the magazine. And others would not fire again because the failure to cock would result in allowing the hammer to ride up behind the bolt too slowly to achieve ignition. (There are two reasons for this: first, nearly every gun mechanism will not allow its firing pin to line up until it is fully locked. Second, the hammer must fly forward under full pressure and strike the firing pin with a solid blow to ignite the primer. Failure of the hammer to deliver the full blow would be the result of letting it simply ride up behind the bolt—as opposed to having it cock properly and be released after the bolt had been secured.)

The function of a disconnector is to disconnect the trigger and sear after firing so that the sear is free to engage the hammer or firing pin. Otherwise the gun cannot be recocked. Relaxing the trigger allows the trigger and sear to again engage so another pull of the trigger will fire the gun. While there are many types of disconnector, most of which work differently, one of the best known is that used on the Browning Auto-5. The workings of this system are shown in the illustrations and will convey the simplicity of the trigger system. While others work differently they all perform the same basic function. (Note: There is also the matter of a double gun's "involuntary" pull as it relates to single triggers. It may appear that this conflicts with the disconnector story, but that's not so. The involuntary pull does not apply here, since the gun's parts are in motion while it occurs.)

SELECTIVE TRIGGERS

A selective trigger is one that can be set to fire one barrel or the other in a double gun. (It also is defined as a trigger used on some military guns where you can select full or semiautomatic fire. The German MG 34 World War II machine gun had such a trigger, capable of delivering full or semiauto fire just by pulling a different part of the trigger.) A recent model of the Beretta over/under shotgun had a similar trigger that allowed you to fire either barrel as you wished by pressing the top or bottom of the trigger. It was pretty ugly and has since been dropped.

Traditional selective triggers are more like those employed on the Browning over/under, the Winchester 101, and other guns; you move the safety one way or the other to choose the barrel you want to fire. Once fired, the gun will then fire the second barrel when you press the trigger again. Others, like the Winchester 21, are less easily adjustable since there is a little button to push or slide, which must be done in advance.

As a matter of fact I think a selective trigger is totally unnecessary. The reason (and this only applies to double guns) being that you should always fire the right barrel in a side-by-side and lower barrel in an over/under gun first. This is because the recoil element lets you get the second barrel back on target quicker.

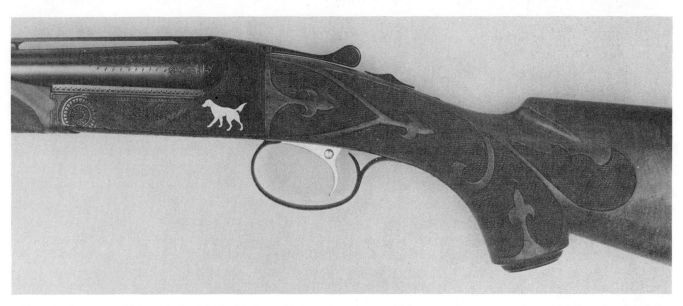

The Winchester Model 21 side-by-side double is a selective trigger gun, which means that you can elect which barrel to fire first. Winchester does this by providing a small button on the trigger itself which is simply shoved either way. Other guns, like the Browning and Winchester 101 over/unders, have this arrangement incorporated in the safety slide.

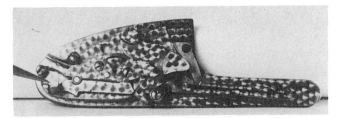

The Victor Sarasqueta sidelock plate with the pointer showing the "intercepting sear." In order to fire the lock, the trigger must raise both knobs. Should firing the other barrel jar the sear out of its engagement, the intercepting sear will catch the hammer and the gun will not "double." Only top grade guns have this feature.

It stands to reason that, in most cases, the first barrel you shoot will be at a closer target than the second, so you want to deliver the more-open choked barrel first. A single-trigger gun is just as good if it's factory set to fire the open barrel first because that's what nearly all of your shooting will be. Most people simply set the trigger this way for the obvious reasons. Another factor is that if you have to stop and think which barrel you want to fire, you can bet the bird's out of range anyway. Bird shooting doesn't usually allow anything but automatic reflex action. Stop to think and you're out of luck.

So I think selective triggers are just so much sales talk and that you don't need them. In the few rare cases where they are an advantage it would be just as advisable to have them as an added option. And that would also lower the price of the basic gun.

In a side-by-side double gun the right-handed shooter wants to fire the right barrel first because, since both barrels are a little off the center line, it will recoil slightly to the left or toward the shooter which makes it easier to get the second barrel back on target. A left-handed person would want it the other way around. With an over/under gun the lower barrel is fired first because its recoil is in more of a straight line and therefore the gun rises less in recoil and the second barrel is again more quickly brought back to the target. Moreover, the lower barrel on the over/under gun is deeper in the massive U frame and develops less strain on the gun's frame.

SOME VARIATIONS AND EXCEPTIONS

There is a type of trigger used by some trap shooters called a release trigger. It's worked by first pulling the trigger and holding it back. When released, the gun fires. As you might suspect, the use of a release trigger takes some getting used to and it's not for the beginner.

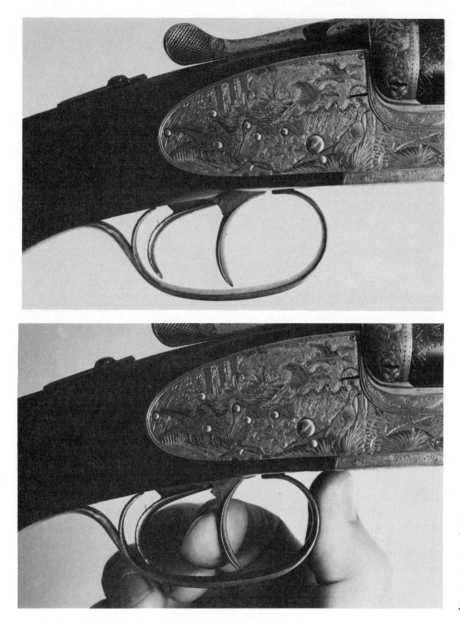

Most of the higher-grade two-trigger double guns have a hinged front trigger that protects the shooter from recoil when firing the back trigger. Note too that the right hand side, facing the camera, of the guard of this Victor Sarasqueta is thicker than normal—another nicety of a fine gun because it's less apt to injure the user.

A variation on the release trigger is seen in some pigeon guns and some guns used in International-style trap. In both cases you use a double gun and fire both barrels. Always. Even if you get the bird with the first barrel you fire the second to keep your rhythm intact. A trigger sometimes used here is a combination of release for the first barrel and standard for the second. It works like this: You load your gun when ready and pull the trigger, carefully holding it back. Then you call for the bird by saying "pull." Your first shot is fired when you release the trigger and the second is fired when you pull it again.

It's a complicated setup, but it certainly provides a very fast one-two shot combination.

SINGLE AND DOUBLE TRIGGERS

Double guns, as mentioned earlier, have a separate lock or firing mechanism for each barrel. Many models, especially the older guns, are made with two triggers, although the present trend is toward single-trigger guns. There are advantages to both. A single trigger allows more room for the trigger finger in the guard, which is important on a chilly day when you wear a glove. The length of pull is the same for both barrels with only one trigger. On the other hand, single triggers are very complicated whereas the two-trigger system is very simple.

Let's talk about two-trigger guns first. The front trigger is always fired first and it should fire the most-open barrel (right or lower). Then you slip your hand back slightly and fire the second barrel. The fastest guns are those with a straight stock, which is often called English style, as opposed to a pistol grip. In fact, I think any double gun should have a straight grip because it gets into action quicker.

You will note that the front trigger usually is a little straighter, the rear one a bit more curved, to facilitate movement from one to the other. And both triggers, even though one protrudes from one side of the frame to the other from the opposite side, are shaped to be centered in the trigger guard. If you've never noticed this, remember you're not supposed to. It's meant to be a subtle thing that works better if it goes unnoticed. Another of the subtle features you may have never noticed is that the front trigger on a quality two-trigger gun is hinged, so it will move forward in recoil when you press the rear trigger. This is sometimes called a yielding trigger and it's meant for comfort. Another little nicety is that the right-hand side of the trigger guard is often thicker than the left, to present a blunt edge rather than a sharp one. Again, for your comfort. You don't see this on all guns, but when you buy a top-grade gun you have a right to expect these little additions and you usually get them.

It might sound at first that you would be hopelessly confused if you owned several guns, all of them with different styles of trigger. The answer is that if you do enough shooting you won't. For example, I have a number of high-power rifles with the military double pull, where you have to take up the slack before the final trigger pull. And I have hammer guns like the .30/30 carbine that you must hand cock as you raise the little rifle when a deer jumps out of a blowdown in front of you. Then I have a number of double guns with two triggers as well as single-trigger guns. The trigger action comes automatically to me on any of these—and it will to you if you do enough shooting. But it must be done by reflex and not by thought. Indeed, about the only time I get confused is when I'm shooting a gun with more than two-shot capacity. I rarely shoot more than two shots because I'm so used to shooting a double gun. Despite that, I have never had trouble with a trigger by changing from one type to another.

A single trigger for a double gun can be a very complicated device; even the simplest of them is complicated. The reason is that you always pull a trigger twice each time you pull it. That's right, twice. The second pull is involuntary and you never notice it. But it's most vital in a single-trigger double gun because two pulls would fire both barrels, and they'd go off virtually at once with painful results. The involuntary pull is a result of the gun's recoil and the single trigger must accommodate this inadvertent pull by wasting it in one way or another. Or by blocking it. The latter method is employed in a number of guns, including the Winchester Model 21, by means of an inertia block. As the gun recoils, the block tends to remain where it is. The net effect is that the trigger recoils under the block and can't be pulled twice. (The effect is the same as swinging the inertia weight forward to block the trigger.) After recoiling, and blocking the trigger against the involuntary pull, the weight is swung back out of the way by a spring and the next pull (which will be deliberate) will fire the second barrel.

This involuntary pull is often confusing. It happens, quite simply, because the gun recoils away from your trigger finger, but there is an automatic takeup when your finger re-engages the trigger. This happens every time you fire any gun. You never notice it because it happens so fast. In fact the only time you ever would notice it would be with a single-trigger double gun where the mechanism was faulty. Such a gun would fire both barrels at virtually the same instant with the result that the recoil would be doubled as both reports blended into one. I've had this happen and it's always something of a shock and surprise.

Involuntary pulls are of no consequence in any gun other than a single-trigger double, because these guns have two separate locks that are capable of firing at the same time. No other

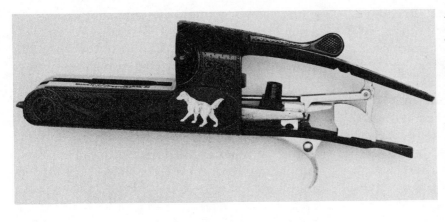

Any double shotgun single trigger must have a means of blocking the second or "involuntary" pull. On the Winchester Model 21 (shown here in Grand American grade) this is accomplished by an inertia block. When the trigger is pulled, the gun recoils and the inertia block, which you see as the large arc above and behind the trigger, remains where it is. This has the effect of the block's moving forward and it gets under the trigger to hold the trigger back to prevent doubling. The inertia block is one of the simpler forms of wasting the involuntary pull and is used on many double guns.

firearm has such a setup and the involuntary pull is so fast that it only affects these guns.

Several gunmakers use a system where the second pull is simply a waste pull; one of the most popular and efficient of these is that patented long ago by James Woodward. (Woodward, one of the finest of all English gunmakers, was bombed out of business during World War II. The Woodward over/under, perhaps the finest of all such designs, was later bought by James Purdey and is still manufactured by the Purdey firm. Original Woodward guns are extremely rare and extremely valuable.) Woodward's single-trigger system is called a swinging-blade system. The mechanism consists of a blade extension on the upper part of the trigger with a similar blade positioned on either side of the trigger blade. The right-hand blade is used to fire the right barrel (lower on an over/under) and the left-hand blade fires the left (or upper) barrel. All three blades rotate around a single pin located at the front.

Located below and between these blades is a slide with several small projections. When the gun is opened and cocked, the slide is moved all the way forward. When closed and ready to fire, one of these projections on the slide causes the right blade to be lifted along with the trigger blade and fire the right barrel. Once fired, the trigger is relaxed involuntarily (because the gun's recoil moves the gun back away from the trigger finger for a moment; then the reverse

happens and you pull the trigger again). When relaxed, the slide is allowed to move back to its middle stop. The involuntary pull now causes the right-hand blade to raise again with the trigger blade, but, since that barrel was just fired, nothing happens and the pull is wasted. Now the trigger is deliberately relaxed, permitting the slide to move to its rear position when it engages the left blade with the trigger blade to fire the second barrel.

There are many other systems of providing for the involuntary pull in a single trigger. Some of them are complicated and all of them are ingenious. With some single-trigger guns it is impossible to dry fire (snapping the gun without ammunition) the second barrel. This will be a gun with the inertia weight. You snap the first barrel all right but then nothing happens. However, if you sharply rap the butt plate with the heel of your hand you'll be able to snap the second barrel because you've made the inertia weight swing far enough to set the mechanism. (Some guns will require hitting the butt on the floor sharply, but not too hard.)

It's easier to learn with a single-trigger gun—something like learning to drive with an automatic-shift car. While I have to admit that I prefer a single-trigger gun, I can work a two trigger just as fast (so long as it's stocked properly) and have no objection to them. The mechanics of a good single trigger are fascinating and I suspect that's part of the charm too.

CHAPTER EIGHT

FIRING SYSTEMS

The purpose of any gun's firing system is to ignite the powder charge which, in turn, burns to develop propellant gas to drive the bullet or shot charge out of the barrel. Very early firing systems were usually a piece of smoldering punk which was stuck in the touchhole directly against the powder. A little later the matchlock was developed and differed only in that it offered a mechanical means of moving the smoldering fire to the touchhole.

Next came the wheellock, a device wound up like a watch mainspring that, when the trigger was pulled, was allowed to spin against a flint to throw a shower of sparks into a pan that contained some loose powder. This was followed by the flintlock, in which the flint itself was fastened in the hammer. When the trigger was pulled, the flint struck a piece of steel to throw sparks into the pan.

Along about 1840, the system of percussion ignition was developed and it has not changed significantly today except that today's ammunition is compact and self-contained. Percussion ignition requires a blow to fire the primer which, in its turn, ignites the propellant powder. The percussion cap was used in a variety of ways during the transitional period from muzzle loading to breech loading. If you consider today's primer the same as an 1840 percussion cap, you will grasp the essentials for they are virtually the same.

Modern ammunition employs two different types of primer: that used in rimfire cartridges, *61*

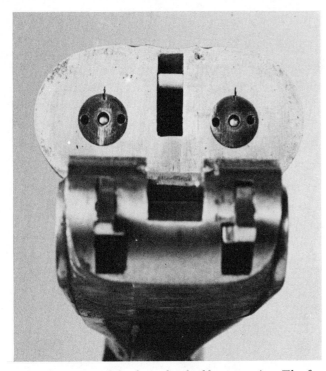

A head-on view of the face of a double-gun action. The firing pins in this gun have removable plates (the small holes are for a special wrench to remove them). The pins also are spring-retracted so that the gun may be opened without the pin noses dragging through the primer.

where the priming compound is spun around the inside of the rim, and that used in center-fire ammunition, where a separate, self-contained primer is seated in a pocket in the cartridge case.

We will dwell more on ammunition later, but, for now, it is essential to understand the two basic types of cartridges. It is also necessary to know that priming compound is used in very small amounts, because it is extremely violent and explosive. There is, in fact, enough power in the primer alone to drive a bullet deep into a gun barrel even if loaded without a powder charge.

The firing mechanism of a rimfire shotgun, rifle, or handgun is constructed to cause the firing pin to crush the rim (any part of the rim) of the cartridge against the breech end of the barrel. On the other hand, a center-fire firing system must strike the primer itself, located in the middle of the cartridge. A rather substantial blow is needed for ignition, and the force and delivery of that blow must be consistent. There are many possible fluctuations in ignition, such

as manufacturing tolerances for the cartridge case, which sometimes vary quite a bit. The same tolerances exist in barrel manufacture. In a center-fire cartridge the primer is composed of several parts, each of which will often vary somewhat. Put all these together and the potential for considerable variation can exist.

For sure rimfire ignition, the barrel must be positioned correctly in the receiver and the cartridge must position itself against the breech end of the barrel with the bolt face snugly behind the cartridge. An accumulation of dirt or grease between the cartridge rim and the barrel will soften the firing pin's blow and cause variations in ignition.

In a center-fire cartridge, rifle or shotgun, the primer must be seated to the bottom of its pocket in the cartridge case, otherwise part of the firing-pin blow will be wasted, because it must first drive the primer all the way into its pocket. Similarly, some primer cups (that's the part you see) are softer, or harder, than others and these variations will have an effect on ignition.

SIMPLE FIRING PINS

By the word "simple," I mean those that are attached to the hammer as a one-piece unit. You don't see many of these, although they exist in many double guns where they are hidden inside the frame. These are relatively simple and straightforward. Many revolvers, especially older models, are made with a one-piece hammer and firing pin. These firing pins simply move forward with the hammer and whack the primer to ignite the powder charge.

Firing pins used for rimfire and center-fire cartridges must have their firing pins positioned differently, for one must strike the cartridge's rim and the other must strike centrally. Most shotguns are center fire so the rimfire type of ignition isn't of great importance here. Of course, certain cartridges are loaded with shot charges, such as the .22 Long Rifle, .22 WMR and you'll see an occasional import for some odd gauge in rimfire ammo.

The next simplest firing pin is the combination of firing pin and hammer, like the Winchester Model 94, where the separate hammer flies up to whack the firing pin which, in turn, delivers its energy to the primer. This system is used in more guns than any other for a couple of excellent reasons: The big hammers employed deliver the substantial blow needed for ignition with no fuss, and they are very reliable. You'll find them on guns all the way from the Browning Auto-5 shotgun to the M1 Garand to the most modern gas-operated shotguns or rifles. There is nothing like that big hammer to provide positive ignition.

There is considerable variation in the firing pins themselves which run all the way from the very short pins tucked inside the frame of a double to the nearly 3-inch-long pin used in the big Browning Auto-5. But that's not important to the system, it's just a requirement of the action length. Naturally, it takes a harder blow (heavier hammer, stiffer spring) to move a long, heavy pin than it does a short pin. These hammer-and-pin combinations usually have the added feature of supporting the primer during ignition when chamber pressure is highest. In any high-power cartridge, the pressure is exerted rearward as well as in every other direction and the firing pin must be securely held down, inside the primer

cup where it has penetrated. If it was not, it would be possible for the high-pressure gas to rupture the soft primer cup and spill gas into the action.

The third common system is that used in most bolt-action guns—the spring-loaded firing pin. It is an excellent system, positive and reliable. Some engineers prefer the massive hammer while some others prefer the bolt action. There really isn't that much to choose from when other things are the same; certain action systems are better adapted to one than the other. You'll find bolt-action shotguns, like their rifle counterparts, use the spring-and-pin combination.

There is also a type of hammer called a rebounding hammer. This refers to those that, having delivered their blow to the separate firing pin, are allowed to rebound to a rest position about $1/8$ inch from the fired position. These occur on older guns and for good reason for it applied to older, lower-pressure cartridges than we commonly use today. It's necessary for the firing pin to be retracted slightly (in most guns) before you can open the action. In a double shotgun, for example, you can't open the barrels

Trap shooting demands instant response from the gun's firing system, especially from handicap yardages where the clay target is often 50 to 60 yards away. Photo shows D. Lee Braun, one of the world's greatest clay target shooters, smoking a clay target at the trap field.

until the firing pins are slightly backed off; else you'd be dragging the pin noses through the primers. This would unnecessarily stiffen opening the gun, would put a strain on the pins that would ultimately result in breakage, and would be hard on the firing-pin hole. So the very first move of the action must be to retract the pin or pins. This is done in two ways, either by forcing them back mechanically or by simply moving the hammer back and allowing a light spring to shove the firing pin back out of the way. Rebounding hammers were common on black-powder single-shot rifles of the late 1800s where the chamber pressure was not nearly as high as that of modern guns.

THE BLOW AND INDENTATION

We can establish certain requirements for the firing system (including the primer):

1. The primer must fire consistently with a blow of a certain energy or weight.

2. The primer must not fire when struck with a blow less than the minimum (that is, the primer must not be too sensitive).

3. The primer, or rim of a rimfire cartridge case, must not rupture or be pierced.

While these limits are required for positive ignition, there is a far narrower range of specifications within which more perfect ignition will

This is a complete firing mechanism, except firing pin, from a Perazzi Comp 1 competitive trap gun. Extremely well engineered and manufactured, it is one of the fastest locks in all gundom. The unit is instantly removable and interchangeable.

result. And more perfect ignition will produce more perfect accuracy. This will explain why the better grades of trap guns are refined to the point where their ignition systems provide the quickest, surest, and (most important) most uniform ignition possible.

Quickness is known in the trade as locktime, and it's important to the trap shooter particularly (skeet shooters to a lesser degree) because he has perfected his rhythm to a degree that when he says "pull" and the target appears, he is on it in the wink of an eye. And when he presses the trigger the gun must deliver Now. Consider the trap shooter shooting from the 27-yard handicap line, which means his targets will be 50 or 60 yards out when he shoots. Every millisecond of delay means increasing range at a distance where the shot cluster is rapidly losing force. His gun must perform when he says "go" or he will fail to break the target.

It can be argued that the rifle shooter has more need of fast locktime than the trap shooter and it can be argued the other way. But correct and quick ignition is of major importance in both situations. That's why the modern target rifle has had an enormous amount of developmental time, energy, and money devoted to its ignition or firing system. And that's why the top trap guns such as the Perazzi, Ljutic, and others have such excellent systems. (It's also why shooters continue to experiment in the quest for better and faster ignition, real or imagined, that will help them score better. Those who seek release triggers and the like are examples. Perazzi, for one example, makes a quickly disassembled entire trigger unit that permits the trap shooter to change the whole system faster than you can read these words.)

Locktime can be timed; it is defined as the time elapsed between the moment the sear releases the firing pin or hammer and the moment the primer is crushed and exploded. In the 1903 Springfield rifle, defined as a rifle with slow locktime, the movement has been timed at approximately .0057 second.

It is claimed by many authorities that the quickest locks are those of a finely tuned, finely made double shotgun employing the traditional v springs. These better actions also provide a hammer stirrup, a small lever connecting spring

On the left is a top-grade Merkel over/under lockplate and on the right the same from an L.C. Smith. Note the far finer workmanship on the Merkel and note also that the lock has intercepting sears to prevent doubling.

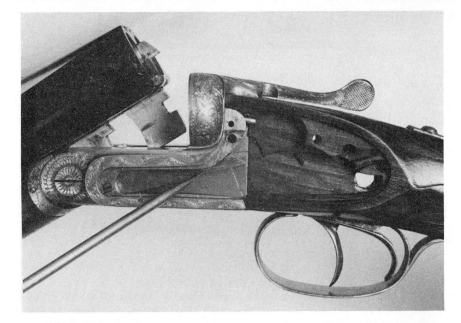

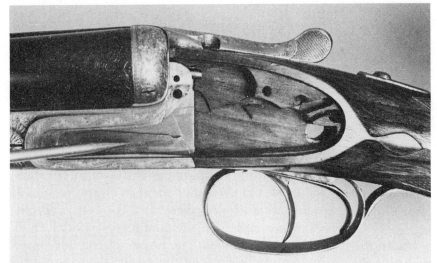

The photo series shows how double gun locks are cocked, in this case a sidelock gun, but the principle is basically the same with nearly all double guns. The first picture shows the action open, barrels down which have forced the cocking bar up at its rear end (see pointer). The next picture shows the gun closed, cocking bar lowered. The last shows the lock plate with the pointer indicating that part of the hammer against which the cocking bar works to cock the gun when the barrels are lowered. This action is called a bar-action sidelock because the spring is fitted to that part of the lock plate that fits in the action bar.

and hammer. The stirrup has the effect of accelerating the spring pressure at the latter part of the hammer movement, when ordinarily the spring's force has slowed because it is under less tension. Thus it may be said that those actions employing a stirrup maintain the spring force throughout the hammer movement while others suffer from loss of spring pressure as the spring is eased.

The speed of the hammer blow depends upon the strength and efficiency of the spring and it further depends upon the angle through which the hammer must fall. It is commonly accepted that, other things being equal, an action in which the striker is actuated by a rotating hammer is quicker than actions in which the striker is pushed forward by a coiled spring as in a bolt-action rifle.

The locks used in double shotguns have a locktime of approximately .002 second. The difference between boxlock and sidelock guns is too inconsequential to mention.

Another factor of importance in the firing-pin blow is the angle of the pin, and often the number of parts between the hammer and primer. Some guns are constructed in such a way that some rather unusual contortions are required to get the firing blow delivered to the primer.

Some firearms—a couple of examples are the Winchester Model 94 and Marlin Model 336—both lever-action "deer" rifles, have two-piece firing pins (which are designed as a safety feature since the two pieces must be aligned, with the action fully locked, before the gun can be fired). Nonetheless, a two-piece firing pin has a degree of lost motion or sponginess, whatever you wish to call it, which should not be tolerated in a firearm meant to deliver exceptional accuracy through a quick action.

If there is a type of gun that has a traditional difficulty in the angle of its pins because of the action itself, it has to be the over/under double. That is because the basic action of an over/under is similar to that of a side-by-side gun; but where the latter has both its barrels lying on the same plane (and so can have each firing system a mirror image of the other side) that is not true with the over/under. The latter requires that one pin be higher than the other. Put another way, the over/under has its barrels turned 90° to the side-

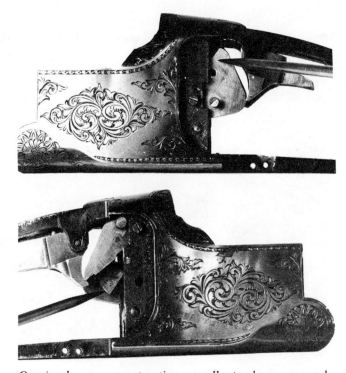

Over/under gun construction usually produces unusual angles for firing pins; rarely are they in a straight line. This Charles Daly is reputed to be the only over/under gun with straight-line firing pins. These photos show how Daly accomplished this near miracle. The pointer points to the striking surface; note that one hammer moves downwards and the other moves upwards.

by-side type, but its firing systems are unchanged. The result is some rather weird contortions in some lesser guns.

To the best of my knowledge, only one action has truly straight-line firing pins and that is the Charles Daly gun, imported from Japan. This system is rather unique as is shown by the illustrations. On the other hand, I do not condemn guns with angled pins. Far from it. I've also shown a sketch of the Remington Model 3200, one of the newest and finest actions developed and already favored by many skeet and trap shooters (it's a bit heavy for a field gun). But there are a number of such guns that do not and cannot deliver a solid blow because of the somewhat unorthodox angles some of them employ.

FIRING-PIN PROTRUSION

An important detail in firearms' manufacture is the control of firing-pin protrusion. It will be ap-

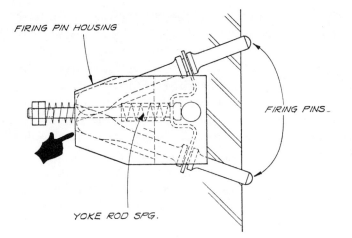

The Remington 3200 over/under gun has angled firing pins as this sketch from Remington shows. While an angled blow cannot be considered as satisfactory as a straight blow, this design is as close to ideal as you can get.

parent that if the pin is allowed to penetrate too far into the primer, it could easily rupture the soft cup and allow gas to spill into the action. On the other hand, should the protrusion not be sufficient, it would result in uncertain ignition. Firing-pin protrusion is usually controlled by the shape of the shoulder behind the striking point. Protrusion is most important in high-power rifle cartridges, where the chamber pressure developed often is several times that developed by a shotgun cartridge. Yet that does not tell the true story, because a shotgun cartridge develops its chamber pressure faster, so the quicker action could rupture a primer more easily in some instances. Normal protrusion is usually between .055 and .065 inch—roughly 1/16th inch (.0625 inch).

This is a good place to point out that most guns should not be dry-fired—snapped without a cartridge in the chamber—because the blow will be stopped by that part of the firing pin that comes to rest in the frame of the gun. The frequent result is battering of the pin hole and/or crystallizing of the pin until it snaps off and renders the gun useless. While many modern guns are made so unlimited snapping won't hurt them, the owner of any fine double gun is advised to get a pair of snap caps, which fit the chamber and absorb the firing-pin blow without hurting anything.

LUBRICATION

Many of today's lubricants are designed for very cold weather and if that's what you use, you won't experience any difficulty. However, occasionally a gun comes along that is loaded inside with grease or perhaps an old-style oil, both of which can freeze in cold weather. The result will be a failure to fire, because the ignition system won't move fast enough to produce the necessary blow. So, unless you are using one of the modern lubricants specifically designed to flow at extreme temperatures, leave firing mechanism dry and lubricate with powdered graphite. In any event, you shouldn't use too much oil on any gun.

TYPES OF SPRINGS

There are three types of springs in general use for firing mechanisms: coil, leaf, and v. There is nothing whatever wrong with any of them, assuming they are correctly made and properly tempered. You will hear and read many references to "modern coil springs" as an improvement over the "older types." The truth is that a coil spring is cheaper and easier to make, and in most cases, it's just as good. But it isn't necessarily better. It is better than a poorly made leaf or v spring and, when you're buying, you will be better off with coil springs in an inexpensive gun. In a high-grade gun, however, you'll generally find v springs and they will work as long as you live, provided you do your part.

Most European made double guns of better quality employ v springs, as shown on this sidelock of the back action type. It is widely believed that such springs, especially when equipped with a stirrup to connect spring to hammer, provide the quickest lock time of any firearm. The reason is that springs lose force as they become extended, but the stirrup tends to accelerate the force.

Today's trend is toward coil springs, because they are easier to make and temper. Unless the gun is a very high grade model you are also far better off with coil springs, because they are less apt to break. This photo shows a modern action, the Finnish-made Savage Valmet over/under.

Leaf springs are not used as much as they were and will be found in relatively few shotguns, whereas the v spring is still used in top-grade shotguns. As mentioned earlier, a v spring when combined with a stirrup and found in a top-grade gun will deliver the quickest locktime in all gundom.

But today's move is toward the coil spring and I find no quarrel with that. It helps keep the cost down, even though it doesn't provide as quick a blow as the v in most designs simply because the spring loses force as it becomes extended. You must understand that these are very fine-line differences. Even the great Perazzi trap gun, consistently among the top winners in world events, uses coil springs to drive the hammers in its ignition systems!

ELECTRIC IGNITION

Attempts to fire guns electrically date almost as far back as Ben Franklin's kite. In 1881, W. W. Greener wrote in *The Gun and Its Development* of an experiment with electric ignition "forty years ago" in Prague. That would have been about 1840

The idea was then, as it is today, to ignite the powder charge by electrically releasing the firing mechanism. One of the more publicized attempts to my knowledge was the High Standard development in about 1960. The company reasoned that U.S. free pistol shooters (used in Olympic and International competitions) ought to use American products. Most Americans use the superb pistols made by such firms as Hammerli in Switzerland. Obviously, the sale of fifteen or twenty pistols for Olympic use would never be profitable and the small amount of publicity would not be worth the investment so the project was shelved. All that electric ignition could accomplish would be a better trigger release and faster locktime. Worthwhile objectives if they can be accomplished, but there must be sufficient market for the product to be viable.

A French firm in about 1954 introduced a double gun that was quite conventional in appearance but had electric ignition. But this gun differed from what we've been talking about since its ammunition was also constructed for electric ignition. This time, instead of releasing a conventional firing pin by an electric charge, the cartridge itself would be fired electrically by delivering a charge directly to a special primer. The system required its own ammunition which spelled its doom.

But electric ignition is far from dead today. Experiments with it continue and they continue with what is known as caseless ammunition, a total unit contained in a combustible cartridge with shot charge included. These cartridges are made by compressing a mass of propellant, in the plastic stage, into the approximate shape of a cartridge. When hard, and it becomes quite hard, the shell can be loaded with a primer, wads, and shot and you have a caseless shotgun cartridge that will be entirely consumed when fired. The obstacles to be overcome in developing and marketing such a cartridge are formidable to say the least, but the results are bright, too, because the heaviest and most expensive single item in a round of ammunition is eliminated: the paper or plastic shotgun hull (or the brass rifle cartridge case). When you consider the military ramifications you can realize what's at stake here, which is why experiments continue.

Nevertheless it will be a long time, if ever, before our basic shotgun ignition systems change to that degree. The systems described in this chapter will remain basic for years to come.

CHAPTER NINE

THE GUN BARREL

When you look at a gun barrel you get an impression of a smooth, shiny steel tube that appears manufactured to extraordinarily close tolerances. Gun barrels haven't always appeared as they do now, they may not always appear that way in the future. Besides, the impression you may have may be far from the truth anyway!

Before we get into shotgun barrels, it might be well to digress for a moment to point out that the main purpose for which shotguns were developed was for shooting birds on the wing. The shotgun has been, and will continue to be, used for other purposes, but basically it is still primarily the wing shooter's gun. Accordingly, in the late eighteenth century, such innovators as Colonel Peter Hawker and Joe Manton saw a formula developed that dictated what a shotgun should be and the load it should fire.

It was held that the gun's weight must be between 6 and 8 pounds, that its barrels should be between 25 and 30 inches long. Its stock should fit roughly a certain shape and dimensions, it must shoot between 1 and 1¼ ounces of shot, and its velocity must be that given by 3 to 3½ drams of black powder. It's astounding to realize that these rules are still applicable two hundred years later! Each of the rules makes sense, so let's take a moment to review them.

If the gun is lighter than 6 pounds it will recoil unpleasantly. If heavier than 8, it will be too heavy to swing quickly. The barrel-length provision was necessary for black powder to develop its full power thrust; it's not necessary today, but the dimensions are still correct to swing and aim properly. Stock shape hasn't changed either since a man is still built the same as he was 200 years ago. The shot charge also remains the same because a charge of that weight is required to offer sufficient pattern for clean kills and a heavier charge will raise the recoil to an unpleasant level. Finally, the powder charge is correct to give the maximum practical velocity to a charge of shot. A heavier powder charge will not deliver higher practical velocity and it would also increase the recoil to an objectionable level.

So there are sound and good reasons why a shotgun has not changed appreciably in 200 years, and it is unlikely to for another 200. True as this may be, the shotgun of today is vastly different from that of 200 years ago—and it's a better shooting gun.

With the rifle we are concerned only with the flight of a single projectile. Everything is devoted to that one single objective. But in the case of a shotgun, we are concerned with controlling the flight of anywhere from 200 to 300 individual pellets. They must be controlled so that as few as possible are wasted. These pellets must be spread out evenly in order to cover an area sufficiently large to strike the target. The larger this area is, the easier it is to hit the target, but the pellets must not spread out too much or they may separate too widely and enable the target to fly "through the pattern" without being hit. The pellets must also retain sufficient striking velocity to penetrate the target upon impact.

It will be seen that the problems encountered in meeting these objectives are more complicated than they are in the rifle.

A shotgun barrel is smooth; that is, it contains no rifling. There is one exception to this: a very few British double guns were made with a trace of rifling near the muzzle (actually in the choke area). Its purpose was to give some rotation to a slug when the gun was used against tough game at a very close range—say a tiger from the back of an elephant for instance. One maker called this the "Explora" another the "Paradox" and I suspect there were some other brand names as well. One sees these guns very rarely, but they do exist.

Early guns were not shoulder fired; the first ones more nearly resembled artillery. Early barrels were wood; a bit too much powder and the barrels burst, so they began wrapping them with wire to add strength. In fact, wire-wrapped artillery barrels were used until comparatively recently. Soon the wooden barrels gave way to metal and then to improved metals as the science of metallurgy developed. The methods by which barrels have been made over the years has been closely allied with machine-tool development. America's Industrial Revolution, when America turned from an agricultural society to an industrial giant, was formed around two industries: firearms and textile machinery. Of the two, firearms is the older, since its ancestry can be traced to the earliest settlers, whereas the textile industry was started in Pawtucket, Rhode Island, in 1790 by Samuel Slater along the banks of the Blackstone River.

A review of some of the methods of making barrels in the old days would serve no useful purpose here but, in a very oversimplified way, a look at the methods used during the early and mid-1800s might prove of interest. Barrels were not bored out of solid steel as they are today; rather they were made by wrapping metal around a steel bar, welding the joints, and then withdrawing the bar. Such barrels are variously called Damascus, twist, stub, or laminated, and sometimes a combination of those names. While there are distinct variations among them, we won't go into the subject too deeply. Early barrels were iron, later ones often a combination of iron and steel. Some of the twist barrels were excellent, being a good combination of steel, with its properties of strength and elasticity, and soft iron. Others were nearly pure iron and would not stand as much pressure as the combination of iron and steel.

The quality of these barrels also depended on the skills of the various workmen who forged and welded them. It was important to keep scale out of the welds—and hard to do. And it was equally important to keep the metal at the right temperature (charcoal fires were used) and hammer it correctly to achieve perfect welds. The hammering had another important effect in that it strengthened the metal by molecular rearrangement. We know this as forging which usually adds greater strength to a metal product.

After these barrels were rough formed on the steel bar, called a mandrel. they were rough ground on the outside and rough bored on the inside. These operations removed most of the roughness, and serious imperfections at this point could be discerned by visual inspection. If they existed here, the barrel was scrapped without further work. Assuming no defects, the barrels were now "proofed," which consisted of loading them with a prescribed load and firing them in the confines of a "proof house." Some barrels burst wide open from poor welds or other defects, those that passed the proof were finished and proofed again. In England and most other European countries where proofing is a government function, this initial proofing is called "provisional proof" and the final proof is called "definitive proof."

As steels improved, the gun industry moved to the bored barrel, cut from a solid steel bar. Initially called "weldless" barrels, they had many advantages over the older methods. Another important consideration about this time was the development of smokeless powder (which came into general use during the mid-1890s) which delivered higher pressures.

Fine Damascus barrels had a handsome appearance because the better barrels were made of several individual bars of iron and steel, each of which was twisted and then welded into a single unit called a skelp. A number of skelps were then welded and forged into the barrel. Perhaps one of the finest appearing (and best) of these was one called a three-iron stub Damascus. These barrels had superb looks with hundreds of tiny, wavy lines not really unlike the lines used on the paper U.S. currency is printed on. Such barrels were favored by many contemporary hunters and gunmakers alike and they died hard. In fact, many of the early weldless barrels were decorated to appear like a fine Damascus.

As mentioned before, it was the man or men wielding the hammers who determined the quality of these barrels so the human element was vital and an obvious result was that some barrels were far better than others. This variation in quality, together with the rapidly expanding use of smokeless powder, ensured that twist barrels simply had to go. It ought to be noted that the better grades of Damascus are quite strong, and while they won't equal a modern barrel, they will give satisfactory service today with proper loads. For the record, no Damascus or twist-barreled gun should be used with anything but black-powder loads. Black-powder shotgun loads are available or you may reload using black powder or its substitute, Pyrodex.

Steel is made both tough and hard for gun use. It's made that way because the requirements for gun-barrel steel are that it must be abrasion resistant, high in tensile strength, and readily machinable. The most common steel in use in guns today is known in the trade as SAE (for Society of Automotive Engineers) 4140, the numbers indicating a precise alloy consisting of chromium and molybdenum. Commonly called chrome-moly, it satisfies the requirements of nearly all gun barrels and many actions today.

Most shotgun barrels really do not need a steel so tough as this chrome moly, but with the increasing controversy about steel shot as a substitute for lead, it is becoming more and more vital that a tough barrel steel be used. Formerly, the steel requirement for shotgun barrels was not nearly so vital. There are very different requirements for rifle-barrel steel, because the pressure, heat, and velocity generated results in far greater friction and more rapid wearing. Along the same line, most .22 rimfire rifles do not require so tough a steel, and as a result, a milder steel is commonly used for them. This is a carbon-manganese alloy that is easier to machine and provides sufficient life for any .22 rimfire barrel. Prior to the advent of steel shot, the same steel was perfectly adequate for shotgun barrels.

The shotgun barrel departs rather drastically from the rifle barrel in a number of ways. It is smooth bored of course and not rifled. Its wall thickness is much thinner because the pressures generated are much lower and its bore is usually much larger. There are many reasons for these differences all of which we'll be going into as we go along. Suffice it to say that the requirements of any gun barrel are that it be strong enough to contain the load for which it is made, and that it have the necessary abrasion resistance to provide accuracy sufficient for the purpose of the gun.

For some reason, or reasons, everyone thinks of a shotgun barrel as a simple thing. Indeed, the whole subject of shotguns is usually considered simple. Nothing could be farther from the truth, for a shotgun is complex and less is known about shotgun performance than rifle performance. There is considerably more romance associated with rifles than there is with shotguns, possibly because there's more romance about a long, precise shot perfectly delivered. Regardless of the reasons, nobody really tries to understand a shotgun as he does a rifle. And that's a shame because the challenges are much more complicated and the flight of a cluster of shot contains so many variables as to defy imagination. What happens to that cluster is determined by the barrel to a very large degree.

INTERCHANGEABLE BARRELS

Most of today's shotguns, chiefly the pumps and autoloaders, have interchangeable barrels. This means that you can buy a gun today with the barrel of your choice; then, later on, you can simply buy another barrel for the same gun of a different length and/or boring with the assurance that it will fit and operate correctly. You can also order, at the time of purchase, either a side-by-side or over/under gun with extra barrels. These combinations are usually in the same gauge, although there are a few exceptions. One gun, at least—there may be more—can be bought complete with barrels for 12 16, 20, 28, and .410 gauges. But that's pretty rare and very costly too. This combination (a Krieghoff Model 32) is meant for the competitive skeet shooter who wants to use the same gun for all gauge matches (and who has a lot of money).

If you've already bought a double gun and want another set of barrels later it will require that the gun be shipped back, for this must be a hand-fitted proposition with the resulting very high cost and probably a long delivery delay.

BARREL FASTENING

While most rifle barrels are screwed tightly into their receivers, the same is not true with shotgun barrels. The barrels of pump and semiautomatic guns are usually provided with what is known as a barrel extension and they are tightly fastened into this part permanently. The extension fits into the receiver (which may be a light aluminum alloy) and, in effect, becomes a part of the action. The breechbolt locks into the barrel extension in such cases. One major exception is the Winchester Model 12 pump gun, which locks into the steel receiver by an interrupted thread requiring a quarter turn to secure the barrel.

The methods by which double gun barrels are fastened are much more complicated. Most conventional doubles, that is the pairs of barrels, are simply hooked onto the frame. The exception to this rule is that of the shallow-framed over/under guns which hook on either side of the barrels rather than underneath. Some over/unders —the Browning and Winchester's 101 for example—hook underneath like a side-by-side double. Others do not. Led some years ago by Woodward and Boss, these guns hook on the side; the result is a much lower silhouette since the guns do not need that bottom lug projecting down. Modern examples of this system are the Beretta, Remington Model 3200, Ruger, and others. The British call this a bifurcated lump— the lump being that part between the barrels of a side-by-side gun into which the lock moves and which hooks over the pin at the front of the action bar.

The two barrels of a double gun must be securely fastened; they also must be arranged so that the shot clusters converge at a distance of 40 yards. The right barrel of a side-by-side gun shoots a little to the right, because it's off the center line. For the same reason, a left barrel shoots to the left. So the barrels must be mounted so the muzzle centers are closer together than the breech centers, which compensates and causes the charges to hit the point of aim at the same distance.

Double-gun barrels are fastened by a variety of methods, the system employed for many years by the English makers of best guns being a system of "chopper lumps." In this system, one half the lump is forged with each barrel blank. After boring and machining, the two are joined by brazing (similar to soldering except that brass is used and much higher temperatures are required and the resultant joint is more secure). The procedure is time consuming but it does provide the best system for joining a pair of barrels. Winchester has gone the British one better with its method of joining Model 21 barrels: The barrels are made the same way except that Winchester cuts a dovetail vertically in the lumps and, when joined, the system is stronger. However, the English look down on that a little bit, claiming that it isn't necessary and that it adds a little thickness and therefore a little weight. Either way is ideal and only best guns are commonly made this way.

Another method employed in double guns is for a separate lump to be made and fitted between the barrels and then brazed in place. This is a quite adequate system, although it will not be found in best-gun manufacture.

The most common method used today is called monobloc and it has many advantages. In the first place, it is the least expensive method while still being as strong or stronger than any other. A monobloc is simply a short section, about 3 inches long, machined out of solid steel, which comprises the entire breech section

Above: *Shown at the top is a set of unfinished 16-gauge L.C. Smith barrels which are chambered, fitted with ejectors, and proofed. (Note proof mark on the flat with the initials NP which mean nitro proofed.) Shown below is a set of 20-gauge L.C. Smith barrels the same as those above except they are finished and have been fitted to a gun.*

Top Left: *Remington's Model 3200 shotgun has a unique method of fastening the barrels. The gun has no conventional side ribs; this is designed to promote more rapid cooling and to allow one barrel to move freely back and forth if it's fired (and heated) more than the other barrel. A relatively few other competition guns are constructed along similar lines but very few field guns are made this way.*

Bottom Left: *The muzzle fastening of Savage's Valmet combination gun. Top barrel is 12 gauge, lower is .308 caliber in this sample. Note that there is an adjustment that can be made laterally (although it is inadvisable to fool with this unless you know what you're doing).*

of the barrels including the lumps. Then the barrel holes are bored out oversize, barrels are turned to fit, inserted, and soldered in place. The result is a solid unit that's powerfully strong and not expensive to produce. You can always recognize a monobloc gun because there's a little line around each barrel about 3 inches forward of the breech, it's generally camouflaged by a bit of engraving. I like this sytem chiefly because it makes the solid double gun possible to manufacture without all the cost of chopper lumping.

Double barrels also require fastening at the muzzle, and, with a couple of notable exceptions, are also fastened along their entire length. The usual method of joining these separate tubes is by brazing carefully fitted separators at the muzzle and at least one midway between muzzle and breech. Then a number of additional spacers are soldered in place and, finally, the ribs are soldered full length to complete the job. The exceptions are the Remington Model 3200, which is only fastened at the muzzle, and the Savage over/under combination shotgun and rifle, which has the same fastening idea as the Remington. The Savage is made in Finland by Valmet. The Krieghoff, a copy of the older Remington Model 32, is also simply fastened fore and aft, as is the Perazzi. The theory behind this Remington-developed system is that since the lower barrel is fired more than the upper, it tends to heat up more. By allowing it to float, that is move forward freely and independently of the upper barrel, it will eliminate any tendency to bend. What this implies is that, with normally fastened barrels, if you only fire the bottom barrel a number of times it will expand and stretch but will be held back by the cooler top barrel. The result will be a slight upward bending of the lower barrel with corresponding raising of the point of impact. To my best knowledge this has never been borne out by performance, although it certainly stands up in theory. It would be different in a rifle, but the point may be academic in a shotgun due to the nature of the cluster of shot, which covers a wide area. An inch or so higher at 40 yards won't mean enough to matter.

Final boring and inside finishing must be accomplished after the pairs of barrels are joined because the heat required for brazing would scale the inside. Top extensions, if any, are fastened at the same time and, in the case of a best gun, are part of the chopper-lump procedure. Such top extensions as are employed by other systems—such as that used by Merkel, Greener, and others—which fit into the frame to be locked there by a cross bolt are also rigidly made a part of this assembly at the time of joining the separate barrels.

WALL THICKNESS

There is a vast difference in the wall thickness of shotgun barrels as will be apparent if you examine the barrel of any production-made pump or auto gun and compare it with that of a best-grade double gun. The production gun's barrel is considerably thicker in its wall thickness. This isn't to make it stronger, although it does that. The real reason is that it's easier to make because a thin-walled tube calls for closer workmanship. Best double guns are made with thin tubes, especially toward the muzzle, because that makes the gun easier to handle. You don't need extra thickness at the muzzle because the pressure is much less there and you want the muzzle as light as possible so the gun's maximum weight lies between your hands.

This difference is but one more of the niceties of a finely made top-grade gun. It has one disadvantage that I can think of; you should never fire steel-shot loads through any double gun. The added thickness of today's pump and autos is ample to handle steel shot, as factory loaded, but the thin walls of a fine double must only be used for the loads for which they were made. And they were made only for conventional lead shot.

INSIDE THE BARREL

The most important elements inside a shotgun bore today are these four: the *chamber*, which is bored out to accept the cartridge; the *forcing cone*, which reduces the chamber to bore diameter; the *choke*, which is a constriction at the muzzle to help determine the size of the shot cluster; and the *bore*, which is normally a long, straight section between the forcing cone and the choke.

Barrels were not always made this way. In fact, the muzzle-loading shotgun had a distinct advantage over the modern barrel. That advantage was that there was no chamber, and therefore no forcing cone was necessary. This meant that the shot charge simply rode easily up the barrel with little resistance or deformation at the breech end.

Once breech loaders became popular they were chambered similar to rifle barrels to provide room for the cartridge. And since the outside diameter of a shotgun hull is larger than bore size, it follows that there must be an abrupt reduction in bore. This reduction takes the form of a sharp taper called the forcing cone. There must also be room for the crimp to unfold which means that there is a space ahead of the unfired cartridge across which the shot charge must jump. It is inevitable that the shot charge will bulge a bit here because it's under tremendous gas pressure to drive it out and, the next instant, it must squeeze down again. No matter how nicely made, this has to affect the flight of the shot up the barrel.

It was believed in the days before about 1874 that a bit of relieving, or opening of the bore, produced more consistent patterns while some barrels were a true cylinder for the whole length. But in the 1873–74 period, choke boring became popular and that changed all the old rules. The original choke boring is variously attributed to two different persons. Most Americans credit an Illinois duck hunter named Fred Kimble, while most Englishmen point out that one of their countrymen named Pape had a patent on choke boring that preceded the Kimble claim. But just who should have the credit is of no importance today; what is important, and uncontested, is that the English gunmaker from Birmingham, W. W. Greener, was the one person who *developed* successful choke boring.

The purpose of choke in a gun barrel is most easily demonstrated by considering a garden hose with nozzle. You can constrict the flow of water so that it throws a small stream of water a great distance. Or you can twist it so it throws a very wide stream a short distance. And you can adjust it to anything in between. Choke boring does precisely the same thing. Generally, the tighter the choke the closer the pattern, which is suitable for longer shots; the more open the barrel, the wider the pattern and the more suitable it is for a grouse that gets up from between your legs giving you a close, fast shot.

We will explore choke in more detail later; the purpose here is simply to explain what it is and how it is made. Choke consists of two parts, one of which is the taper and the second, forward part, is parallel. Interestingly, no two identically bored barrels will give precisely the same results. This is one of the reasons a top-quality gun costs a lot of money. When a customer orders a gun to deliver, say a 50-percent pattern at 40 yards, this is exactly what he expects to get. And that's what he will get, but the gunmaker must cut and try, cut and try some more until the gun is shooting precisely as ordered. There is no way he can bore the barrel to a certain dimension and have it shoot exactly as ordered. This will help explain the high cost of best-quality guns and the great competitive trap guns that consistently win matches.

A machine-made gun, on the other hand, is made to different standards because the market would not stand such high costs. So these barrels are choked to a standard size and stamped as indicated. If you do some testing at the pattern board you'll find that some barrels marked modified or even improved cylinder will actually deliver full-choke patterns. There are a number of complicated reasons for this which we'll explore later.

Choke in better-grade guns is bored; that is, the barrel is bored to provide the full-length bore up to the choke where this section is bored and carefully polished. Very time consuming. Some years ago, a production engineer learned that you could simply bore out the barrel for its full length and then squeeze the muzzle down from the outside. The operation is called swaging, but it's more often referred to as jug-choking. It serves the purpose for any machine-made gun, even though it's a far cry from a fully machined choke that's been hand regulated.

It is possible, although it's a costly custom job, to put choke back in a barrel if it has been removed (such as by cutting a barrel off) or if it is desired to tighten the choke. This is done by recess choking, which means the bore is opened slightly for a distance behind the choke, which has the effect of allowing the charge to expand to larger than bore size before being choked.

There also are chokes on the market that can be fastened to any single-barrel gun and provide different adjustments, again like the garden hose. One of the most popular of these is known as the Poly-Choke, installed by cutting the barrel to whatever length you want, then threading it and screwing on the device. It is used by many shooters. Another, similarly attached, device is the Cutts Compensator, put out by the Lyman sight people. This differs from the Poly-Choke in that it has interchangeable tubes for adjustment.

Still another method of adjusting chokes is a development used in several Winchester shotguns and known as Winchoke. This simple device consists of small tubes that are inserted inside the barrel. When you buy the gun, you get a set of three different choke tubes. Something along similar lines is offered with the Perazzi MT-6 over/under Olympic trap gun. This is the first time any successful method of adjustable choke has ever been offered with any double gun to my knowledge. Its main difference from the Winchester system is that the Perazzi is hand finished all the way—and this is reflected in the price, too.

The usual American chokes are: full, modified, improved cylinder, and skeet, in descending order with skeet being the most open. You also can effectively control choke by trying various brands of ammunition and various loads within the brands. This is an ever-changing situation and no categoric statements can be made about it. A gun may deliver 50-percent patterns with Winchester, 60 with Remington, and something else with Federal, everything else being the same. And if you think this confuses you, I assure you that it continues to stagger the manufacturing engineers who live with it all the time, too.

Among the many confusing aspects about a shotgun bore are such considerations as should it be mirror smooth inside? Or should it be rough? Common sense would tell you that it ought to be as smooth as smooth can be—polished like a mirror. Not only is it nice to look through such a barrel, but it's also the way it should be made for best shooting. But that's not necessarily so. A case can be made for having a bore that's roughed up a bit. This has been demonstrated in a variety of methods including some by old-timers who made a practice of urinating through the bore of a new gun and allowing it to rust! Along similar lines, some have cut circular rough marks in the area just behind the choke. Heresy? Maybe, but you can make a case for the result and the reason is quite simple: With a smooth bore there is no resistance to the wad column, which is being urged ahead by the expanding gases. When the shot leaves the muzzle, the wads are still pushing and they tend to disrupt the center of the pattern producing what is called a blown pattern, meaning one that has a big hole in its middle. The roughened bore, especially if it's rough near the choke, slows the wad column down enough to let the shot cluster get clear of the barrel unmolested. And the theory has been proved enough times to give it considerable merit. One of the most interesting things about this theory is that after all these years there is still disagreement. There has been little change in the shotgun in more than 200 years; you'd think things like this would have been resolved long ago.

RIBS

The rib on top of a shotgun barrel, or lying between the tubes of a side-by-side double gun, is an aid to sighting. It's also rather expensive to make and install, which is why the cheaper guns don't have a rib, just a bead at the front.

There are three basic kinds of rib: ventilated, hollow, and solid. Both of the latter look alike, but the hollow is lighter and is preferred. The purpose of a ventilated rib is to allow heat dissipation, otherwise the purpose of any rib is the same—to provide a sighting plane. It is often thought that a ventilated rib (usually shortened to simply vent rib) is the most highly desirable addition. This isn't necessarily so at all. Vent ribs have been made popular by advertising copy to the point where a lot of shooters think they're just the ticket. But the vent rib is really a mistake on any game gun because it has a nasty habit of picking up lint, twigs, pine needles, and other such foreign trivia and it rusts easily underneath, where it's hard to get at. Moreover, it tends to bend easily if you bang it against any decent-sized twig. So the vent rib is meant for skeet and trap guns, not field guns. The latter should be fitted with either a hollow or solid rib, preferably a hollow one for the weight reduction.

Ribs are pretty standard in width although some recent trap guns have overly wide ribs that appeal to some shooters.

PRESSURES

Operating with far lower pressures than rifles, shotgun barrels' walls are much thinner and the result is that shotguns can be made fairly light and still be strong enough. You can take a relatively small rifle cartridge, like the .22 Hornet, and load it to develop as high as 50,000 units of pressure. Your typical shotgun load operates at around 10,000 units. The result is that you do not require the mass of metal to hold the pressures. The chief reason shotguns develop such low pressures is that they hold a straight cartridge, which allows the pressure to get right to work and move out, as compared to a bottle-necked high-power rifle cartridge like the .300 Winchester Magnum for example. In the latter, the gases are turned back by the shoulder and build high pressures rapidly and consequently need a lot of wall thickness to hold things together.

BARREL LENGTH

Shotgun barrel lengths are pretty well established; most common barrels are between 24 and 30 inches long with a few variations. Some makers are limited and list all 26-inch barrels as improved cylinder, 28-inch as modified, and 30-inch as full choke. Others give you a lot more choice. Other things being equal, a shorter barrel can be gotten into action faster than a long tube. The ideal game gun, to my way of thinking, has a barrel no longer than 26 inches, and I'm speaking of a double gun. You must remember that if you have a pump or auto, the added action length makes the overall gun much longer than a double.

By federal law a shotgun or high-power rifle must have a barrel no shorter than 16 inches long (14 inches for a .22 rifle) measured by sticking a rule down the barrel against the closed breechbolt. Therefore, you cannot saw off a rifle or shotgun barrel shorter than those dimensions or you have an illegal gun. But no sportsman has use for a shotgun with a barrel any shorter than 24 inches as a minimum for best balance, although you might want to go a little shorter in barrel length if you are using a pump or auto in the dense grouse and woodcock thickets.

The longest barrels are generally found on trap guns, where 32- and 34-inch lengths are fairly common. If there is any real advantage to these lengths over 30 inches I'm unaware of it. But many of the better shooters use them. For many years Marlin has made their Goose Gun, a bolt-action 12-gauge gun, with a 36-inch barrel and it has sold extremely well. Based on that success the same company produces a 38-inch and a 40-inch barrel for their Model 120 pump gun. The extra-long barrel may have a certain mystique, but it surely can't perform any better than a shorter tube. I've shot the Marlin 40-incher and it does surprisingly well. It aims nicely at trap targets, it seems to have less recoil, and it has very little noise. Still, it's far too long a tube to make any sense to any knowledgeable shooter.

Now and then one sees some rather unusual things on the shooting line, rifle or shotgun or pistol. One of them is the astounding modification Simmons has done to the Remington Model 3200. I've shown a picture of this for its interest. You might think it looks ridiculous (and maybe it does) but it has been used by at least one All-American trap shooter to rewrite the record books. Target shooters of all types have experimented with all manner of things and many of them have proved worthy of adoption by the major manufacturers. I hope they never quit experimenting. If there's a lesson to be learned it's that you should never condemn anything until it's checked out.

If there is any standardization about barrel length in terms of what is best, I have yet to hear of it. First, though, it's necessary to realize that pumps and autos are vastly different from doubles because the length of their actions must be added to the total length of the gun. A double gun with the same barrel length will be about 4½ inches shorter.

Shorter lengths are more acceptable today than they were 40 or 50 years ago, the chief reason apparently being that shooters began to try them and found they worked. There is no appreciable loss in velocity, but there is a decrease in weight and an improvement in handling. However, it's important to note that a gun should not just have its barrels bobbed off without making the necessary stock changes to be compatible. Going from 30 to 28 inches would make no difference worth noting, but anything shorter would be another matter entirely. All this applies chiefly to double guns. I would suggest that a length of about 26 inches is best for most upland shooting, although that can easily go an inch or two either way if you prefer. For waterfowl, 28 or 30 inches is usually preferred, although any gun suitable for upland gunning is perfectly satisfactory for decoyed ducks.

I have known some excellent ruffed-grouse hunters who use semiautomatic guns with extraordinarily short barrels—20 or 22 inches—with great success. A grouse gun must be moved and fired fast, fast, fast, and patterns ought to be wide open. When you're in heavy cover, as you usually are, there is no room to swing a long barrel and moreover the bird is gone so fast there's no time to swing it either. So the use dictates the need in some cases. Personal preference has a great deal to do with the choice of barrel length.

Just about the shortest practical length for any gun barrel is that of the 20-inch riot gun now used by law-enforcement personnel and, I believe, originally used in World War I in trench warfare. These guns also saw duty in World War II for guard duty, there being nothing to gain the respect of a prisoner more than a 12-gauge shotgun loaded with buckshot. Such a gun is sometimes referred to as an alley clearer for obvious reasons.

The primary aspects of barrel length with which to be concerned are handling (weight and balance), pointing, and ballistics. Only you can answer the first two, but be assured that ballistics are virtually the same for any length. The slight differences will be within the tolerances for the loads anyway, which is to say that a 30-inch barrel with a load developing velocity at the low end of its tolerance will be no faster than a fast load

with much shorter barrel. You may consider this a tossup.

These three factors add up to confidence in your barrel or barrels and that's what it's all about. When you have confidence you can shoot your gun and this is an indefinable something that we cannot pinpoint, nor can we tell you how to find it.

HEADSPACE

Headspace is rarely discussed in shotgun circles but it's just as much a factor as it is in a rifle. In fact, there's one occasion when it becomes pretty important. Headspace is the fore-and-aft space in the gun barrel for the cartridge. Since all shotgun cases are rimmed, it is the rim that governs headspace. And since shotgun ammunition is made by virtually every nation in the world, and guns are too, it follows that there are tolerances.

That means you can get a minimum rim thickness and chamber it in a gun with maximum chamber specifications. That's no danger in any gun properly made but here's what can happen. (It is usually felt most in double guns.) Say you have a difference of .015 inch, fifteen thousandths of an inch (or 1/64th)—not very much but enough to make the gun recoil more heavily than normal. When the firing pin strikes, it drives the case forward all the way and then the actual firing drives the case backwards sharply until it slams the action face. That small amount of movement is enough to make quite a pronounced difference in recoil. When a set of barrels is a little off the face, as is true of some older guns, and you have a rather deep chamber, that gun can kick hell out of you.

One gun that is said to be immune from this is the French Darne, because it opens by withdrawing the breech face directly to the rear. The barrels do not lower, as in conventional doubles, and there is considerable mechanical advantage. I'm told that this allows the makers to chamber more tightly than other double guns and that, for this reason, the Darne does not recoil as heavily as most doubles. But I've been unable to get my hands on a Darne to test it. The importer, located in Victoria, Texas, claims all his mail goes to British Columbia. Must be so because he

Today's gun manufacture is accomplished by the most sophisticated machinery on the market. This operation, for example, is entirely controlled by the complicated device seen at the right. It's called "tape control" and that means a tape, which has been programmed, controls the machine. The man shown is simply setting up the machine; once set, it will run automatically. Such manufacture assures much more precise parts and the final result is a far better firearm. This photo was taken in the Marlin plant, the newest in the industry (built in 1970).

doesn't answer me, so I can only report this as hearsay evidence but will add the comment that it could be true, based on what I know of the gun's operation.

PROOF MARKS

Virtually all European guns bear proof marks and, since most guns made in Europe are double guns, let's confine this discussion to double guns, both side-by-side and over/under. These marks appear on both the barrel and action flats. Over/unders have to be marked a little differently due to the nature of their construction. (They do not have flats such as a side-by-side gun has, so the markings appear inside the u frame.)

These marks are not random inspector's stamps, nor are they symbols of some ancient incantations that can be ignored. Properly interpreted they can tell you a story, a story that you should pay attention to. They'll tell you, for example, whether the gun has been proofed for smokeless (nitro) powder, the bore size, the chamber length, the maximum load (in most cases), and the degree of choke.

Since these matters vary among the nations, and have been updated many times since government proof houses were first established, the marks used are far too lengthy and involved to include in this book. My purpose in introducing the subject is to alert you, should you ever consider the purchase of a used European-made double gun, to the fact that these exist. Your dealer should explain them to you clearly and explicitly and, if he doesn't know what they mean, don't buy the gun. No reputable dealer in such guns will refuse to tell you exactly what he is selling and this is especially important because so many of the older guns were meant to be used with much lighter loads than are currently used here. If you fired a Magnum 2¾-inch load in a light double gun made for the 2-inch or 2½-inch load commonly used in England, you'd very likely destroy a good gun. You should also know whether or not such a gun is of any use to you because this ammunition can only be obtained at considerable cost and trouble unless you reload it yourself.

BURSTS

A burst gun barrel, or ringed barrel, usually if not always is the result of some object in the bore. This can be snow, mud, dirt, a 20-gauge load mistakenly dropped into a 12 gauge with the latter loaded and fired behind it, or most anything else you can think of.

In years gone by, when only one barrel of a double gun was fired a number of times without using the second, it was fairly common for the load in the second barrel to loosen and some of its components to move out into the bore. When the barrel was fired there was a burst or a bulge. Now that muzzle-loading shotguns are becoming popular again, it might pay to heed the warning learned the hard way by many old-timers with muzzle loaders and early cartridge doubles. If you fire only one barrel and reload, you should develop the habit of *always* reramming the second charge. The same caution might be considered when using reloads. If your cases have been crimped several times they may be a bit weakened and it's a good idea to check when you reload. These cautions apply to double guns only.

CHAPTER TEN

THE GUN STOCK

It's quite possible that you will hear more prejudices, more opinions, and perhaps more references to ancestries when listening to or entering into a discussion of gun stocks than with any other aspect of firearms. And that is more true with rifles than it is with shotguns. Why? I suspect because of two reasons: 1) most people think a shotgun is a simple thing; and 2) most shooters just don't know any better.

Actually, a shotgun stock is of far more importance to the gun than is a rifle stock. It serves a totally different purpose, since the shotgun is fired by pointing, not aiming. Therefore the stock must fit the shooter properly if he is to shoot well. This is basic. Once your target appears, whether feathered or clay, you must swiftly mount the gun, get on target, and press trigger all in a single fluid motion. You cannot make any adjustments or any accommodations if you hope to connect. When you fire a rifle, on the other hand, you have time to adjust and to aim deliberately. (There are a few exceptions, but they are rare, when it's necessary to snapshoot a rifle like a shotgun.)

Let's review some of the terms we'll be using in our discussion of gun stocks.

Butt: The rear end of the stock, generally from the action back, and often referred to as the buttstock (especially on any gun with a 2-piece stock).

Buttplate: A protective pad covering the rear surface of the butt. Often steel, plastic, or

The top grade, most expensive shotgun produced in America, the Winchester Model 21 Grand American. Custom built, this particular gun has a very fancy grade of American walnut stock and is made to the buyer's specifications. Stock is with pistol grip and has a beavertail forearm.

rubber, the buttplate is sometimes called a recoil pad (if soft and cushioned). Often, better-grade shotguns have no separate buttplate, but are checked directly on the wood.

Heel: The top of the butt with gun in normal position.

Toe: The bottom of the butt with gun in normal position.

Comb: The top line of the buttstock, the front end of which is called the *nose,* the rear the *heel* as already defined.

Cheekpiece: A raised portion along the side of the stock extending from the comb down in varying shapes (which is designed to be an aid in aiming with a scope sight and is rarely found on a shotgun).

Monte Carlo: A top line (comb) with a dip down to the heel that lowers the buttplate while keeping the shooter's eye level relatively high.

Drop: A distance, measured at comb and heel (two measurements), from a continuation of the line of sight.

Pitch: The angle formed by the buttplate and the continuation of the line of sight.

Length of pull: The distance from the center of the trigger to the center of the buttplate (measured from the front trigger of a 2-trigger double gun).

Cast-off: The amount the buttstock is out of line with the bore's centerline—to the right.

Cast-on: The same as above but to the left. Normally a right-handed person requires a small amount of cast-off, a left-handed person a small amount of cast-on.

Forearm: The part of the stock lying forward of the action, sometimes called a fore end.

Inletting: The fitting of metal into wood.

MATERIALS

Stocks are made of a variety of hardwoods. Sometimes the nature of the gun to be built dictates the type of wood demanded. By this I mean that a finely fitted sidelock double gun, which requires the removal of a lot of wood, requires tougher wood than many other types of gun. The wood used must be capable of holding the action in place during recoil, sometimes for many thousands of shots. A wood that splits easily, or that warps freely and does not have stability, is of no use in a gun stock.

Gunmakers learned long ago that the most desirable wood for gun-stock use was walnut, because it has a combination of strength, weight, and stability that is equaled by few other woods and exceeded by none. There are, however, two distinct types of walnut: These are English walnut (*Juglans regia*), which is native to all of central and southern Europe and the Near East; and American or black walnut (*Juglans nigra*), which, except for English walnut, is the best stock wood available.

Now let's clear up some of the confusion that has always been rampant regarding stock wood. First, English walnut is the very best material available anywhere at any price. It alone possesses the most desirable hardness, closeness of grain, and beauty of figure that make it the first choice of anyone who knows anything about guns. However, English walnut is usually called

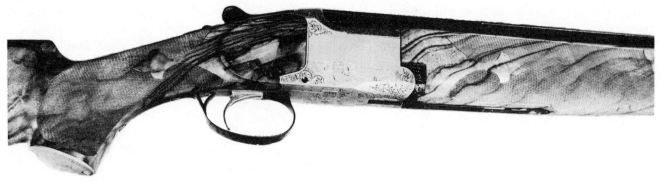

A Browning over/under custom stocked by Joe Balickie shows the contrasting colors in a super piece of English walnut. Note also the generous, perfect checkering executed by Mr. Balickie, one of the leading stockers in America.

French walnut, largely because that country has produced most of this wood for many years. The same wood has been called a wide variety of other names including Circassian walnut among others. English walnut is the proper name and that's the name of the edible walnuts with which we are all familiar. Many early colonists brought seedlings to America with them. Today, many of these trees are grown in California under irrigation which yields lots of nuts and some reasonably good wood for gun stocks. I say "reasonably" good because this wood does not compare with that from a tree grown slowly in the harshness of high altitude and in soil with little richness that makes it grow slowly. The force-fed, irrigated American variety will have coarser grain and it will not have the figure and color of its European cousin that grew the hard way.

The most magical of all names in gun-stock wood is Circassian walnut, a term highly promoted by gunmakers a few generations back. True Circassian walnut is the same species of tree that grows in France or California; the only difference is that it comes from an area in the USSR north of Turkey. No gun-stock wood has come from this part of the world for many years; in fact, most stock wood sold as Circassian came from France anyway. Circassian always was more myth than reality. Which is neither here nor there, for the wood is equally good.

European walnut picks up its color—some of which runs from nearly white, through the reds and oranges, to brown and black streaks—from the minerals in the soil. This will tell you quickly why two identical seedlings, one planted in an irrigated walnut grove in California and the other near a mountain top in France, will produce vastly different wood. The latter will be far superior, especially in terms of its coloration and grain characteristics.

Grain is a far different thing from coloration. Grain is the direction in which the fibers lie and it is what gives the stock its strength and stability. Color lines do not always follow the grain line, although they usually run close to that followed by the grain. You get the finest grain, and often the finest colorations, from wood cut near the butt of a tree. An ancient walnut tree that's 3 or 4 feet or more thick at the butt will, when properly dug out of the ground and correctly sawed, produced dozens of exquisitely figured gun-stock blanks. The areas around burls and branches often yield interesting grain patterns.

You can picture some wood buyer standing on the slopes of a mountain far from civilization and next to an ancient walnut tree somewhere in France or northern Italy. He buys the tree, directs its felling (which must be done just so, else the tree may split), then directs digging out the butt to a depth of several feet. This then is pulled, pushed, and dragged to the sawmill where it must be carefully studied before any cutting. Alas, however, the chances are that the buyer is buying for a furniture company rather than a gunmaker. In this event, hundreds and thousands of potential top-grade gun-stock blanks wind up as furniture veneer.

As this is being written, in 1976–77, there is little European walnut available in higher grades. And what is available is priced very high. I have no idea what the dollar will be worth as you're reading these words, but in terms of 1977 dollars, the highest-grade English walnut gun-stock blank (that means the roughly sawn stock wood with no labor expended) is valued at from several hundred to nearly a thousand dollars, depending on the exact grade of the wood itself.

The American black walnut tree is second in preference; it produces a good stock and is used by most American gunmakers. Some American walnut has fine figure and some has good coloration too. No matter how good American walnut is, or how pretty, it is coarser than European—which means it isn't as strong. And you can usually cut American walnut checkering to not more than about 18 lines per inch while some makers cut up to 28 lines in good English walnut. There are, however, some guns that ought to be stocked with American walnut despite the superiority of English. An American classic like the Winchester 12 pump gun just wouldn't look right if it wore a fancy English walnut stock.

Despite the ravages of gunmakers over 200 years and furniture makers and occasional other users, there is still a surprisingly sufficient supply of American walnut available. Most of it today comes from the Ozark Mountains area. Even though gunmakers are gobbling up prodigious quantities of trees annually, the supply continues to hold up. Yet, you can read in old accounts that during the early 1800s, the "supplies of walnut were being exhausted" and some substitutes were being used. Substitutes are still being used today. There is an item in the trade called a "promotional" brand—meaning that it is the same basic model as, say, the Ajax Model 100. Except that it isn't stamped Ajax; it may be stamped Centurion Model 10. But it will be exactly the same as the famous and popular Ajax 100 except it will have a "walnut-finished hardwood" stock, which means birch or elm or sycamore. It also means a lower price tag and the manufacturer doesn't care what the retailer charges for this promotional-branded gun while he prefers that the Ajax 100 continue to retail at its "suggested price." You will often get a good buy, in terms of a solid, dependable gun, with one of these promotional guns.

The same thing is often true with private-branded guns, guns that are also virtually identical to some famous models but that appear unders Sears' "Ted Williams" brand or Western

Auto's "Revelation" or whatever. Depending on the specifications made by the private-brand buyer, this gun may or may not have a walnut stock.

There are a lot of other woods that have been used for gun stocks over the years, some of them acceptable, some of them excellent but so rare as to be improbable, but many of them unacceptable. (There is little point in expending a lot of costly labor on the wrong kind of wood.) Stocks have been made of maple (hard, rock, or sugar maple), apple, pear, myrtlewood, cherry, beech, and many other woods. A large number of Kentucky rifles were made with maple and some with cherry stocks. Neither wood is as good as walnut, although there are some who will argue that point; the selection of wood can be very subjective.

The gun you buy will probably have an American walnut stock if it's one of the better grades of American gun. If it's a very high quality import the stock will be English walnut and the same if it's a quality American custom gun. If it's a lesser brand you will probably have a birch or elm stock. (Those are generalities and subject to change.) Some of the wood being used on today's "finer" imported guns is a shame. I have seen, on today's market, gun-stock wood that is English walnut all right but that is so plain and of so poor a color that the manufacturer really ought to hide his head in shame rather than market the product and ask the prices he's asking. I acknowledge that good wood is hard to get, but there is no excuse for offering some guns at a suggested list of more than a thousand dollars that have stocks about as handsome as a pine plank.

In a recent visit to Abercrombie & Fitch, I noticed that their A&F-branded shotguns, all side-by-side double guns, had nice walnut stocks. The incredible thing was that there were about thirty or more guns in the rack and they all had similar grain. It turns out the guns were Japanese made and that those good Japanese workers are now *painting* the grain in plain wood before finishing! The result is really attractive—it's a sort of smoky gray coloration and it does a lot for the looks of these guns. The same finish is evident on an SKB gun made in Japan, so the practice is fairly universal over there. This is an acceptable

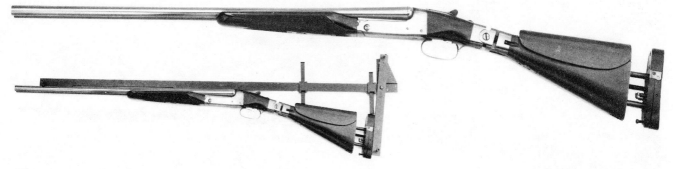

The try-gun used at the Orvis Shooting School is adjustable in almost any direction. In use, the instructor adjusts its elements until he is satisfied the fit is precise. Then the measurements can be taken with the device shown and the results translated into a custom-fitted stock. It is important to note that the use of a try-gun calls for an expert gun fitter; otherwise the results will be worthless.

way to improve a plain piece of wood. But if someone ever decides to refinish such a stock he's in for a surprise!

Over the years there have been some substitutions that we ought to mention just in passing. Most of them relate to rifles, but one never knows what will occur next and they may someday be applied to shotguns. One of these substitutions is the laminated stock, first used I believe by the Germans on their Mauser military rifle. Walnut being in short supply, they began using laminated stocks made up of strips of wood a little thinner than 1/16th inch. The result was a serviceable stock though far from a pretty one. There were many experiments in this country for a few years by benchrest rifle shooters in the belief that they could offset warping tendencies by gluing alternating strips of wood. And at one time Remington offered a rifle with laminated stock using alternate layers of walnut and beech. The contrast was terrible looking.

Another departure from convention that hasn't yet found its way to shotguns is the Remington use of nylon in its Nylon 66 .22 semiautomatic rifle. In this little rifle, the entire action and stock are molded nylon with a steel barrel and steel breechblock, the latter sliding back and forth in nylon. Quite an impressive development although lacking the soul and character of a good piece of wood.

SHOTGUNS ARE FOR WINGSHOOTING

The first thing you should remember is that wingshooting was developed by the English

sportsman and his gunmakers. It is safe to say that the world's greatest wingshots have been English, or those trained in the English method. Good wingshooting calls for a stock that fits the user, meaning that it is only necessary for the gunner to shoulder and fire and everything else will be automatic. The gunner must do his part, but he can't do it with an ill-fitting gun.

A fitted gunstock is accomplished by using what is known as a "try-gun." The stock is adjustable in every direction and its proper use is for the fitter to make the necessary adjustments and then take the customer to the shooting grounds where he will be observed in actual shooting situations. Once the fitter is satisfied with the adjustments, the measurements are recorded and the customer may have his gun made to those dimensions. It should be added that those who can correctly fit a stock are very few in number.

If you ever visit London, I suggest most strongly that you visit Holland & Holland, Ltd. and ask to be fitted. They will give you your stock measurements which you can have made by any American gun stock maker and you'll have a stock that fits you. There are a few try-guns in America; at Winchester, at Orvis, at Abercrombie & Fitch, and perhaps a few other locations. There is usually no obligation involved; that is, if you are fitted by Holland & Holland you don't have to order a gun there. (In 1977 dollars, they start at about $10,000 and the waiting period is nearly that many years.) If you visit the Orvis school in Manchester, Vermont, they also have a shooting school and a try-gun. They'll take your order and can supply a good

Top: *A Browning Auto-5 showing an older type of pistol grip. Today it's called a semi-pistol grip and was popular a few years ago. It is not as full as the grip of today and not quite as satisfactory.* Bottom: *Trap shooting calls for a specialized gun with slightly longer stock and somewhat higher comb. This is the Perazzi single-barrel trap gun, which is one of today's favorites. Such guns are expensive because of the precise workmanship involved.*

Standard factory equipped stocks are meant to fit "Mr. Average Man." They do a pretty good job. This is the butt-stock of a Remington Model 1100 autoloader just as you buy it at your local dealer's.

double gun made to your measurements in Europe.

The double gun stock ought to have a straight grip. This is usually called English style, its main attribute being that it's faster than anything else. And that applies whether the gun has two triggers or a single trigger. You can get it up and in action quicker. Pistol-grip stocks do not belong on a double gun, even though most American doubles have been made this way for reasons that must be lost in obscure history.

A shotgun buttstock (that is, the length-of-pull as measured from the center of the trigger to the center of the butt) should be longer, about an inch longer, than that of a rifle stock. The reason is simply that such longer length aids in rapid shouldering and pointing. Similarly, shotgun buttplates should be smooth. If a rubber pad is used it ought to be smooth surfaced so it won't catch on the clothes. *Nothing* must interfere with

the fast and automatic reflex of shouldering the gun when a bird bursts from cover.

The forearm of a double gun takes one of two basic forms, a beavertail—which is wide and flat, like the tail of the animal from whence came its name—and the usual small forearm that the English have traditionally put on their game guns. These game-gun forearms are often, and irreverently, called splinter forearms, because there is so little wood there. That's a lousy reason to attach a deprecating name to a part of a fine game gun by people who don't have any understanding of what a gun ought to be. The game-gun forearm is ample and adequate. In fact, it looks better than a beavertail, the only redeeming feature of the latter being that it provides more wood to hang onto in shooting a few rapid rounds of skeet or trap when the barrels become warm.

Most English shotguns are made with straight grips, very few with pistol grips. In fact the straight grip is often referred to as English grip. (We're speaking of double guns since the English really don't recognize anything else.) The straight grip originated with two-trigger guns because it makes it far easier to slip the hand back and fire the rear trigger that way. But, and this is important, a straight grip also is a faster gun to bring to your shoulder and fire. *All* double guns should have straight grips in my opinion, side by sides and over/unders alike.

The pistol grip is a different proposition on a rifle because it helps you guide and hold the rifle

Many people ask what's the difference between trap and skeet. This photo showing both layouts will help explain it. Two skeet fields appear in the foreground; shooters fire from each of eight stations around the semicircle. Targets fly from both high and low houses and are pre-set to cross at a certain point. The flight of a skeet target is always the same. Trap shooting is done on the two layouts at the rear. Shooters fire five shots from each of five stations; targets come from the same low house, but the angle is constantly changing so you can not predict the flight until the target appears.

in recoil and this becomes more important as the chambering of the rifle increases in power. It's also not important whether pump and autoloading guns have a straight or pistol grip. After all you have an action that adds about 4 to 4½ inches to the length of the gun, which makes it a totally different proposition. I find pumps and autos more comfortable with the pistol-grip stock, but I also must admit that my bird shooting, with one exception, is done with double guns. That exception is waterfowling around salt water, where I'd rather expose a pump or auto to the elements and spray than a fine double.

I have always believed the appearance of a sidelock double gun was superior to the boxlock. While this feeling is fairly universal, there are more boxlock guns because they're a little simpler to manufacture and a hell of a lot easier to stock (although any double gun is very hard to stock). There are some boxlock guns on the market with dummy side plates that are meant to resemble a sidelock and give it the same flowing lines. The genuine sidelock is recognized by the ends of several pins that are visible in the lock plates.

USE DICTATES SHAPE

Shotgun stock shape, as well as dimensions, are dictated by the use to which the gun is to be put.

A game gun should be stocked essentially the same as a skeet gun although the total weight of a game gun is usually lighter. A trap gun is stocked entirely differently. Those special guns for live-pigeon shooting are stocked much like a trap gun, but there are slight differences hardly apparent to the eye.

Since those are the principal uses of a shotgun, let's examine the uses in a little more detail. I said that a skeet gun was stocked like a game gun but was usually heavier. That's because you don't carry a skeet gun, unlike a game gun, very far. You also shoot it a great deal more, since there are 25 shots in each round of skeet and you need a bit more weight in the gun to soak up some of the recoil. Depending on what you hunt and where you hunt, it's unlikely you'll fire more than a few shots a day when you're hunting. (There are obvious exceptions, such as dove shooting on a day when they're really flying and hot action in a duck blind, although today's limits don't let you do much shooting unless you're a lousy shot.)

When the game of skeet was started back in the early 1900s in Massachusetts, it was intended that the game be as close to field shooting as possible. When you called for the clay bird, you were expected to have your gun down and not to bring it up until the bird appeared. Then the rules were changed to allow you to shoulder the gun before saying "Pull." The modern game of International Skeet has returned to the old rules and your gun must have its butt positioned below your elbow when you give the "Pull" command. That's the way the game ought to be, since it poses a little more of a challenge. The beginner, or the observer, will conclude that trap shooting is easier than skeet. And so it will be at the beginning. But trap is the harder game.

The skeet field is set up so that both traps throw the targets through a 3-foot circle at a certain point on the field. Thus the targets always follow the same path, even though the shooter moves from station 1 to station 8 through each round. Trap shooting on the other hand is considerably different. The trap (there are five sets of three traps in International Trap) is on a continuously oscillating arm that is also raising and lowering itself continually. As a result, you don't know just where the trap is when you call "Pull." It may be a hard bird to the deep right, low down or high. Or it may be left and low. You won't know until the bird appears at up to 100 miles an hour. You can get a left-flying bird out of the right corner of the trap house, too. And in the International game you don't know which one of the traps will deliver the bird. It is the unpredictability of trap shooting that makes many strong men weep.

If you're starting out, you'll find that it's easier to begin to break 15 or so birds out of 25 at trap than at skeet. But once you get the hang of skeet you'll find it easier to be a steady performer. You should soon be breaking more than 20 in skeet after a little practice. But that's not going to happen so easily with trap.

This may not seem to have much to do with stocks, except that the use does dictate gun design. Hence the skeet gunstock should be the same kind of a stock you'll need for a fast-handling game gun. When a partridge blasts out nearly from between your legs and wraps itself around a tree, scaring you half to death, the quicker you can mount your gun and shoot the better your chances. Skeet's the same kind of a game. Trap on the other hand, while it calls for quick shooting, also calls for more deliberation. A good skeet shooter gets on the bird fast. Very fast. That's because it's easier to break when it's closer; before the wind can start to play tricks.

The trap shooter gets on his bird fast but then he's deliberate because he must compute the flight, which isn't as automatic as in skeet. So the trap gun must be different.

The following table gives, in inches, the most common stock dimensions for American guns. The figures are from Winchester specifications for popular models and I've added in parentheses the figures given by Remington where they differ. Where both manufacturers use the same figures they are not repeated.

	Length of Pull	Drop at Comb	Drop at Heel
Field gun	14	$1\frac{1}{2}$	$2\frac{1}{2}$
Trap gun	$14\frac{3}{8}$	$1\frac{3}{8}$	$1\frac{7}{8}$ ($1\frac{3}{4}$)
Skeet gun	$14\frac{1}{4}$ (14)	$1\frac{1}{2}$	2 ($2\frac{1}{2}$)

Notice that the skeet and field guns are fairly close in their buttstock dimensions—in the Remington brand they are the same, as a matter of fact. But the trap-gun stock has quite a bit less drop at the heel and a little less drop at the comb. These discrepancies may not seem like much, but they are significant.

STOCK FIT

It will be obvious that the physical makeup of the shooter will have a bearing on his shotgun stock to a larger degree than is true with a rifle. The extra-tall person, or one with sloping shoulders or extraordinarily long arms, will need more drop at the heel than is usually offered in standard stock dimensions. Likewise the extra-short man and most women. Women also need the toe cast to the side to avoid absorbing recoil by the breast. And the person with a very full, or very thin, face may be helped by a special stock with full or scooped-out combs, depending on the precise nature of the face. There are many things the custom stockmaker can do to help the person who can't fit into the "Mr. Average American" factory-offered gun stock.

Another oddity is a cross-over stock for the person who shoots from the right shoulder but who either has a left eye as the "master" eye or perhaps has lost the sight of the right eye. Such a stock, sometimes called offset, is bent to allow using the right shoulder but with the left eye.

How can you tell if your gun stock really fits you? I don't think the average person can tell

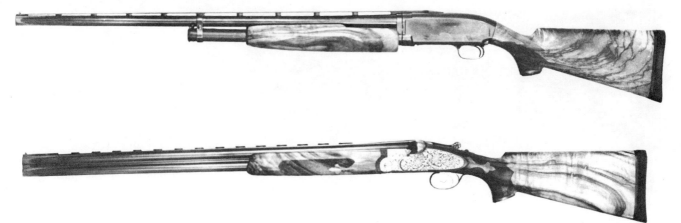

Joe Balickie stocked both these guns in English walnut, an extremely fine grade of walnut. Top is a Model 12 Winchester pump gun and bottom is a Beretta S-5 trap gun. Note that a solid rubber pad has been used on both guns.

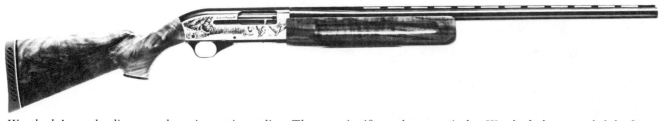

Weatherby's autoloading gun shows interesting styling. The most significant departure is that Weatherby has extended the fore-arm to hide the usual protruding magazine cap. You have to use a coin, or cartridge rim, to loosen the cap but that's a small price to pay for the different look.

this. You can get some idea if you mount the gun with your eyes closed and then open them quickly. The gun should point where you want it to and your head should rest so the eyes are in correct position. Of course, you'll be wearing the clothes you wear hunting. (And that introduces another variable because you'll wear less some days than other days. And some days you'll wear gloves too, and they'll make a difference.) When you're making such a test you are very conscious of what you're doing. And you can't do that in the field, which is why it's best to have your measurements taken by a skilled gun fitter. As I said earlier, they are few and far between. You can visit the Orvis Company in Manchester, Vermont. Or write and ask Winchester if they'll measure you if you visit New Haven. Or visit Reinhart Fajen in Warsaw, Missouri. James Purdey Ltd. usually sends a fitter to the U.S. once a year and he's available at Abercrombie & Fitch stores across the country. There are probably other try-guns and fitters equally proficient and

most custom stockmakers who specialize in shotgun work can do the same job. But there are not very many and you'll have to go out of your way to seek them out. It will be worth it.

Aside from the relatively few bolt-action shotguns being made, all shotguns have a two-piece stock. And that's a break for everybody because, other things being the same, it's easier to find shorter stock blanks than those of rifle length. And a shotgun is less fussy as to warpage and barrel bedding which are problems in the rifle end of the business.

There are basic guidelines every stock must follow. Let's first discuss the custom-fitted stock, for this is the highest order of gunsmithing. The first requirement is that it fit the customer and otherwise be to his specifications. The next is that its lines complement the metal parts of the gun. To use a simple example, you would build a totally different-looking stock for a Winchester Model 21 20-gauge double than you would for a Winchester Model 12 12-gauge pump gun even

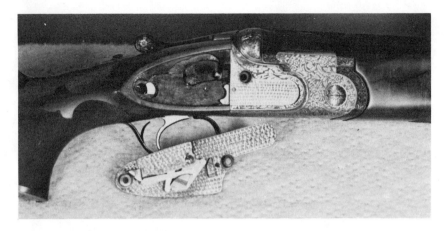

Really good inletting means removal of the barest amount of wood necessary for proper functioning of the parts. This Beretta sidelock gun by Joe Balickie indicates flawless work.

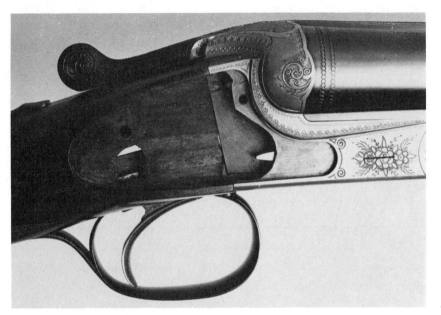

Another sidelock, this one from Europe, where the quality of inletting is excellent but not in the class of Balickie. More wood than necessary has been removed and there is a slight gap between the frame, center, and the wood.

though they were both made for the same man. Moreover, each custom stockmaker has his own ideas, which means that no two such men are going to turn out identical-looking stocks for the same customer, even though both will be made to the same measurements. The touch of each man will be evident, and this does not mean that one will necessarily be better than the other.

Custom shotgun stockmakers are fewer in number than rifle stockmakers. I'm not sure why this is so but will venture the guess that more customers want custom-stocked rifles and that fewer gunsmiths want to work on shotguns. To tell the truth there are not too many stockmakers who are capable of making a good shotgun stock. One of the reasons for this is that few customers know their measurements. Another reason is that few gunsmiths have the ability to cor-

rectly inlet the action of a good double gun, and few should even try it.

INLETTING

The act of cutting out the wood to fit the metal is called inletting, and it's a straight mechanical operation. There is no excuse for inletting being anything but a mirror image of the metal parts. If you examine the inletting of a good double gun you'll see just what I mean by these words. You must remove the barest minimum amount of wood—just enough to permit the parts to move freely—and you must establish tight bearing against the portions where the wood will take the thrust of recoil from the metal.

Action inletting is done by first stripping the frame of all parts and inletting that first. Then install the bottom tang to the frame and inlet those pieces following which the internal parts are added and space provided for them and their operation. Naturally these steps can't be taken in a production gun but the result must be close to the same. If the custom maker had to make ten or twenty stocks at a time, he'd set it up on a production basis too.

Inletting is done before any shaping by the custom stockmaker, who then establishes his drops, pitch, and other guidelines from his customer's specifications. Rough shaping is done with such tools as spoke shaves, band saw, gouges and chisels, and even, sometimes, a sharp hatchet. Final shaping is usually done by fine spoke shave, draw knife, and files making certain that specifications are met and that the lines blend in with the metal. Finishing is done with progressively finer sandpaper until the wood is as slick as glass, after which the pores are filled with either a filler or the final finish itself depending on the workman. Once the pores are filled, the checkering pattern is laid out and master lines are cut whereupon the finish is completed and the checkering cut. A bit of finish is scrubbed into the checkering with an old toothbrush and the job is complete.

The importance of good stock shape cannot be overestimated, and this applies to any firearm. One of the reasons is that we spend far more time looking at and handling our guns than we do shooting them, so it follows that a lot of our enjoyment comes from this phase. It is also true that it's just as easy—and no more costly—to shape a stock properly as it is to shape one poorly. Few factories have shown much imagination in stock shape and where some have departed from the traditional they have usually worsened the design. Aside from being a little straighter, that is with less drop at comb and heel, American shotgun stocks have changed little from those that were popular around 1900. The change to a straighter line helps keep the gun from rising in recoil, making it more pleasant to shoot, and quicker to get back on target for repeat shots.

A Monte Carlo stock is often found on trap guns; its purpose is to better position the head by lowering the butt slightly. A Monte Carlo is that drop at the heel of the stock which you find on

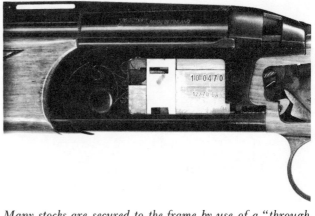

Many stocks are secured to the frame by use of a "through bolt" as is this Valmet. A through-bolt is the strongest method of attaching a buttstock, is easier to do in production, and is no better than a first class job of inletting.

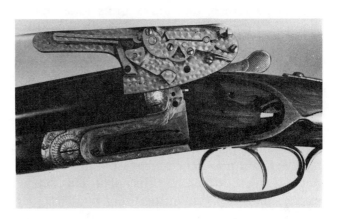

Another top quality inletting job, this one from Spain's Victor Sarasqueta in a fine 12 bore side-by-side. Compare the parts on the lockplate with the inletting cuts (and remember there must be clearance for the parts to move!).

trap guns almost exclusively (and a lot of rifles as well where it has no purpose at all). You might think that stock shape is less important to the trap shooter than to the bird hunter. After all, the trap shooter is permitted to mount his gun and get set and ready before he commands "Pull." But stock shape is still important—in fact it's very important. Recently I've been shooting a Perazzi Comp I which fits me very nicely and with which I can shoot a fair round of trap. The other day I shot a round of trap with a new Winchester Model 12 trap gun and it kicked hell out of me. My thumb kept ripping into my lip until it drew blood. This is not criticism of the Model 12, but it points out that this particular gun does not

A handsome Browning restocked by Al Biesen in a good piece of English walnut. Note the generous checkering pattern, which offers an excellent grip as well as very handsome lines.

fit me. I let another shooter fire a round with it and he did fine, liked the gun very much.

CHECKERING

Checkering is important to a stock because it provides an aid in gripping. That's its purpose, but since you're going to have checkering it may as well look nice, too. Many guns today come through with that impressed checkering that looks bad and acts worse. Some of it is slicker than plain wood. But, happily, gunmakers are gradually going back to the old cut checkering, which does offer a good grip.

The appearance of checkering is directly proportional to the pattern selected. Some like it fancy, some just like it functional. I've always believed that good checkering should be ample but not overly done, and just plain checkering rather than skip line or anything of that fancy

This is a style of checkering pattern not seen too often. To the uninitiated it appears quite ornate, to the knowing stockmaker it's an easy pattern to checker because it breaks up the checkering into small areas. I checkered this one myself, on an old Merkel over/under 16-gauge gun. Not too many stockmakers use the idea, although it's a good one that really looks good.

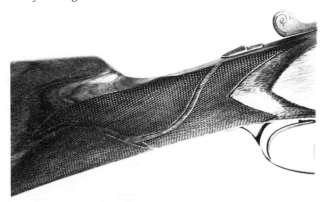

nature. (In fact, skip line was invented to cover up shoddy work on some European guns some years ago. A few lines of cheap engraving were also used for the same purpose.) Checkering patterns should also complement the metal lines and what's right for one gun isn't necessarily right for another. But checkering is time consuming and you won't find generous patterns on low-cost guns.

The usual rule of checkering is that the diamonds should be 3 to 3½ times as long as they are wide. This is sometimes changed to provide a more elongated diamond, especially on some guns made in Europe. Diamonds are usually brought up to a sharp point, but you will occasionally see a fine English stock on which the diamonds are left flat on top. This is hard to accomplish, for you must stop cutting each groove at the same precise depth; on the other hand, when you're making your diamonds with points, you will continue to have a point even if you cut too deeply. I've never cared much for the truncated diamonds and you don't see them very often. They do not offer as good a grip either.

In examining checkering, peer at it from a rather long angle, against the light, because this will disclose if any diamonds are not finished up to the point. On any quality gun you should expect nothing short of fine checkering.

The biggest sin in checkering is to run past the edge of the pattern and produce a groove in the stock outside of the pattern. It's one of those "oops I slipped" things that is so easy to do but so hard to correct. Borders are often cut around patterns to help reduce the incidence of such overruns, there being no other reason for a border. It follows that the best checkering is that with no border and no overruns. This is what you should demand when you pay top dollar.

When a top stockmaker errs in his pattern — say he chips off the top of a diamond — he must resort to surgery. That means he must drill a small hole where the errant diamond appears, fill it with a plug of the same wood, and match the grain. Then carefully he must file the plug down to the surface and recut the checkering over the plug. When finished it will never be detected. While it's a nasty job, it will save a stock on which many hours of work have been lavished and in which a considerable investment already has been run up.

Good shotguns, like good rifles, ought to have checkered stocks. In fact, they should have a bit more area covered than in the rifle stock. It is extremely difficult to checker large areas; keeping the lines straight is a damned hard thing to do. Your line is several inches long if the checkering wraps itself clear around the forearm and you must maintain the perfect separation and straightness for each line cut. This is why it's a lot easier to break up the checkering area into panels. I have shown a couple of examples of how I've done this on guns I've stocked. The panels give the appearance of being quite fancy; in actuality it's far simpler to checker these smaller panels than the larger area. You have more places to make overruns, but you also have a much better chance of keeping your lines straight. I show these for that purpose; the checkering isn't that good and I know it. After all, I was a metalworking gunsmith, not a stockmaker, and while I can make a fairly decent stock, I'm not in the expert class.

Sometimes carving is substituted for checkering and, if you like it, it can be just as functional. Perhaps the most commonly seen carved stocks are those on German and Swiss Schuetzen rifles. These were single-shot rifles of superb accuracy and built exclusively for offhand (standing) position shooting, which was known as Schuetzen shooting and was popular here around 1900. Shooters at a Schuetzenfest did some great shooting, some long storytelling, and consumed vast quantities of beer.

BUTTPLATES, GRIP CAPS, FOREARM TIPS, SWIVELS, MONOGRAM PLATES

The gun stock is not completed unless it has a buttplate; the remaining items listed above are either nice but not necessary or inappropriate.

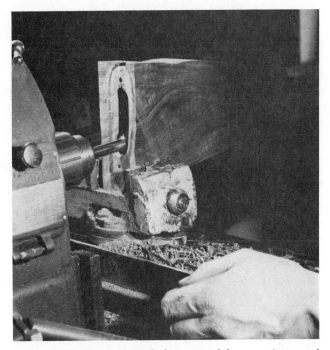

Sometimes it's necessary to lighten a stock by removing wood from the butt. Here, Al Biesen is doing just that. The stock can be finished one of two ways: either with a butt plate to cover the hole or by carefully fitting and gluing a wooden plug and checkering the whole butt surface.

A buttplate is meant to protect the butt of the stock from abuse and chipping. It should be made of a fairly thick material and should be reasonably hard. Should a gun be dropped a short distance, in a way that it will land on the toe of the butt, a soft buttplate will bend and you'll probably chip out a piece of wood. Guns of heavy recoil often wear a rubber pad and such pads come in many styles. The best-looking rubber pad is the smooth one that's about ½ inch thick. The less desirable pads are those known as ventilated pads which pick up dirt, dust, and dozens of other loose objects. Years ago pads were made of what we used to call hard rubber, a material that is gone today, having been replaced by various plastics. Many best-grade shotgun butts have no pad at all; the wood is finished like a pad and checkering in the wood itself finishes the stock distinctively. You are not supposed to mishandle such a gun.

Occasionally you'll see a fancy buttplate that's skeletonized in some form or another. These are perfect devils to install but they add a bit of class.

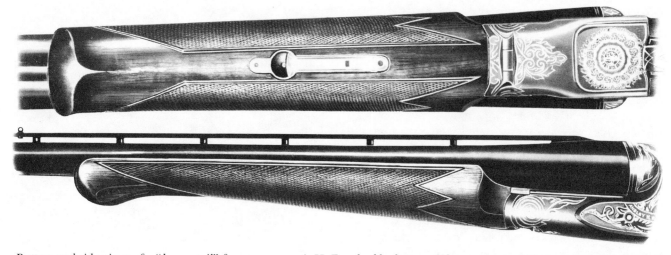

Bottom and side views of a "beavertail" forearm on an A. H. Fox double shotgun. The exaggerated tip, known as a "schnabe," was fairly popular many years ago. Beavertail forearms are usually used in shotguns with which a lot of shooting is done, such as skeet or trap guns to keep the hand away from hot barrels and, in rifles, where a target grip is desired.

I made and installed one on a gun of my own many years ago that was made out of a commercial plate and I assure you I'll never do another, because it was an awful job to get it in position. The wood is checkered in between.

Buffalo horn was used as buttplate material at one time by some European gunmakers and is still seen on occasion. Horn is another material that has largely been replaced by plastic. Often a thicker buttplate is used to lengthen a stock in a perfectly legitimate way for a new owner or for whatever reason. This is often accomplished by the substitution of a thick pad; other times it's accomplished by a piece of buffalo horn an inch or so thick.

Grip caps serve the same general purpose as buttplates, although they're less important for function. They do function though and a well-shaped grip cap is a decided addition to the looks of any firearm. These caps are made of steel, plastic, or buffalo horn and sometimes of a very contrasting wood, like ebony. You can buy small blocks of ebony, sometimes buffalo horn, from such gunsmith supply houses as Bob Brownell or Frank Mittermeier. These are heavily waxed to prevent splitting and may be used for forearm tips or for grip caps. You can often make a forearm tip, then a grip cap from the scrap.

As with buttplates, plastics are in nearly uni-versal use among the major gunmakers for grip caps and they often stick their logo or something similar in the cap. The American public has gotten used (brainwashed) to seeing the manufacturer's name emblazoned across his products. Ever see a Ford pickup without the name FORD across its rear end like a billboard? And every other car made here has the same nasty billboard, as have many other major appliances. I think this is a form of bad advertising and downright poor taste; but you can't avoid it unless you return to the Stone Age in your living habits. In any event, I don't think these things belong on a gun.

A monogram plate located on the underside of the stock near the butt always looks neat and classy. It doesn't do a damned thing for the gun but it pleases the ego of the man who owns it. You can have your initials engraved there. That's what the plates are for, but they aren't always engraved. These are usually made of gold or silver although I made those I've installed out of pre-Lyndon Johnson nickels, which are very close to German silver and take a nice polish without tarnishing. These nickels were filed to an oval shape, then bent to conform to the bottom line of the stock shape. The edges were beveled and the coin inletted carefully into the wood. Once it was deep enough, I drilled a hole and fit a wood screw, rounding its top so it just

Sometimes the Europeans find it hard to separate rifles from shotguns. It's a common practice to install sling swivels and even a cheekpiece is not totally unknown on a shotgun. The gun shown is an hermaphrodite anyway — one rifle and one shotgun barrel (note the rifle sights).

met the bottom surface of the monogram plate. Then I removed the screw, tinned (with solder) the screw top and monogram plate bottom, wound the screw back in, and placed the plate in position. I then applied heat with a soldering iron until the solder grabbed and the plate was in place. Filed down to the wood's surface and finish sanded and polished, the result looked nice indeed. Sometimes such plates are made in the shape of a shield or you can get more imaginative if you want.

Many Europeans like to install swivels on a shotgun. And in case anybody ever asks you, it's very hard to change the minds of these makers. Even when guns are made for the American market, and when the distributor tells the maker *not* to install swivels, the guy will usually drill and tap two little holes up front and two big holes in the buttstock. He will fill the metal holes with tiny plug screws and will fit wooden plugs in the butt, but he'll be damned if he'll turn out a gun without providing for swivels. There is no use for swivels on a shotgun. At least that's the American opinion, and it's the English opinion too; it's just on the Continent that they have this silly habit. Slings are for rifles, not shotguns.

CHAPTER ELEVEN

SHOTGUN SIGHTS

With a couple of exceptions, the sights on a shotgun consist of simple round beads, because shotguns are not aimed precisely as a rifle is, but rather are pointed and so become an extension of the shooter's arm. A claim could easily be made that the fit of a shotgun's stock is as much the gun's sighting equipment as the actual bead sight or sights.

First, let's discuss the exceptions. One of these is the sight of the rifle type, provided on barrels for slug shooting. Most makers of pump and semiautomatic guns provide special barrels for such shooting that can be interchanged in a matter of moments. These barrels are equipped with an adjustable rear open sight, like that furnished on most factory rifles, and a compatible front sight. Often a sling strap is also furnished when the slug gun is bought as a unit. (In that event, the buyer can buy interchangeable barrels for bird shooting; which one comes first doesn't matter, because everything except the barrel is identical.)

Many hunters who live in areas where slugs are required for deer hunting buy an inexpensive bolt-action gun and fit it out for slug shooting exclusively. This consists of fitting a blade front sight and often a peep rear sight (most of these bolt guns are drilled and tapped for receiver sights). Or they mount a scope of low power. The result is a shotgun that is well suited for deer hunting, and is usually used for that purpose exclusively.

The shotgun scope is an item that comes and

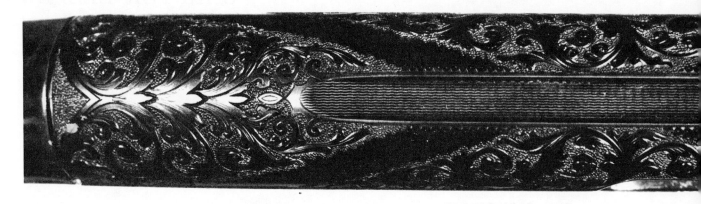

goes in the market pretty much with each generation or two. An industry spokesman once confided to me, when I asked why anyone would make a shotgun scope, "because it sells scopes." At that time, the scope in question was a 1X model especially made and marketed for shotgunners.

As this book is being written Weaver has a scope known as the Qwik-Point. The Qwik-Point unit is an interesting device that places a blaze orange dot out where the game is and it's supposed to make aiming much easier. It is likely that this device, which is not really a scope, will help some shooters. One man of my acquaintance wrote that he'd made a test on blackbirds, quite a pest in many parts of the country, and that it helped his shooting significantly. That's not very scientific, but it does point out that some devices help some shooters for some indefinable reasons not based on fact. I've tried the Qwik-Point but by no means enough to offer any concrete opinions about it except that it is very high and I think awkward. Certainly it detracts from the appearance of a gun. Moreover, as we've said before in this book, shotguns are pointed, not aimed, and a device of this type is better suited to aiming.

Some years back, right after World War II, there was a shotgun sighting device called the Nydar. It consisted of a glass lens resembling a magnifying glass about 2 inches in diameter that was mounted on about a 45° angle. Fitted in a base, the unit was screwed to the top of the gun's receiver (requiring the drilling and tapping of a number of holes). This Nydar was quite the rage for about a year or so but shooters apparently found it wasn't worth beans and it's long gone.

Another recent offering from Weaver is called the Accu-Point, which can be mounted on any single-barrel gun carrying a steel rib. Only 6 inches long with a small tube 3/16 inch in diameter, the Accu-Point is actually an optical sight, because it has a tiny lens element inside the tube. In use, it places an orange dot where the pattern will be. Whether this will prove any more successful than most of the other devices is hard to say but I would doubt that it will.

The main reservation I have about aids to sighting, such as some of those described, is that they work against the basic concept of shotgun pointing. That is, they encourage *aiming*, as with a rifle. But a shotgun is not a rifle and is not intended to be used as such. I believe the shotgunner is well advised to forget about any such devices and concentrate more upon gun fit and practice.

The basic sights on any shotgun consist of one or more of the following: ribs of any type, beads, and a slight groove running down the receiver top on pump and autoloading guns.

Ribs come in a variety of widths; a recent trend in trap guns is a rather wide rib. Most game guns, however, are pretty standardized in terms of the width of their ribs, and whether or not a wider rib is really an aid to shooting is probably in the area of personal preference. Ribs also appear in a variety of different elevations, or height above the bore. Target shooters often prefer a higher rib but this too depends upon the individual shooter and his stock. The man who brings his head down tightly against the stock requires a rib of a different height, and stock with less drop, than the man who traditionally shoots with his head more erect. Most of

The shallow groove running down the receiver top could easily be called the rear sight on a shotgun. Shown is the groove on an ornate factory engraved Remington Model 1100. Some claim the shooter's eye is really the rear sight. Most shooters don't try to define a rear sight, however.

the less-expensive guns do not have a rib at all, because ribs are an added cost factor. These lower-cost guns usually have a single brass bead near the muzzle, fastened by drilling and tapping a hole directly into the bore, screwing in the sight, and then smoothing the inside. Ribbed guns have their bead or beads screwed into the rib. The higher-grade guns have ivory beads and, as you come down in price, you begin to see white plastic beads. Some guns have only a single

bead at the muzzle, others have a second, smaller bead near the center of the barrel.

Whether a shotgun has a plain barrel with no rib, or whether it's a ribbed gun with two ivory beads, or anything in between, the rationale is the same: these are merely devices to *aid* the gunner in pointing. Assuming a gun that fits correctly, the shooter mounts his gun swiftly and without any thought to what he's doing. Once instinct tells him it's time to shoot he presses the

The Simmons Company in Olathe, Kansas, caters to trap shooters; the top gun sports their Olympic ventilated rib, which can be custom fitted to your barrel. The higher rib helps dissipate heat waves and is an aid in getting on target faster. The lower gun shows a special barrel that Simmons calls the "Un-Single," and you'll note it has only a lower barrel, the short tube on top being purely for weight and balance (it's adjustable). The purpose behind this is that most O/U shooters only fire the lower barrel in trap singles because the recoil is in a straighter line. This arrangement may look weird, but it's been used to set some pretty hot scores in championship shooting.

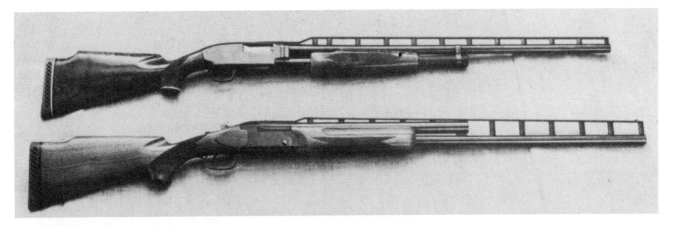

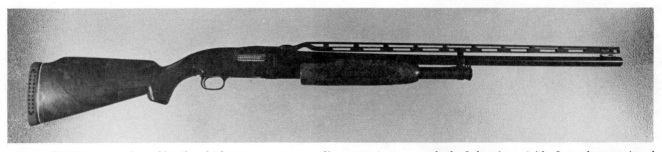

Here is the Simmons adjustable rib, which you can custom adjust to your own method of shooting. Aside from the occasional shotgun scopes placed on the market, these aids from Simmons are really the only "sights" you can say that shotguns have.

trigger—and he must do all this unconsciously. He must position the gun and determine the proper forward allowance (lead) totally by instinct if he hopes to connect. To illustrate this point, you will often score a hit on a bird that flushes from almost between your legs by quickly mounting the gun and snap shooting. That's a very difficult target indeed. But you must shoot *fast*—and if you've practiced enough and your gun fits, you will probably connect. On the other hand, let's say you're crouched in a goose pit and you spot a lone bird coming directly to your blind. You watch him approach for seconds that seem like hours and you think about how fast he's flying and in precisely what direction. Exactly how high he is and just how much forward allowance you should give him. Should you shoot while he's still approaching, while he's exactly opposite, or just as he's going away. All

these thoughts are going through your mind as you're trying to plan the shot and ought to get this bird easily; in fact, since it's going to be such an easy shot you might even be able to taste him a little bit. The frequent result is that you completely miss such an easy shot simply because you've had too much time to think about it. When the total surprise of your first shot miss is clear you rapidly throw two more charges at him and these are just as likely to be misses also.

My point here is that shotgunning is a combination of reflexes, practice, gun fit, and correct load. You must know where your gun is pointing in relation to the target. Sights, except as a subconscious aid to pointing, have very little to do with shotgun shooting. Other devices are simply gadgets placed on the market from time to time that may help some shooters but are not an aid to the experienced, good wingshot.

AMMUNITION & BALLISTICS

INTRODUCTION

Part Two of this book concerns itself with ammunition—what it contains and how it performs inside the gun, how its projectile, or projectiles, perform once they're airborne, and what happens when they arrive at the target. This is the science of ballistics; internal ballistics for the goings on within the gun, external ballistics for the rest of it.

As a science, ballistics is deep, mysterious, and highly steeped in some of the highest order of mathematics. We'll avoid that sort of thing because it's of interest to hardly anyone except the professionals. What really counts is the practical business of what happens, and we'll explore this in some detail, in language that will help you to understand why your particular gun does what it does. Or, perhaps, why it doesn't do what it ought to do.

Before getting started, however, a few definitions, so we know what we're talking about when these terms come up. There will be other terms, but these will serve as a start.

Cartridge. A cartridge is a complete unit consisting of the paper or plastic case, primer, propellant powder, and shot charge. Note that we are using the term correctly for shotgun ammunition. Shotgun cartridges are usually called shells, but they are correctly called cartridges.

Primer. This is the very tiny component that is exploded by the firing pin's blow and that, in turn, ignites the powder. Primers are sensitive, powerful, and very small.

Powder. The propellant. When ignited, it burns to generate gas, which propels the shot charge.

Pellets. The round pellets used in a shotgun charge. The word shot may be substituted.

Caliber or **Gauge.** A term used to measure the bore of a firearm but having no relation to its power or performance.

Magnum. The word simply means big, as in a magnum of champagne. The word can be (and has been) employed so loosely that it has little real meaning and is not necessarily descriptive.

In rifles and handguns, Magnum usually means a cartridge with considerable power. But in shotgunnery, the word merely means a load with a bigger payload. A Magnum shotgun cartridge contains more shot, and more powder, since it takes more propellant power to deliver more shot. The velocity of Magnum shotgun loads is approximately the same as that of standard loads.

CHAPTER TWELVE

AMMUNITION GENERAL

Ammunition, in general, consists of center-fire and rimfire types. Today, with the pellmell rush back toward the basics of muzzle loading, we have that to contend with as well. In fact, that may be a logical place to start because it's the least confusing.

Long ago "ammunition" consisted of powder and shot for a muzzle loader. The powder being black powder, the only kind available, and the shot being round pellets essentially as they are today. To use the muzzle loader you poured the required amount of powder down the bore and seated a wad and shot charge on top of the powder. Ignition in the earliest days was by sticking a smoldering wick of some sort through a little hole in the breech that touched and ignited the powder. The next refinement was the wheel lock, which spun against a flint to throw a shower of sparks into a pan containing a pinch of powder that fired the main charge. This was soon reversed and the result is what we call the flintlock, which clamped a flint into the hammer and, as the flint came down, hit a vertically standing piece of steel called the frizzen, which caused the sparking. The pan lay under the frizzen and contained the same pinch of powder.

There is a lot of present-day interest in flintlocks and percussion-cap guns. It may be a large step backwards, but vast numbers of people are shooting these guns and having a lot of fun doing so. You can buy excellent guns using flint ignition today and they operate just as simply as I have just said.

Perhaps one of the greatest inventions in the gun world was the percussion cap. And the shortest lived. Invented about 1840, the percussion cap replaced the flint and lasted only until the development of "fixed" ammunition— meaning the self-contained cartridge as we know it today. The first successful modern cartridge was used in about 1854 so you can see that the percussion cap didn't last long, though its impact was monumental.

In percussion-cap ignition you eliminated the flint system. You replaced the pan with a little part, called a nipple, which stuck up and rearwards and contained a small hole that extended into the barrel where the main charge lay. Instead of the shower of sparks on which the flintlock depended for ignition, a small cap containing fulminate of mercury was placed over the nipple. The new hammer had a concave face that fitted over the nipple and came down to whack the cap, whereupon the fulminate exploded and drove a hot fire into the powder to ignite it. Today, they're making cap-and-ball (percussion) guns (as well as flintlocks) faster than at any time in history—except for a couple of early wars—and shooters are gobbling them up like mad. It's a bit hard to perceive the attraction for these oldies but it's real.

The first modern cartridge was developed by the Frenchman Louis Flobert. It was exhibited at the Paris exposition in 1851 and consisted simply of a small pinch of "percussion cap material" with a small bullet perched on top. Flobert showed the cartridge along with a small rifle he had developed for target shooting. The development caused little stir, but it was observed by two American visitors named Horace Smith and Daniel Wesson. They returned with the idea and added a very small charge of black powder to the combination. Thus was born, in 1854, the .22 Short cartridge (today's .22 Short is hardly changed from that 1854 cartridge, at least in outward appearance). The .22 Short was the first successful modern cartridge. Entirely self-contained, it was what the military call a "fixed" round.

The history of ammunition development is hard to separate between that for rifles, handguns, and shotguns. Smith & Wesson's .22 Short cartridge was first used in revolvers and, since that company owned a patent on the cylinder with bored-through charge holes that it vigorously defended, it soon obtained a stranglehold on the handgun market.

Meantime, rapid development in ammunition was taking other directions. The rimfire cartridge was excellent for low-pressure cartridges, but its basic weakness was that its rim had to be crushed by the firing-pin blow for ignition. This meant the cartridge case material had to be soft enough to crush—and too soft to hold high pressures. The result was the center-fire cartridge, and development went on at a fast pace; the same principles of center-fire ignition apply to rifles and shotguns, although there are differences. The principal difference is that a shotgun primer must be hotter than that for most rifles. It has farther to travel (through the base wad) and the powders used in shotguns are usually harder to ignite. It may be stated, with little fear of challenge, that the shotgun cartridge of today is very little different from the first such cartridge to employ a rolled-paper tube. The method of priming is different, but not much else has changed. We still use the same kind of a charge of shot, we still use a wad column between the powder and shot and a means of igniting the powder. So what's new with shotgun ammunition?

Not very much indeed. Shotgun velocities cannot be increased. There have been a few changes in the makeup of pellets, although some shooters prefer shot made harder by plating it with copper or nickel. There have been many changes in the case itself with most of today's loads being in plastic hulls but with some competitive shooters preferring paper. Wad columns today are largely a one-piece plastic unit which is an improvement in most cases (but not all) and powders are smokeless rather than black. Otherwise the shotgun cartridge has changed very little over the years.

STEEL SHOT

The "steel shot" issue raised its head in the 1960s when some people began to complain that ducks were dying of lead poisoning. They claimed that certain bottom-feeding ducks occasionally picked up a spent lead shotgun pellet lying on the bottom in shallow water. Ground up in the bird's gizzard during the digestive process the lead might poison the bird and result in death by lead poisoning.

There is no question that this can happen. There is no question that it has happened. The only question is the magnitude of the problem. And there is no way in the world the problem can be precisely identified. It is also true that this occurs most often in shallow waters with a relatively hard bottom. Lead pellets may sink into mud to where no duck can reach them and deep water is no problem for these species of birds and their feeding habits.

But the outcry, largely led by antigunners and aided by others, was either that duck shooting should be stopped entirely or that the gun industry should develop a nontoxic pellet. That sounds plausible, development of a nontoxic pellet, but it raises more problems than it solves. In the first place, there is no metal (other than lead) combining the necessary attributes for such use. Only lead is abundant and relatively cheap. Only lead has sufficient specific gravity to maintain velocity and is hard enough, when correctly alloyed, to retain a reasonable degree of roundness. The only other metal with sufficient ballistic qualities is gold but gold lacks other obvious requirements such as abundance and reasonable price. As a substitute, and having no real alternative, the ammunition makers began experimenting with steel.

In the fall of 1976, certain areas in the Atlantic Flyway and other isolated areas across the United States were designated as steel-shot areas, meaning that you could not shoot ducks there with anything except steel-shot loads. While the final story is not in, I have learned from friends that the whole thing has been a joke so far. Steel-shot ammunition was nearly unavailable locally and the federal wardens simply ignored the whole thing. The program is supposed to be extended into all flyways in the near future and will extend the problems and controversies along with it.

Steel shot is far less efficient than lead in terms of killing power. That's because steel is lighter than lead and the pellets, even though they are driven at higher muzzle velocities by a heavier powder charge, do not retain downrange killing power. And this brings up another interesting fact: too many shots are taken at ducks at ranges too far for lead pellets. The use of steel shot would simply compound this problem, because it's unreasonable to think these gunners will improve their shooting skills. There is no question that, if all hunters restricted their shooting to within 40 yards, steel shot would be an acceptable ballistic substitute. But you can forget this. Skybusting, which is defined as shooting at waterfowl out of range, is hard to cure.

Nobody really knows how many ducks are really killed by lead poisoning. And nobody will ever know, because the subject is impossible to research. It is known that a switch to steel pellets will increase crippling due to the lower killing power of these pellets at more than 40 yards. Many industry people feel as many ducks will die from steel-shot-inflicted crippling as are now being poisoned. Neither means of death is desirable because the bird dies slowly and is lost in either event. Nobody wants to see lost birds, but there is no simple solution to waterfowl problems. I believe the leading waterfowl problem is habitat depletion. That the bulldozer (and the land developer) eliminates more ducks than anything else. This is another issue but it's all part of the complex problems that arise when you start to tamper with nature.

Another important objection to steel shot is that it is hard on gun barrels. Factory-loaded steel-shot loads contain special plastic shot collars that offer additional protection (more than that used with lead loads). Even so, the pellets are harder and have the capability of hitting the choke harder than a charge of lead shot. I understand that this is no problem with most guns of present manufacture, but it may be with many older guns. And nobody ought to use these loads in any good double-barreled gun unless its manufacturer specifically states it may be so used.

The handloader is cautioned—in fact he's solemnly warned—that there are *no* components available at this writing for reloading shotgun ammunition with steel shot. So if you're toying with handloading steel shot—don't do it! If and when these components become available they must be used as directed by the manufacturers without substitution. It is most vital that you realize there are no substitutes; especially that air-rifle shot or ball bearings must not be used.

A rule of thumb with steel shot is that if you are now using #6 lead shot for decoyed ducks, you should move to #4 steel. Move up one size in other words. For this reason, the companies have made #1 shot available in steel for those who have been using #2 lead shot. (There is no #1 lead available.)

There are and will continue to be constant experiments to find a more suitable substitute than steel. For example, copper has been tried with the result that copper poisoning proved as insidious as lead, although slower to develop. It is my opinion that steel shot is not any answer to the problem; in fact I'm not sure it has been proved that a problem actually exists. That ducks die because they occasionally pick up a stray lead pellet is known. How many ducks do so is not known, consequently you might call this a problem of unknown dimension. To try and solve such a problem with a hasty solution, which is also of unknown dimension, is pretty stupid. If indeed there really is a problem of sufficient magnitude to call for an answer, then it seems to me a logical solution would be to isolate the areas of shallow, relatively hard bottom where lead pellets could be picked up by ducks and 1) restrict these areas to steel shot only or 2) close them entirely and make them refuges. That would eliminate the problem but I suspect that suggestion is too simple for the bureaucratic mind. The relatively small areas involved would not constitute a big sacrifice for sportsmen and it might be a good tradeoff.

While it cannot be called the positive last word on the subject, at least one company has made a concerted, and expensive, study of the situation. The company is Winchester-Western and the tests were made at the company's Nilo Farms, which is an experimental and demonstration shooting preserve near Alton, Illinois. "Nilo" is Olin, the name of the parent company, spelled backwards.

These tests were quite exhaustive and were conducted by widely respected biologists and conservationists, men whose reputations are above reproach. Still, the tests have been criticized but, to date, there is nothing more scientific to offer any rebuttal. Until such time, these studies will stand.

THE NILO SHOTSHELL EFFICIENCY STUDY

by

John Madson and Ed Kozicky

After eight months of field testing and data analysis, Winchester-Western has concluded the most intensive study ever made of relative shotshell efficiencies in duck hunting.

Conducted at Nilo Farms, Winchester-Western's experimental and demonstration shooting preserve near Alton, Illinois, the project involved 2,400 pen-reared mallards shot at varying ranges with steel, lead, and solid copper shot pellets.

The purpose of the testing was to compare performance of lead shot substitutes that might reduce lead poisoning losses of waterfowl. The closely controlled study was designed by Winchester-Western Conservation personnel and statisticians of the U.S. Bureau of Sport Fisheries and Wildlife and the University of Wisconsin. Other cooperators in the test included the Illinois Natural History Survey and wildlife technicians from the conservation departments of Illinois, Colorado, Iowa, Kansas, Michigan, Missouri, Nebraska, New Mexico, South Dakota, and Wisconsin.

The test was of shotshells with #6 steel, #4 steel, #4 pure copper, and #4 lead shot. The special steel and copper loads each contained 1⅛ ounces of shot. The #4 lead load, in the Super-X Double X Magnum, contained 1½ ounces of shot and was used as a "control" load because its pellet count was similar to that of the #4 steel load. All shotshells contained "grex," a granulated polyethylene that filled the spaces between the shot pellets.

Test mallards were secured to a special transport device that was driven electrically down a 100-foot track. Limit switches actuated an electronic timer and the solenoid that fired the full-choke, 12-gauge shotgun, which was clamped in a rigid mount at ranges of 30, 40, 50, 60, 70, and 80 yards. All variables such as wind drift of shot, temperature, wind velocity and direction, speed of the transport device, and other factors were carefully monitored.

After being fired upon, living birds were tested for coordination. Ten days later, after being held in pens with food and water, the birds were tested for flying ability. All were ultimately classed as "bagged," "crippled," or "survivors" and were sent to the University of Wisconsin where they were fluoroscoped to check broken bones and locations of embedded pellets. In addition, 20 percent of the ducks (480) were completely defeathered to determine entrance and exit wounds and pellet penetration.

Field testing at Nilo began on November 6, 1972, and was concluded March 17, 1973.

The Nilo work confirmed the hypothesis that the effectiveness of a shotshell in waterfowl hunting depends on three factors: (1) the striking energy of each pellet; (2) the efficiency with which the pellet delivers its energy; and (3) the number of pellets striking the bird's vital areas. It was found that lead, copper, and steel shot pellets of the same size were similar in efficiency of energy delivery, and in the number of pellets striking the bird's vital areas. However, the striking energy of the pellet was about proportional to the density of the shot metal.

The most practical measure of shotshell efficiency was determined to be the number of birds bagged per bird crippled. The study revealed that #4 lead shot was more efficient than #4 steel, #6 steel, and #4 copper at 40, 50, 60, 70, or 80 yards. The four shotshells were comparable in performance only at 30 yards.

The breaking point in shotshell efficiency began to appear at 40 yards, where the #4 copper load crippled 3.16 times as many mallards as did the #4 lead load in bagging a given number of birds, the #4 steel crippled 4.31 times as many, and the #6 steel crippled 6.75 times as many ducks as did the #4 lead load.

Rate of crippling varied inversely with the density of the shot metal. It had been suspected that steel shot might have only a narrow zone of crippling; that is, it would lose energy so fast that it would not be a serious crippler at longer ranges. This was not the case. The #6 steel shot, for example, was comparable to #4 lead shot at 30 yards but lost its killing efficiency rapidly beyond 30 yards and continued to cripple mallards at a level of 10 percent or more through 80 yards.

The pure copper shot proved more efficient than steel and performed well at all ranges. However, pure copper is toxic to mallards. Copper poisoning takes much longer to appear than does lead poisoning, but is just as deadly.

One of the basic goals of the Nilo study was the development of a mathematical formula into which the ballistic data of any 12-gauge, 2¾-inch shotshell could be entered, quickly obtaining an estimate of the relative efficiency of that shotshell in bagging ducks.

Such a formula was developed, enabling workers to calculate the relative efficiency of a shotshell design without repeating the actual field testing. This has been done, with no indication that ballistic engineering can bridge the gap between the performances of lead and steel in bagging mallards—a gap that is due basically to the difference in the specific gravities of lead (11.34) and iron (7.86). It resolves to this: It takes energy to kill a duck, and a lead pellet delivers more energy than a copper or steel pellet of the same size.

While the Nilo field work was under way, Winchester-Western ballisticians were firing thousands of rounds in test barrels. Six full-choke barrels were tested for choke deformation with various shot metals: two with copper, two with steel, and two with lead loads. Five thousand rounds were fired through each barrel.

After 5,000 rounds of steel shot, bulges of .0057″ to .0065″ were clearly visible on the outsides of two test barrels at the chokes. With lead and copper shot, bulges measuring from .0005″ to .0014″ developed at the chokes. (A bulge

begins to be visible after about .0010″ to .0015″ increase in barrel diameter.) About 40 to 50 percent of the total 5,000-round deformation with steel shot occurred in the first 500 rounds.

Patterns did not change significantly during the testing, and it has been found that there is no significant pattern change for barrels with less than .010″ deformation of the choke. Deformation of the six test barrels was considered to be a cosmetic change only, and did *not* compromise safety or pattern performance. However, the thin, soft barrels of some double guns are another matter. A steel-shot bulge in a double-barrel shotgun occurs more quickly, will be more severe, and the barrels may separate. Severe choke deformation with steel shot can also occur in modern single-barrel guns with barrels of thin and/or soft steel.

The Nilo study makes it possible to estimate total crippling losses of waterfowl if steel shot is required for hunting. To do so, however, we must consider current crippling losses with lead shot, and the ranges at which ducks are shot.

For the years 1955–71, the average annual bag of ducks was 10.6 million. About 20 percent more than that, or about 2.1 million, were lost as cripples with lead shot.

A 1971 study by the Michigan Department of Natural Resources indicates that about 75 percent of the shots fired at ducks are from 45 yards or less.

By comparing such information to the Nilo data, it is estimated that the total annual crippling loss—in bagging the average 10.6 million ducks per season—would greatly increase if the use of steel shot were made mandatory. And how does that compare with current losses to lead poisoning?

In considering a steel-shot requirement for waterfowl hunting, the Bureau of Sport Fisheries and Wildlife faces a tradeoff: the reduction of lead poisoning losses for an increase in crippling losses.

The Nilo study reveals that threat of one alternative: that the hunter would bag fewer waterfowl, and cripple more, with the use of steel shot. The other alternative is less clear, and it is essential that the Bureau obtain current, valid information on lead poisoning losses before requiring the use of steel shot for waterfowling.

The steel-shot controversy may be ended by the time this book is printed but I think that's unlikely, for the use of steel shot is being forced in all flyways. The results of all this may be grist for analysis, and we can be sure that the sportsmen will be heard from. At this stage of the game, nobody knows what's going to happen. But nobody in the gun world thinks much of the idea.

At present, steel-shot ammunition is offered by Winchester-Western, Remington, and Federal only in 12-gauge, 2¾-inch shells, in sizes 1, 2, and 4 shot. In addition, Winchester-Western

APPROXIMATE NUMBER OF PELLETS IN PRESENTLY AVAILABLE LEAD AND
STEEL SHOT LOADS

Shot Size	No. of Lead Pellets in 1¼-oz. Load	No. of Steel Pellets in 1⅛-oz. Load	No. of Steel Pellets in 1¼-oz. Load	No. of Steel Pellets in 1½-oz. Load (3-in. Shell)
6	280	Not offered	Not offered	Not offered
4	169	212	235	282
2	110	138	153	183
1	Not offered	114	127	152

offers a 3-inch steel-shot load in the same shot sizes. Because steel pellets weigh less than lead pellets of the same size, there are more pellets of a given size in steel-shot loads than in lead loads.

In 1977 Federal added a line of "premium" rifle and shotgun ammunition. According to the company, the line has been introduced with the serious hunter in mind and the shotgun ammo comes in three types: Magnum for waterfowl, turkey, and fox; Hi-Power for waterfowl and large upland game; and Field Premium loads for upland birds and small game.

All the Premium Federal loads are loaded with extra-hard shot, copper-plated to resist deformation. Magnum cartridges have a granulated plastic buffer material in the shot charge to help resist deformation at the point of acceleration. The company claims superior patterns, shorter shot strings, and maximum penetration on game. I've tried some of the Field Premium loads but my tests surely are not sufficient to prove or disprove all the claims. However there's no doubt these will be superior loads for the purpose intended.

As reported elsewhere in this book however, it is debatable whether tighter patterns are a blessing for most upland game species. I rather think not, and it's my opinion that widely dispersed patterns at close ranges are far wiser on birds that are shot within 20-30 yards than trying to maximize pattern density. But, I hasten to add, there are several schools of thought on that.

Federal's Premium Magnum loads are in 10, 12, and 20 gauges including a 10-gauge 3½-inch Magnum that brings Federal into the 10-gauge ballpark along with Remington and Winchester. There is no point in listing all the shot sizes and other options that are offered in these loads because they will doubtless change as time goes by. Federal does point out, correctly, that the use of extra-hard, copper-plated shot will provide cleaner and deeper penetration as well as tighter patterns. They also claim "more useful" patterns from any degree of gun choke. I would challenge that last statement. As you might expect, these Premium loads will carry a higher retail price than standard loads. This is a good move, I may have my reservations about the Field loads as noted above but there's no question about the waterfowl load advantages.

CHAPTER THIRTEEN

SHOTGUN GAUGES

The measurement of gauge is a hangover from artillery days, when a five-pounder was a gun that had a bore size measuring the same as the diameter of a five-pound lead ball. A 12-gauge shotgun is the same size as a lead ball weighing $1/12$ pound. And so forth. This is true with all gauges down to size .410, which is measured in decimals as are rifle calibers. But it's no longer necessary to cut a pound of lead into equal spheres; the dimensions are standardized around the world as follows:

Gauge	Bore Diameter (in Inches)
10	.775
12	.729
16	.662
20	.615
28	.550
.410	.410

The shotgun cartridge has undergone considerable refinement over the past few years and more will be said about this as we go through this book. For now, suffice it that most cartridges used to be made out of rolled paper and brass heads. That wasn't very long ago, because the changes started to show up in the early 1950s. The first change I recall was Remington substituting a plastic tube for the paper. Then Winchester added a shot collar that surrounded the shot charge to protect pellets from sliding along the barrel as the charge was fired. Soon the changes were coming so fast that keeping up was hard. The whole case is now (in most instances) totally plastic except for a metal head for extraction, and the waddage has also been changed to plastic. But one can't be totally sure today that plastics are really the best after all. Some very experienced trap shooters are reverting to the older paper cartridges. No matter how you slice it, the answer isn't really in yet.

Over the past few years there have also been other developments that have made the 20 gauge virtually equal in payload to the old 12, the new 12 equal to the old 10, and so on. The result has been that fewer gauges are necessary and it now appears that the 16-gauge gun is going down fast. This is rather a shame, in my opinion, because I've always liked a 16-gauge gun.

Actually, one needs far less shotgun power than most gunners use anyway. The guy who knows how to shoot and sticks with field loads is going to bag his share of game as fast as, maybe faster than, the guy who shoots the biggest Magnum. The British (you can learn an awful lot from the British wingshooter) knew this years ago when they built nice, neat, light, 12-bore (bore and gauge mean the same thing) guns to fire a cartridge only 2 inches long. These short cartridges handle ¾ ounce of shot, which is a light load but perfectly adequate if your gun patterns properly—and if you know how to shoot. I don't necessarily recommend that you go to a 2-inch load (you would have to import them anyway) but you surely don't need anything more than field loads for any shooting whatever.

I do not profess to be a good wingshot, but I've been in many a goose pit in Canada and held my own with my companions. My goose loads have always been a standard 1⅛-ounce field load of #4 shot; for decoying ducks nobody needs anything heavier than field loads with #6 shot. Yet the trend is to power and more power. Right now there are a number of 10-gauge Magnum guns hitting the market. And I'm told they are selling like mad. Ithaca has an autoloading model, Marlin a bolt action at a far lower price, and H&R a 10-gauge model of its single-action gun at a lower price yet. These guns are selling despite the fact that you only get ⅛ more ounce

of shot in the load. One eighth ounce of #2 shot is only about 10 more pellets than a 3-inch 12-gauge Magnum offers.

Do you seriously think for a moment that the addition of just 10 more pellets is going to bag a goose for you? No serious gunner thinks that. Unfortunately, only the serious will read this book, or any other words on the subject. It's the innocent, the naive, the stupid who fall for the big 10 gauge and will try to bring down a flock of geese from 5,000 feet elevation. This is called skybusting, or sometimes worse, and when it happens near your pit after you've carefully set out your decoys in the dark before dawn and a flock appears to be coming to your blocks only to be scared away by a skybuster you never knew was there, that makes the blood boil.

Some years ago there were huge shotguns in such gauges as 8, 4, and even 2. As a matter of fact, the 8 gauge was popular for waterfowling not that many years ago. I have a 1921 Winchester catalog that lists several 8-gauge loads using bulk or dense smokeless powder (bulk powder was listed in drams only at the request of the powder manufacturers). These big cartridges were loaded with 1¾ ounces of shot in BB and 1 to 4 sizes so you can see they were intended only for waterfowl. When you consider that today's 12-gauge 3-inch Magnum load handles 1⅞ ounces of shot, you can appreciate that the big 8 gauge was not necessarily more powerful than today's guns. But this doesn't really tell the whole story.

Just because the 12 and 20 gauges overlap today in terms of shot loads it does not necessarily follow that they perform as well. The reason is given, for instance, that a 16 gauge is no longer needed because 12s and 20s can do all the 16 does. But this fails to take into consideration the length of the shot string when a large charge of shot is driven out of the relatively small 20-gauge bore. This is a subject we will explore more deeply, but it's important here to note that a shot cluster has three dimensions—not just two—and that third dimension can be just as important as the others.

Not only is it an oversimplification to say that a 3-inch 20-gauge equals a light 12-gauge load because it handles as much shot—it is also false.

Shown at the left is the 12-gauge Magnum 3-inch load of 1⁷⁄₈ ounces of shot. At right is the 10-gauge, 3¹⁄₂-inch Magnum, which handles 2 ounces of shot. The only difference in load is a mere ¹⁄₈ ounce of shot, scarcely enough to warrant going up to the big ten. For any practical purpose, the 12-gauge 3-inch Magnum is its equal.

Shotgun cartridges come in various lengths although the standards today are established pretty well. There was a time when you could buy nice, light guns chambered for shorter cartridges like the 2¹⁄₂ or 2⁹⁄₁₆ inch in 12 and 16 gauges. Today's standards are 2³⁄₄ and 3 inch in 12 and 20 gauge and 2³⁄₄ in 16 gauge. The owners of some of the older guns can, if the barrels are thick enough, have them chambered a little deeper to accept the longer, modern cartridges. Or they can reload and trim cases to the shorter length. It is a shame that these older cartridges have been dropped but there have been good reasons for doing so. It reduces the inventories necessary and reduces the number of items that must be manufactured. Regrettable though it may be, your shotgun ammo today would cost much more if the companies were

still obliged to carry as many items as they did not too many years ago.

You measure the length of a shotgun cartridge *after* it has been fired and the crimp is unrolled. What appears to be a cartridge measuring 2³⁄₄ inch is really a 3-incher when it's fired. Unless there is room in the chamber for this crimp to unroll or unfold, it will occupy space in the forcing cone where both shot and waddage must pass through. If this opening isn't wide open it will restrict passage and boost pressures enormously. It is a must that proper cartridges be fired in barrels clearly marked with the proper length of the cartridge you are using. Incidentally, European guns are marked in millimeters along with the gauge. The figures 12, 16, or 20 mean that is the gauge. The number 65 indicates a chamber 65mm long (2⁹⁄₁₆ inch) and 70 indicates 2³⁄₄ inch.

DRAM EQUIVALENT

Nearly 200 years ago, when the rules for shotguns were established by Joe Manton, it was determined that any shotgun load should consist of a charge of shot weighing from 1 to 1¹⁄₄ ounces of shot and that it should be propelled by from 3 to 3¹⁄₂ drams of black powder. Any heavier charge of shot required more powder to achieve the desired velocity and this produced more recoil. Enough more to be uncomfortable. And the mere addition of more powder, unlike in a rifle, would not produce more velocity because the laws of physics do strange things to the flight of a sphere.

Manton's "laws" of shotgun and load are still correct and will remain so as long as we live on the earth. When black-powder loads began to fade and smokeless loads to come into popularity, the latter were labeled "dram equivalent," to indicate that the amount of smokeless powder used was the equivalent of that number of drams of black powder. Why this listing has persisted is beyond me. There is no reason for it, and no excuse. The manufacturers do not need to list these numbers because nobody pays any attention to them or knows what they mean—or cares. It is past the time when this ought to be dropped. And I think that time will come, perhaps soon. It's only necessary to provide "high velocity," "field," and "target" designations and there does, at long last, seem to be a trend in that direction.

SIMPLIFIED PRACTICE RECOMMENDATIONS

The purpose of a series of "simplified practice recommendations," which was undertaken in 1925, was to establish a list of loads for ammunition that are in general demand and widely used. Those represented on the committee include the ammunition manufacturers, the distributors (that is, representatives of the largest wholesalers), and the users (normally, these are representatives from the National Rifle Association, Department of Commerce, and Bureau of Standards).

From 1925 until 1960 the number of individual shotgun cartridges offered was dropped from 4,067 different loads to 163 — a 96-percent reduction. There have been loads dropped since 1960 as well. This has value, even though someone's pet loads have been dropped, and I must confess that I have had certain disappointments in the results of these moves and so it's not all that easy to be objective. For example, I have a pet Merkel 16-gauge over/under gun which I restocked many years ago and which has long been one of my pet bird guns (in New England a "bird" is a ruffed grouse). But this gun is bored for the 65mm or 2⁹/₁₆-inch cartridge, which was dropped from the line some years ago. While I still have a few shells left, enough for a couple of more years of good hunting, I suspect I'll then have to have Champlin deepen the chamber (Champlin being the distributor of Merkel guns, and an excellent gunsmithing firm). Between the light 12-gauge field loads with 1 ounce of shot and the heaviest 20-gauge 3″ Magnum loads carrying 1¼ ounces, the spread covers everything needed. This sort of thing doesn't hurt the new guy just coming into the market; he can make out fine. But it does bother the rest of us who might have owned favorite guns or used favorite loads for years.

Another gauge that was quite highly promoted a few years ago and now is going downhill is the 28. This is a fine little gun; it's mostly used

for target events but is a fine bird gun in the hands of a skilled wingshot. It wasn't accepted as a bird gun by the general public so it's being ignored except by some skeet shooters in their special events.

The same can be said for the little .410 which is an almost entirely misunderstood gun. It's a gun for the expert because its charge is so light. You need to be an expert shot to put that small pattern where it will do some good. But most people seem to believe it's a "starting" gun for kids because it recoils so lightly. This is a very false reasoning for the simple reason that no beginner is going to be able to hit anything save a sitting tin can with the .410 with any degree of regularity. If he misses enough times he'll soon tire of the shooting sport and we'll have lost him. Start these kids with a 20 gauge with field loads. Don't ever start them with a .410 unless you yourself have enough ability to make it work for them.

BIG BORES OF YESTERYEAR

In W. W. Greener's *The Gun and Its Development,* 9th edition, some comments were made relative to big-bore shotguns used during the period 1881–1910. The 8 gauge is regarded as the "best all-round gun for sport shooting," in a double weighing 11 to 12 pounds with 34-inch barrels. It is suggested that this gun will have enough power to kill ducks to 150 yards, but its "available range" is 80 to 100 yards, with No. 1 shot.

Greener further states that a 4-bore gun is usually the largest made to be fired from the shoulder. These guns were usually made in single-barrel style, weighed from 15 to 18 pounds, and best results were obtained with a load of 9 to 10 drams of black powder and 3¼ to 3½ ounces of shot. There were a few 2-bore guns made but Greener states they were a paper-cartridge-case proposition and not much bigger than a 4 bore with brass case and that the guns did not shoot as well as a 4 bore.

At one time there were quite a few 8-gauge doubles made and used in America. They were strictly for waterfowl shooting, being far too heavy to carry in the field. The largest bore legal today for waterfowl shooting (which comes under federal migratory bird regulations) is 10 gauge, so even if you have one of those fine old 8-gauge Parkers, you can't use it legally in the duck blind.

These gems are interesting for a couple of reasons. One might say that men could handle bigger guns then than today and at the same time, these guns delivered a charge of shot that exceeds anything loaded today. The standard 8-bore load, according to Greener, was either 2½ or 2¾ ounces of shot. Yet, from my 1921 Winchester catalog, the heaviest 8-gauge load listed is a black-powder load with 2 ounces of shot and 1¾ ounces with smokeless powder. That compares with the Magnum 10-gauge load of today with 2 ounces of shot and the 3-inch Magnum 12 with 1⅞ ounces. You can see that the British duck hunter might well have been tougher than his American counterpart. While I think that Greener was wrong to encourage anyone to take shots as long as 100 yards, he does document actual experiences with letters. (The question is: How accurately was the range estimated?) There is no justification in my opinion for anyone today to take a shot at any bird at a distance more than 50 or 60 yards, and not even at that distance unless he is an excellent shot and knows his gun's performance with the load being used.

BORE DIMENSIONS OF ODD GAUGES

4 gauge	.935 inch
8 gauge	.835 inch

Shotguns in 4 and 8 bore are obsolete; they both largely disappeared after smokeless powder came into general use. Both were virtually restricted to waterfowl shooting because of their weight and their huge loads of shot (up to 3 ounces in 4 gauge), which are unnecessary for any short-range shooting. Rifles in 4 bore were widely used in Africa for dangerous game where loads, using brass cases, often employed lead bullets weighing as much as 1,880 grains (more than ¼ pound) with 12 to 14 drams of black powder for a muzzle velocity of about 1,300 feet per second. These rifles kicked about as hard on the butt end as they did at the target.

The 10 gauge appeared close to dying a few years ago but has now been resurrected—largely by Ithaca, when that company marketed its Mag-

10 autoloading shotgun to handle the 3½-inch 10-gauge Magnum. The Ithaca has been followed by other 10-gauge guns and Remington and Winchester have developed better loads for the big 10 because of the recent popularity.

At one time during the 50s and 60s, Winchester conducted extensive research on 14-gauge aluminum ammunition. It was finally abandoned in favor of plastic 12-gauge loads, although hundreds of thousands of rounds of ammunition were made and fired in test programs. The objective of this testing was to develop a "gun of 20-gauge weight but with 12-gauge performance." I'm told the loads performed extremely well because the case mouths were so thin that very little forcing cone was required. Aluminum 12-gauge loads were also considered but, due to the thin case walls in comparison with paper or plastic, they would have required different chamber dimensions. It was obvious that rampant confusion would have resulted with two different sizes of 12-gauge cartridges on the market.

The reason the 14-gauge development was abandoned was twofold: There were not enough advantages to warrant marketing a new gauge, and there was no reason to require the sportsman to buy a new gun.

GAUGE POPULARITY

Some insight into the popularity of the various gauges, and the flip-flopping that has taken place over the years, is seen in Greener's *The Gun and Its Development*. According to this celebrated English gunmaker, the 20 bore "has been strenuously advocated by writers in the sporting papers, but there are very few sold . . . the proportion is perhaps one 20-bore to twenty of 16-bore." And, in the next paragraph: "The 16-bore was at one time a favorite with Continental sportsmen, who now for the most part prefer the 12-bore; for use in England probably not one gun in 500 is made 16-bore." (Both quotes appear on page 376 of the 9th edition.) I don't know if this was true in 1881 when the book was first printed, or if it was true in 1910 when the 9th edition was printed. Still, it is an interesting insight into gauge popularity nearly a hundred years ago.

We do know that the 16 gauge achieved considerable popularity on the Continent subsequent to Greener's writing and, of course, we know the vaulting popularity the 20 gauge is now undergoing. We might also learn something from the fact that the 12 gauge was popular then, is popular now, and has been the all-time favorite ever since records were kept.

An important lesson I think we might well learn from the older English gunmakers is that, rather than go to 16 or 20 bore for a lighter gun, it's a smarter idea to go to a light-loaded 12 instead. This was why the British went to their 2-inch 12-gauge cartridge with less than 1 ounce of shot. And they built wonderfully light doubles to fire that load that outperformed equal loads in 20 gauge. I think we should consider going that route, for the results are superior to those obtained by smaller bores.

You might ask that, since 1-ounce loads are available in 12-gauge field loads, why bother with the shorter chamber? The answer is that the gun can be correspondingly lighter. If you shoot an ordinary gun with the light load it will be pleasant to shoot but unnecessarily heavy to carry. Of course, I suppose if a 2-inch or 2½-inch 12-bore gun was placed on the American market, a lot of idiots would stuff 2¾- and even 3-inch cartridges into them and do serious damage. Nonetheless it is an interesting prospect.

CHAPTER FOURTEEN

CASES AND PRIMERS

Cartridge cases are divided into two broad categories: metallics and shotgun. Metallics deal with rimfire and center-fire rifle and handgun cartridges and all are commonly made of brass. Shotgun cartridges on the other hand are generally made of a rolled cardboard tube which was the standard from its invention by the Parisian M. LeFaucheux in 1836 until the 1950s when plastic cases became popular. Today, most cases are plastic but there is also a return to the older paper tube in many instances. One of the leading and most noteworthy being in the world of trap shooting where many shooters prefer a paper case.

The shotgun cartridge, whether paper or plastic, is a tube with thick base section providing sufficient space for the load of powder, wads, and shot and with a metal head to provide extraction. It has been essentially the same since 1836 although there have been many changes that are not apparent to the eye. As early as the 1500s, men used the principle of firing a number of small pellets from a gun barrel, instead of a single projectile, to increase the chances of hitting a small moving target. Those were muzzle loaders of course and the method of loading was pretty much the same as that for rifle or musket: A measured charge of black powder was poured down the barrel, then a wad was seated over the powder to separate the powder from the shot charge and to seal the bore. Wads were followed by dumping a measured charge of shot pellets down the barrel and another wad over the shot to hold it in place. And that is essentially what the shotgun cartridge of today still consists of except that it contains its own primer.

The paper tube case is made by rolling several thicknesses of special paper with paste between each layer. A tube must meet certain rigid specifications: It must not split; it must expand to fill the chamber and thus seal the bore; it must have enough elasticity to contract after firing to make extraction easy. It is essential that every tube contain the same amount of moisture to provide consistent performance from shot to shot. (A tube will vary in size if its moisture content varies, which you may have experienced if you've ever had ammunition under water or dropped on the ground overnight; you usually can't chamber such a cartridge because it has swelled.)

Inside this tube, at its rear or base end, is placed another roll of paper that is called the base wad. Base wads vary in thickness to accommodate different charges, a low base wad being used for high-velocity loads (with more powder and more shot) while a high-base wad is used for lighter target and field loads because they have lighter charges and require less volume for the load. To hold tube and base wad together it is necessary to provide a brass head that crimps everything together into a single unit. The head also provides a seat for the primer and a rim for extraction, ejection, and headspace. The term headspace means that the thickness of the rim itself should be equal to or slightly less than the provision for it in the gun barrel. Headspace in a shotgun is the same as that for a rimmed rifle cartridge such as any of the .22 rimfires or the .30/30 Winchester. This dimension is quite critical.

In somewhat oversimplified terms, that explains the paper shotgun cartridge. It has, however, largely been replaced by plastic cases. During the 1950s the world of shotguns was introduced to plastic, or the other way around if you prefer.

The 1836 LeFaucheux development consisted of a rolled paper tube. Its most important departure was that the device included "pinfire" ignition (which was also applied to rifle and pistol cartridges). The pinfire system consisted of a centrally located primer, much as in today's am-

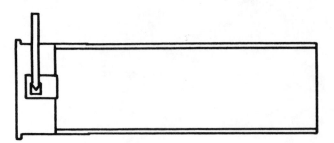

Le Fauchex pinfire shotshell cartridge, about 1836. Note that it greatly resembles a modern cartridge except that it contains its own "firing pin," which is struck from outside the gun by a hammer.

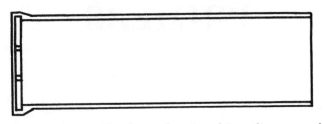

Lancaster's cartridge featured a pierced iron disc, smeared with priming compound, fastened inside case head; early 1850s.

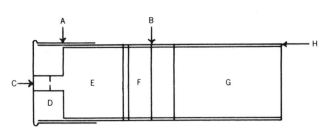

Details of a typical paper shotgun cartridge: A, the brass head. B, cylindrical paper tube. C, Battery cup containing primer. D, base wad. E, powder charge. F, filler wads. G, shot charge. H, crimp. There would be an over-powder wad between the powder and filler wads and an additional paper wad over the shot when a roll crimp was used.

munition, but this primer was activated by a pin that extended outside the cartridge head laterally. In use, the cartridge was loaded in the gun with the pin sticking up and extending outside the breech where it could be struck by the hammer. Then the pin drove into the primer and fired the cartridge.

In the 1850s, a couple of refinements on the pinfire system of English origin were marketed. The first of these was the Charles Lancaster system consisting of a paper tube and a solid-headed cartridge case inside of which was a small iron disc pierced by several holes and smeared

One of the earliest uses of plastic in shotgun cartridges was this Remington development. In this earrly "test," various cartridges were run through a clothes washing machine with result as pictured — the plastic came through nicely while the older paper cases are a shambles. The next plastic development was Winchester's shot collar and from then on the race was on.

with priming compound. When the firing pin struck from the rear, as in today's guns, it ignited the priming mix whereupon the flame shot through the holes and into the powder charge.

The second British improvement was by a man named Needham and used a combustible paper cartridge with a zinc base enclosing the primer. This cartridge required a side-opening gun and, when fired, the entire cartridge was consumed except for the zinc wad. When reloaded, the zinc wad was shoved forward to act as a top wad for the next shot. Ingenious although primitive, these inventions fell by the wayside when two colonels, Boxer and Berdan, developed their superior primers. Col. Hiram Berdan (of Civil War Berdan's Sharpshooters fame) developed a primer that was adopted in Europe and is still used there. Col. Edward Boxer (of the British Army) developed a very similar primer which has become the American standard. These primers are basically different only in their anvil arrangement, the Boxer anvil being in the primer while the Berdan is machined in the case. Shotgun primers are different from those for rifles and the types used around the world today are similar while those used in rifle ammunition are different.

The first plastic cartridge ever marketed, to my knowledge, was a Remington which consisted of a plastic tube that was merely substituted for paper. Everything else in that first case was essentially the same. The next step was from Winchester, when that company simply added a plastic collar to surround the shot charge to help prevent deformed shot from the ride up the barrel. From then on the developments came thick and fast. Today we have cases made from a single plastic extrusion and, while they have a metal head, it isn't really necessary at all. Apparently the loading companies do not feel the market is yet ready for an all-plastic case. One of the most important changes wrought by plastic has been the one-piece wad and shot protector. Of course, the so-called pie or folded crimp was applied to shotgun ammunition before the days of plastic. This turnover replaced the old over-shot wad and rolled crimp to hold the wad in place. The function of the over-shot wad was, of course, to hold the shot in place. But it also had another important function — to hold the shot back for a few milliseconds until the desired pressure was built up.

The plastic case is really a boon to most shooters, certainly to all hunters. It can be reloaded

The components of an early plastic cartridge. From left to right: base wad, plastic tube, brass head, primer, and completed cartridge. Today, everything except the primer is made in one piece of extruded plastic, except that a metal head is added for looks. The metal head really isn't required for function but the market isn't ready to accept a case without a "brass head."

more times. It is tougher than paper and will stand higher pressures. It can be made at lower cost and will not swell from moisture. And it provides a better crimp. This is not to say it's really any better in terms of performance, but it is a more practical case for most shooting purposes.

LOW BASE, HIGH BASE, LOW BRASS, HIGH BRASS

These are terms that are very often confused, and it's not hard to understand why. For the sake of simplicity let's talk about a standard 2¾-inch 12-gauge cartridge. Cases of this same length are loaded with such varying loads as 1⅛ ounces of shot in target and field loads and down to 1 ounce in some "light" field loads. The same length cases are also loaded with as much as 1½ ounces of shot in Magnum loads. That's a difference of ½ ounce of shot — or 50 percent more than the lightest load. Since more powder is required to drive the heavier charge, and since the outside dimensions of the case must remain the same, the inside must compensate for these wide discrepancies in the loads. Therefore the lighter loads, using less powder and shot, have a high base wad and are known as "high-base" cartridges. Similarly, the heavier loads require more space and use a low base to provide that room. There also are variations in the wad column, but that's another element entirely.

Usually, though not always, a low-base wad cartridge is accompanied by a higher-brass head to provide added support. Normally, high-brass heads are associated with the low-base wad and heavier loads. The brass heads on today's market range from slightly more than ¼ inch for one

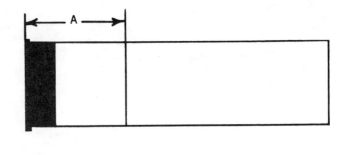

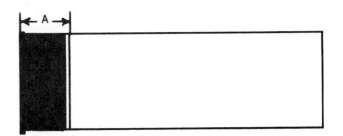

High-brass shotgun cartridge (top), with brass height shown as A, is usually associated with low base wad (shaded area) which allows more space for heavier loads and powder charges of high-speed loads. Bottom cartridge is low brass, high base wad (shaded) for target and/or field loads. These designations are going out of favor with modern plastic ammunition primarily because the modern plastic wad can accomodate both heavy and light loads with complete satisfaction.

British load to a high of 1¹⁄₁₆ inch for one Canadian load. This might change tomorrow, however.

Brass heads are often brass-plated steel, and, as we have said, are not even really necessary with plastic cases. Another trend today is to let the wad accommodate the differences in loads and most plastic cases are identical. Hence the low-base, high-base definitions are rapidly becoming history since the advent of plastic cases

A typical target or field shotgun cartridge with low-brass head (outside) and high-base wad, the latter because both powder and shot charges are light. However, most modern cartridges are the same internally and the difference is quite effectively taken up by the plastic wad columns.

A Holland & Holland Ltd. Paradox load. The English made a few guns with a short section of rifling at the muzzle and the guns shot well with shot charges and with such slugs as this one. Other proprietary names were used by other gunmakers but the principle was the same. This is a solid brass case, heavily crimped over the slug. Its major use was for dangerous game at close quarters, such as tiger hunting in India from the back of an elephant.

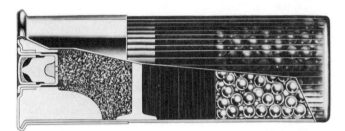

The elements of a high-velocity shotgun cartridge are shown in this photo. It has a high brass head, and a low base wad (inside) to permit a larger powder charge, and its wad column is fairly short to accomodate the heavy shot charge. Note the primer—called a battery cup in shotgun lingo—with its long anvil, which is necessary to reach through the base wad. This is an early preplastic era case.

and the one-piece wad column. Both can accommodate the wide variations in loads and charges with total satisfaction.

You will occasionally see a brass shotgun cartridge because they once were quite popular for reloading. While their use is mostly a thing of the past, there are some available today. They are capable of many reloads and they are crimped by using an over-shot wad which is simply placed on top of the shot and sealed in place by a material called water glass, which is usually a mixture of sodium silicate and hot water and is used in preserving eggs. It hardens and holds the wad in place with sufficient force to provide satisfactory performance. One additional note about brass cases is that some shooters make .410 brass cases from .444 Marlin rifle cartridges. The size is roughly the same and, I'm told, the results are very good, although I have never tried this myself. Some European shotgun slug ammunition is also loaded with brass cases. The reason for such loads is that they are used in the tropics where an efficient, moisture-proof seal is

required. The Holland & Holland Paradox cartridges were loaded this way and were intended to be fired in a shotgun that had a trace of light rifling in the choke area.

In nearly all shotgun cartridges the front end of the case is rolled, turned over, crimped, folded, or whatever you wish to call it to hold the shot in place and to provide some resistance to movement until the powder charge can build its pressure. The exception to this is chiefly the brass case sealed with water glass. Most modern cases are crimped with the folded, or pie, crimp, some having six and some eight portions. This is widely regarded as a superior method of crimping because it eliminates the top, or over-shot, wad which is in the way of the pattern when the shot cluster leaves the gun barrel.

We are living in a period of intense change in shotgun ammunition, with special regard to the case itself and the wad column. There is no way to predict what the future may have in store, although there have been many experiments with caseless ammunition for shotguns as well as rifled arms. Caseless ammunition is that in which the case itself is combustible and actually forms a propellant. The case, in this event, is made of smokeless powder that has been formed into the shape of a case. (This is done while the powder is in a semiliquid or plastic form, when it can be pressed into any shape desired, and the result is a case of considerable strength but one that will

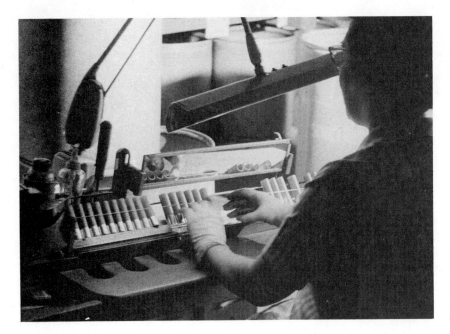

Finished, but unloaded, shotgun cartridges undergoing visual examination. Note that a mirror reflects the inside to the inspector as the cartridges move by on a conveyor.

burn under the proper circumstances.) The unit is completed when a bit of priming mix is placed in the conventional location and sealed in place with more combustible material. A wad column to cushion the blow of the gas pressure is added, then a shot charge and an over-shot wad, which in this case is frangible, meaning that it bursts into dust particles on firing and won't get in the way of the pattern.

I think all this is far into the future. Beyond my time at the very least. There are considerable military advantages to caseless ammunition, weight and cost being among the most important. The advantages to a caseless shotgun cartridge are less apparent since the shotgun is primarily a sporting proposition the leading military application of which is guard duty. It will be a long while indeed before a bird shooter retires his pet Purdey, Boss, or Merkel to use a modern shooting machine firing caseless ammunition.

What probably will continue is the improvement of plastic cases. These are plenty good right now but I suspect they'll be improved as time goes on. Still, there's something about plastic that cuts across the grain. It's one thing to find an old, fired paper hull from years gone by in the field that has been discarded by a hunter. But it's quite another to spot a fired plastic case because you know that thing is going to still be lying there when the Pyramids are gone. I think

hunters ought to pick up their plastic empties and not leave them lying on the ground.

Many gun clubs have a rule that if a fired cartridge drops on the ground, it becomes club property. That's because the cases are valuable for reloading. Shooters using double guns can catch their empties before they are ejected and some firms catering to trap and skeet shooters make special gadgets that fit the side of the receiver on a semiautomatic or pump gun to catch the empties.

PRIMERS

The primer is a tiny pinch of a violent chemical that explodes when hit or crushed. Its flame then saturates the powder charge and ignites it to develop the gas pressure that drives the shot charge down the barrel. Primer mixture is so sensitive that it is handled moist in all stages of manufacture, only being allowed to dry after it's safely in place either in the primer cup or inside the rim of a rimfire cartridge. The amount of priming compound necessary isn't any larger than the small amount you could get on the very end of a toothpick. If you placed this on a flat surface and hit it with a hammer it would explode.

Early primers were made of fulminate of mercury, one of the most violent chemical mixes known to man. I understand that fulminate of mercury is still used in such things as artillery shells, bombs, and the like, but it's no longer used in small-arms primers. The primary object in getting rid of the mercury in the old fulminate of mercury primers had more to do with rifles than with shotguns, for mercury weakens brass and so rifle cartridges fired with primers containing mercury had to be discarded and could not be reloaded. Mercury also has another disadvantage in that it tends to decompose when stored for long periods. Again, not so big a factor except for military rifle ammunition, but a fault nonetheless.

A later favored priming mix was potassium chlorate—just as violent but without the mercury. But potassium chlorate did contain salt, similar to common table salt and containing all the moisture-collecting properties of table salt. That's why you had to clean a barrel after every firing; each shot would leave a salt residue that, if left, would collect water and rust the bore before too many hours passed. Since the only thing that dissolves salt is water, such cleaners had to be water itself or a water-based cleaner. All primers in use today, with a few rare exceptions, are nonmercuric and noncorrosive.

The story of the noncorrosive primer began at the Remington plant in Bridgeport, Connecticut, in 1926, when a chemist named James E. Burns dropped in to visit on his way to Florida. Burns had recently left the U.S. Cartridge company and had a revolver in his pocket with six primed cartridge cases (no powder, no bullets) which he proceeded to fire six times, making six loud snaps but causing no damage. He then told the Remington people to put the revolver, just as it was, in a very damp place and leave it there until he came back. They took him at his word and placed it where the entire outside of the gun became deeply rusted. A month later Burns returned and wiped out the bore and charge holes which he showed to the Remington officials. The bores were bright and shone like new.

Burns had discovered a substitute priming mix for potassium chlorate. While it required another two years of experimenting before the primer was marketed, what Burns had done was to eliminate fouling by primer residues by using lead styphnate with tetrazene as a sort of exciter for the styphnate (earlier primers contained about 20 percent ground glass to help ignite the priming mix). Thus was born the first noncorrosive primer which Remington called Kleanbore and which other manufacturers quickly adopted. (The reader is cautioned that my advice is to clean your guns just the same. My own practice is to clean shotgun bores after the season or after a rainy hunt or a day in the salt marshes duck hunting).

Every primer must contain three elements: a sensitizer to explode and start the procedure, a fuel, and an oxygen producer. The ideal primer is one that both ignites the powder charge and starts the bullet out of the case. (There is more power than you'd believe in that small primer.)

Primers must not only provide sure ignition, they also must provide *consistent* ignition. There are a vast number of factors that affect performance and ignition—consistent ignition—is one of them. As a result, there has been a great deal of effort expended in recent years to develop and produce consistent primers.

The shotgun primer is called a battery cup. While it acts essentially as a rifle or handgun cartridge's primer does, it is larger in diameter and longer. It must be longer to reach the deeper pocket in which it is seated. Actually, a shotgun cartridge's battery cup is more than twice the diameter of a large rifle primer and nearly five times longer.

A point that becomes most important if you are a reloader is that there are differences between primers. You must be certain to use the correct-size primer as specified for a given load in whatever handbook you are following. Some cases require different sizes, others different strengths, so be certain you follow directions and do not experiment by mixing your primers.

CHAPTER FIFTEEN

PROPELLANTS

We have discussed the fact that the priming compound explodes. And that the result of that small explosion is to ignite the propellant. Powder burns. It does not explode. There are varying requirements for today's gunpowder and it requires a different kind of powder to drive a charge of shot, a large-diameter pistol bullet at moderate speed, a small, high-velocity rifle bullet at tremendous speed, or a heavy artillery shell many miles. The same basic kind of propellant can be used for each, but many modifications must be made to provide a suitable powder for each of these, and many more, specific uses.

The gun barrel has often been compared to an internal-combustion engine in which the piston is replaced by a bullet or shot charge (and where a new "piston" is required for each shot). The gun barrel however more closely resembles a diesel engine than the internal combustion because the gasoline-operated engine is driven by an explosion. A diesel on the other hand develops a relatively slow thrust throughout the piston stroke. So too does the gun work, for we cannot generate the necessary chamber pressure with an explosion; rather we must make this pressure build gradually in order to gradually accelerate the flight of the shot charge down the barrel, otherwise the result would be disaster. The pressures developed in the barrel would be beyond the ability of the barrel to contain them. Similarly, different situations occur in the many different types of gun, and the propellant chosen for each individual cartridge and bullet weight must be compatible with those components, the guns in the field chambered for that particular cartridge and for the uses to which such guns and ammunition will be employed.

BLACK POWDER

The first discovery of a fuel that would burn without atmospheric oxygen was the mixture of charcoal, sulphur, and saltpeter which was known as gunpowder for several hundred years. During that long period its composition changed little, although its appearance and methods of manufacture changed. Later it was formed into rough grains and graded by sifting; still later it was compacted by forming it into cakes under considerable pressure before being broken up for use. These efforts helped control combustion speed so that the pressures generated by combustion were distributed more evenly as the projectile traveled the length of the bore.

SMOKELESS POWDER

It is generally claimed that the invention of a Frenchman named Pelouze in 1838 sealed the doom of black powder as a propellant. Pelouze discovered that an explosive could be made by "nitrating" cotton, which means treating cotton with nitric acid. That's an oversimplification of course, but the result is an explosion known as guncotton. Or, to put it another way, the result was a nitrocellulose, cotton being of the wood-fiber family and nitro referring to nitric acid.

The active agent in any explosive of this type—as in smokeless powder—is the nitrogen atom in combination with two oxygen atoms (NO_2). Originally, the combination contained potassium, which fouled a gun barrel. Then the chemists found they could remove the potassium by means of sulphuric acid and join the result with a simple hydrocarbon like glycerin. The result was nitroglycerin. Uncertain and awkward to handle as a liquid, it was mixed with sawdust or some other porous substance, molded into sticks, and became dynamite.

Instead of glycerin today we use cellulose in the form of wood pulp or cotton, treat it with nitric and sulphuric acids, and we then get nitrocellulose—the chief ingredient of smokeless powder. But this material is too light and loose to

pack into a cartridge so it is dissolved with ether and alcohol or acetone to make a plastic mass that can be molded into rods resembling spaghetti. This process was discovered by a French government chemist named Vieille in 1885. That, basically, is how smokeless powder, the nitrocellulose variety which we also call a single-base powder, is made. There is also a double-base powder which came about in 1878 when the Swedish chemist Alfred Nobel thought of dissolving guncotton in nitroglycerin. Nobel made a huge fortune out of his discovery and, apparently appalled at the thought of what he had discovered, left his fortune to benefit mankind by what we know today as the Nobel Prizes.

In any event, the Nobel invention is known as cordite and it is, for our purposes here, a smokeless powder containing both nitrocellulose and nitroglycerin—which makes it a double-base powder. Some double-base powders are harder on a barrel than single-base powders, but this is more generally found with British cordite than with American double-base powders. For the record, the line of DuPont powders known as IMR (for Improved Military Rifle) are single-base powders. A few of the powders in the Hercules line are double base, otherwise most of the powders available to the American reloader are of the single-base variety (that is, nitrocellulose).

There is still another type of powder known as Ball Powder, an invention in the early 1930s of Western Cartridge Company, now part of Winchester-Western. Ball Powder is made essentially the same as any other nitrocellulose powder (which it is) except that it is made into an emulsion that forms small droplets on the suface that can be removed in that form. The process greatly reduces time and cost in manufacture. Still, Ball Powder is basically another form of nitrocellulose containing a small addition of nitroglycerin and is a double-base powder.

Although only three types of smokeless powder have been mentioned, these three types can be manufactured in an endless variety of rates of burning. By which I mean that you need a much faster burning powder for a shotgun or pistol cartridge as opposed to a big Magnum rifle which requires a very slow-burning powder, comparatively speaking. Any of these types can be manufactured to deliver a desired burning rate.

Long ago it was discovered that, as with pieces of wood, small-size grains burned faster than larger grains. Take a piece of 2×4 pine 6 inches long and split it into a couple of dozen pieces and it will burn a good deal faster than if left whole. The same exact thing happens with gunpowder, because you are increasing the exposed surface of a given amount of powder. The greater that surface, the faster it will burn. Colonel Rodman of the U.S. Army discovered that you could perforate powder grains, which would increase the rate of burning even further. Now you had an exposed area inside the grain of powder and burning was from both within and without.

Burning rate, then, is controlled by the size of powder grains or, more precisely, by the amount of surface area exposed. It is important to keep this in mind because the same basic type of powder is used in 16-inch naval rifles as is used in shotguns. But the individual powder grains for the big artillery are many times the size of even a 12-gauge Magnum cartridge. Burning rates are further controlled by coating the powder grains with graphite. So, with nitrocellulose (single-base) and with nitrocellulose/nitroglycerin (double-base) powders we control the rates of burning by the size of their grains, by the amount of surface area, and by a retardant coating of graphite.

One further point about Ball Powder: It too can be controlled and this control is exercised by rolling the spherical grains, while in plastic form, into flats like little pancakes. These can be rolled thick or thin, or they can be left in tiny spheres. Ball Powder also is coated to retard burning.

Powders must also be mated to their loads with extreme care. It is very easy to use the wrong powder with disastrous results. (To use an extreme example, if you loaded an artillery piece with fast-burning pistol powder, you would blow the gun and its crew clear to hell and beyond because it would develop pressure far too fast to move the projectile before maximum pressure was achieved.)

Powder is made in huge lots or batches and, while extreme control is exercised, the lot may or may not turn out exactly as desired. For example, let's say DuPont wishes to make a new lot of a powder for handloaders, say SR7625, a popular low-pressure shotgun powder (these powders are called "canister lots"). Their supply of SR7625 is low and must be replenished. So they manufacture a lot of powder with the hope that it will turn out to be SR7625. It may or may not. DuPont won't know until the powder is manufactured and tested, retested, and tested some more. Because every lot must be exactly like every other lot. Should the lot fail to duplicate SR7625 exactly it is given another number and will now be sold to one of the ammunition-loading companies which, in turn, will experiment with this powder to mate it to one of their batches of ammunition. It will be loaded to achieve specified pressures, velocity, and accuracy in a particular load.

There have been times when a powder manufacturer manufactured a canister lot of powder and then could not duplicate it to restock dealers' shelves! That's one of the reasons a powder is occasionally "taken off the market." There was not necessarily anything wrong with the powder, but it simply could not be duplicated with the precision necessary for a canister lot. The lot of canister powder you buy tomorrow will exactly duplicate the lot you bought in 1948.

One of the problems with gunpowders is that they occupy a limited space in the cartridge case, held back by the projectile. When the powder is ignited it begins to generate gas, and the gas begins to move the projectile which leaves more space for the gas to occupy. Then the gas, filling this void, tends to lose pressure simply because the same amount of gas now occupies more space. The solution lies in the perforation of powder grains. As a powder grain burns from the outside, it gets smaller and smaller which reduces the burning area and so reduces the amount of gas given off. But by burning from within, the surface keeps expanding and more gas is given off. Thus the thrust against the projectile is maintained and, with the proper blend of powder, is actually increased so that the thrust against the projectile is maintained all the way to the muzzle.

The correct powder for a given load can be achieved by regulating the size of the grain, including the size of the perforation. In some cannon powders, each grain sometimes has as many as seven perforations. When we use the term *progressive* powder, we mean a powder that will rapidly build its pressure (called the pressure curve) to start the projectile moving but which will then maintain that thrust all the way to the muzzle at which point the pressure will have dropped substantially. A pressure curve builds steeply, then gradually tapers down as the projectile reaches the muzzle, but the push keeps pushing all the way down the barrel. Another advantage to progressive powders is that they develop maximum velocities without attaining extraordinarily high pressures. Such high pressures can be hard on a gun mechanism; they also are generally accompanied by very high temperatures.

Powders used in shotguns and pistols, while progressive to a degree, are much quicker than those used in rifles. One reason for this is that these powders are usually (but not always) small, very flat, and thin grained. That means they burn much faster. Burning rate is also a function of the heat within the cartridge case, which builds when a projectile is harder and slower to move. For example, it takes much longer to move the 1⅞-ounce 12-gauge Magnum load than it does to move a 1-ounce field load.

With a shotgun or pistol, where the bullet or shot charge starts to move more quickly than in a rifle, the gas must also be built to develop quicker, in order to provide the thrust necessary.

BULK POWDERS

In the early days of smokeless shotgun loads it became apparent that a quantity of smokeless was required to exactly duplicate the results of black-powder loads. That is still true, incidentally, because the performance of black-powder loads was and is the same as their modern counterparts. Since the reloader in those days measured his black-powder load by bulk—filling a little scoop level full—it was advantageous to have a smokeless powder that would equal black, bulk for bulk. Not only would this give the reloader the same performance from his load, but it would also mean that he could use the same scoop and, since the powder would occupy the same space in the cartridge, there would be no changes in the wad column. These powders became known as bulk powders and they were so labeled and sold. Reloaders knew that they could buy "bulk smokeless" and load it the same as

they loaded black powder. That was a particularly significant advantage, because smokeless powders were new and reloading was not the sophisticated operation it is today.

The opposite counterpart of bulk powder is dense powder, powder with the capability of developing much more gas for its volume than bulk powder. A smaller quantity of dense powder will do the same work as a larger amount of bulk and therefore must be used according to established and recommended loads. However, the terms "bulk" and "dense" are now seldom used; the modern reloader works from carefully prepared tables supplied by the powder manufacturers but he still works with a wide variety of powders with wide-ranging characteristics.

A satisfactory powder for shotgun use should develop its pressure faster than that in a rifle but not so fast as to jolt the shot load too severely. Its propulsion should be developed by a slow initial thrust and, once the wad and shot start to move, this pressure can be built rapidly. Of course, once the shot begins to move, its stationary inertia has been overcome and less pressure or thrust is needed to accelerate it rapidly. For this purpose the powder used must be progressive in its burning rate to properly increase the velocity of the charge as it travels down the barrel.

DRAM EQUIVALENT

This ancient term is a hangover from the days when smokeless powder was first introduced and was loaded bulk for bulk with black powder. Black was always measured in drams while smokeless is always measured in grains avoirdupois. There are 7,000 grains in 1 pound avoirdupois, and 27.34 grains equals 1 dram by *weight*. This means that you must not expect 1 dram's performance from 27.34 grains of smokeless powder. I mention this comparison only for its relative value, not as a suggestion that anyone load powder (except bulk smokeless) by the dram method.

Dram equivalent is a term that has certainly outlived its usefulness. It is totally meaningless today and the ammunition makers would do everyone a favor if they dropped the term completely. No ordinary hunter knows what it means and, while the target shooter can interpret the term, he also has no use for it.

CHAPTER SIXTEEN

SMOOTHBORE SCIENCE

When a shooter tries to hit a target that appears too suddenly and moves away too swiftly for him to take aim properly, he must compensate for his unavoidable error by the many pellets in a shot charge, which are fired typically in a disperse pattern. The odds of hitting this target depend on three variables: the target, the shooter, and the pattern. The shooter has no control over the target. It may be a clay target (which can be broken by only two pellets); it may be a tough bird requiring four or five larger pellets for a kill. The skill of the shooter is up to the shooter himself and can be controlled by nothing else. The pattern delivered by the gun is something else again. This can be controlled to a degree and the object is to control that pattern to a degree that will maximize the odds in favor of the shooter.

Now, once again, let's repeat the definition set down by gunmaker Joe Manton 200 years ago: It must shoot 1 to 1¼ ounces of shot and it must shoot them at a velocity obtained with a charge of 3 to 3½ drams of black powder. It is a wise definition. It has been broken time and again and it will be broken again in the future. But a heavier shot charge must be accompanied by a heavier powder charge to drive the heavier charge to the same velocity. And those increases either must increase the weight of the gun (which will prevent fast handling) or result in recoil punishment that is unnecessary. Furthermore, any good wingshot knows that he doesn't need a heavier load. It's only the inexperienced and naive who fall for this myth, and then they do no better with them than they would with the Manton formula.

A shotgun cartridge is different from that of a rifle or handgun cartridge primarily in that it delivers a charge of individual round pellets, the exact number of which depends on the size of the pellets and the weight of the charge. Since the shotgun cartridge is a straight case, it conforms more or less to the straight rifle case, meaning that you can use a faster-burning powder because there is no shoulder to turn back the gases and develop enormous pressures. Thus a shotgun operates at far lower pressures than a rifle does.

The flight of the shot pattern, once it emerges from the barrel, is dependent upon what happens to it while it is riding up the bore. Some kinds of shotgun shooting demand a wide-open pattern designed for close-range shooting. Some examples are skeet, ruffed grouse, decoying ducks, quail. This is where you must shoot quickly, at relatively close range. On the other hand, other situations demand a dense shot pattern that will produce clean kills at greater distances. Some examples are trap shooting, live pigeon, pass shooting at ducks. Sometimes you'll be hunting a bird that's tougher than some other birds; a typical example is the pheasant. He is a big, tough bird and, after the first few hours on opening day, proves very hard to hunt. There too you'll need a closer pattern.

Pattern is controlled within the gun barrel; once the charge is airborne there is no further control over it. Moreover a shot pellet is spherical, the poorest ballistic shape of all—and there's nothing whatever that we can do about that either. So, even though the results occur some distance from the muzzle, they are still controlled by the cartridge and by the barrel.

WADS, SHOT, AND LOADS

The projectile in a shotgun is a charge of many small spheres and it is necessary that these be kept in a container—or in some way be kept together as completely as possible until it clears the bore. When the gun is fired, the shot is kept in place by the walls of the barrel and the wads moving behind the charge.

Let us first look at loads as they appeared from Joe Manton's day until today, when we use the one-piece wad column and plastic cases. The earlier shotgun cartridge, when loaded, consisted of a charge of powder over which was placed an "over-powder" wad. This was a small cardboard disc that served to keep the powder away from the wad column, because the latter was slightly greased. Atop the over-powder wad was the wad column, sometimes called the filler wads. These wads served several purposes: They sealed the bore against the thrust of the propellant gas; they served to cushion the shot against the sudden pressure coming from the rear; they helped scrape the bore of the fouling of the last shot; and they gave the bore a slight coating of lubricant. Of no small importance, they also served to fill in the necessary space between powder and shot that would permit a proper crimp despite the load employed.

The shot charge was placed on top of the waddage and a thin top wad was then placed over the shot charge whereupon the crimp was rolled into the paper case. Each of these components had a role, or several roles. Today's principles are the same except that we have a one-piece wad that contains enough spring due to its construction that it will accommodate any reasonable charge. That has eliminated the over-powder wad and wad column and there is no longer any over-the-shot wad because the plastic case is crimped in the now-familiar "pie crimp" which eliminates any need for a top wad and roll crimp. Despite these changes things still work the same. In firing, there is resistance from the shot charge, which tends to remain where it is (inertia). There is also intense pressure from the gas building up in the rear and the result is to spread the wad slightly and so to seal the case and bore (after the wad and shot moves into the bore itself).

Before plastic, wads used to be made of felt, which had the most consistent characteristics, although many other materials were tried. One of the materials tried, and used by reloaders, was Celotex, the common wallboard material, which was cut in a special drill-press cutter.

CRIMP

The obvious reason for crimping the front end of a shotgun cartridge is to hold the shot in place. This is indeed one of the crimp's roles but there's another, less obvious, one that is of major importance. Crimp holds the shot charge back until sufficient pressure has been built to allow the full ballistic strength to build. If it were not for the crimp, the shot charge would begin to move too quickly — before the full pressure developed — and maximum velocity would not be achieved.

Shot pellets, with the exception of the larger sizes such as buckshot, are formed by dropping molten lead from a tower 180 to 200 feet high. The pellets become round and drop into a large tank of water. From here they are gathered and sorted by sieving to collect pellets of the proper size. They are checked for roundness by being rolled down a long sloping surface at the bottom of which is a gap. Those pellets that are perfectly round have gained sufficient momentum to jump the gap. Those that are not have not, and they fail to jump the distance, so they go back upstairs to be remelted.

When a shotgun is fired, the pressure on the shot is tremendous. The result is that the pellets are pushed against each other in every possible manner as well as against the sides of the barrel. Being shoved from the rear they are rubbed against the side of the barrel and, depending on the smoothness of the bore, they are abraded and deformed. Pellets are also deformed from being pushed against each other. And when the charge meets the choke, it is further squeezed and more deformation takes place. The net result of this is that any pellet that is deformed will fly in a different path. So will any other pellet whose last shove was in any direction other than straight ahead. You can see that the charge begins to spread rapidly once the protective walls of the barrel are left behind.

In 1962, the Winchester-Western people developed the first breakthrough in shotgun cartridge design. It was a pretty modest beginning, but it started the ball rolling and the result is today's plastic cartridge. That first development was a simple shot collar — a small piece of thin plastic that was designed to fit around the shot charge and ride up the barrel with the charge to protect the pellets from scraping against the barrel. This development was so interesting, and the thinking behind it so important, that I have included some of the rationale here because of its subject matter.

In the spring of 1922 a new name was born — Super-X — and with it came one of the finest shot shells that money could buy. Yet, this was but a beginning, for it was followed in subsequent years by the super-seal crimp, which for the first time eliminated patchy patterns caused by over-shot wads; the cup wad, which for the first time sealed off the shot column from the hot propellant gases; and many others. . . .

This is the story of the development of the Super-X Mark 5. It is told in the following pages in two parts: The first outlines the solid base of technological knowhow on the performance characteristics of shot-shell clouds; the second then relates how this knowhow was used as the basis for an intensive research and engineering effort and how this all led to final development of Super-X Mark 5. . . .

The secret of the Mark 5 lies in a piece of polyethylene plastic, deceptively simple in appearance, which looks like, acts as, and so is called, the shot collar. It does several things: It helps absorb the violent punishment the pellets are given when subjected to more than 2 tons of setback force during firing; it acts as a barrier between the fast-moving shot column and the torturous abrasive effect of the barrel wall; and, as the pellets are hurled from the muzzle, it holds them together for one additional instant of time, just enough to launch them all in a straighter, truer path. What this all means to the shooter is that this denser, more homogeneous cloud of shot can reach out appreciably further to make a kill. The true effect of the polyethylene collar can perhaps best be explained by the fact that it gives an increase in performance nearly equivalent to one full quarter ounce of shot. . . .

SHOT SHELL PATTERNS AND SHOOTER'S ODDS

The shooter wants, above all other considerations, to hit and kill a target. The true performance characteristics of a shot shell, therefore, are improved by increasing the probability, or odds, that a target will be hit, and also by increasing the probability that a target, once hit, is killed. Accordingly, the first part of the discussion will describe the relationships between kill probability, pellet dispersion, and the uncontrollable elements such as aim error and target size and vulnerability. . . .

THE NATURE OF PELLET DISPERSION

The principles underlying the dispersion of a large number of pellets in a shot-shell pattern can best be illustrated by a description of the typically erratic path of a single pellet through the atmosphere.

A lead pellet subjected to the forces of acceleration and to deformation resulting from friction against the bore is not generally a true sphere when it hits the atmosphere. Roughness and deformation will therefore cause the aerodynamic pressures over its surface to be unbalanced. As it first hits the atmosphere, this unbalance of aerodynamic pressure will cause a slight lateral component of force which will, in turn, give the pellet a small lateral deflection. The pellet will also begin to rotate slowly about its center, and as it changes its attitude in flight, it will be given a second lateral deflection in a different direction. This process

Figure: 1
Each of the steel balls, dropped from above, bounces off the array of steel pins and is thereby given a large number of random lateral deflections. The result is the bell shaped or "normal" distribution.

continues, and so the pellet is given a number of lateral deflections which will vary randomly, in both direction and magnitude.

The unique erratic path of any given pellet is most aptly visualized by the use of the device shown in Figure 1. (This device, which looks like a Chinese pinball machine, was built to illustrate random statistical processes, and is known by statisticians as a "statistical quincunx." For our purposes, however, we call it our "black box.") When a steel ball is dropped through an aperture at the top, it will land on one of the pins in the top row. It will then promptly bounce off onto one of the pins in the second row. However, the spacing is such that the second pin will be hit by the center of the ball. As a result, the ball has a 50-50 chance of bouncing off to the right or to the left. The ball hitting the third row of pins will again be subject to a 50-50 chance of going to the right or to the left. This same process then continues until the steel ball has bounced off a pin in the last row and finally falls into one of the many channels at the bottom of the box. If the pellet is dropped from the center of the aperture above, it is possible for it to land in any of the various channels. Moreover, if two pellets are dropped, one after another, they will most likely not end in the same channel even if aimed at the same point. This illustrates the complete independence of the paths of any two pellets. When a large number of steel balls are dropped all from the exact center of the upper aperture, the multiplicity of random processes will cause the pellets to travel each individually of

the other but nevertheless all tending to fall in the bell-shaped pattern shown in Figure 1.

There is an exact analogy between the motion of a steel ball through the matrix of pins and the flight of a lead shot-shell pellet through the atmosphere. This analogy is shown graphically by reference to Figure 2 which represents one typical shot-shell pattern. At the bottom of this figure a step-diagram shows the number of pellets lying in consecutive 2-inch strips laid vertically across the target. There are, for example, 28 pellets in the strip that runs through the center of the target; 26 pellets in the first strip to the right of the center one; and so on. The step-diagram pictures the actual pellet distribution across the target in this typical case. It will be noted that if a large number of patterns are similarly analyzed, it will be found that on the average, the distribution of pellets across the target will describe an identically shaped curve. This bell-shaped curve is mathematically describable and is identical to the curve which is generated by the black box shown in Figure 1.

A mathematical analysis of the process, graphically illustrated in Figure 1, leads to an exact mathematical formula which says that the distribution of pellets across a pattern should conform to this normal law of distribution. Although the shape of this distribution could be derived by theoretical considerations, it was found necessary to determine whether or not actual patterns conformed to this type of distribution. Accordingly, an analysis of hundreds upon hundreds of shot-shell patterns with all types of ammunition fired from various types of choked barrels were made. The procedure was pretty much as illustrated in Figure 2. Strips were laid across patterns both horizontally and vertically, and the number of pellets in each strip were counted. The results of this very thorough analysis led to four conclusions:

1. Pellets fired from a full-choked barrel gave patterns which invariably produced a very accurate representation of the "normal" distribution in both vertical and horizontal directions. It was found that although tighter patterns gave a more peaked curve as opposed to disperse patterns, nevertheless, the basic shape of the curve was always identical. (In the same sense that two equilateral triangles, although of different size, have identical shapes.)

2. Patterns fired from modified chokes were close to this normal distribution, but patterns fired from a cylindrical-bored gun had more concentration in the center of the pattern, less concentration away from the center, and again an excessive number of pellets at the actual fringes than would have been the case with a pure normal distribution.

3. An analysis was made on these patterns to determine whether or not there was more "patchiness" than would be allowable on the basis of random statistical variation. Patchiness was measured by simply taking discs of various diameters, 3″, 4″, 5″, 6″, etc., and seeking to find spots in the shot-shell patterns, inside the 30″ circle, where a disc could be placed without covering any pellet holes. It was found that with patterns fired from a full-choke barrel, there was no more patchiness than would normally result from statistical chance. (This is probably due to the action of the super-seal crimp.) There was, however, a little more patchiness than would be warranted by statistical variation in cylinder-bore patterns.

4. A similar analysis showed none of the patterns fired from the various types of chokes gave any observable degree of "shot clumping." (This is probably due to the action of the cup wad in preventing the hot gases from fusing pellets.)

CAUSES OF DISPERSION

Since the pellet distribution is "normal" at all ranges, its only characteristic that changes with range is the size of the cloud; i.e., the dispersion. The way this changes with range is one of the fundamental aspects of the hit-probability program.

In the search to determine quantitatively the relative effects of several variables on accuracy, a program of unusual interest was undertaken. Its purpose was to isolate the relative contribution of gun and ammunition on total dispersion. The experimental method of isolating these components was based on two hypotheses. The first hypothesis is to the effect that the dispersion of pellets on a target is due to three basic components of dispersion: vertical dispersion due to variations in time of flight from pellet to pellet; the dispersion due to all factors causing slight displacements of

the line of flight at the instant the pellets leave the muzzle; and the dispersion due to the in-flight displacements of the pellet by the force of air resistance, as just described. The second hypothesis is that the relative proportion of these factors to total dispersion determines the relative pattern size, or tightness, at various ranges. This may be more clearly illustrated by two extreme examples:

1. If the only source of dispersion of the pellet charge is due to factors causing slight displacements of the line of flight at the instant the pellets leave the muzzle, then the point of impact of each pellet on the target is predetermined as soon as the shot charge leaves the muzzle. This extreme case might be exemplified by a man firing a shotgun in a complete vacuum, such as if he were standing on the moon. In this situation, since each pellet would be traveling in straight lines, the size of the shot shell pattern at 40 yards would be exactly twice the size of the pattern at 20 yards, etc.

2. In the other extreme case, it is assumed that there is a complete absence of any influences tending to deflect pellets from the true line of aim until they have left the muzzle. This extreme situation might arise if the shooter were possessed of a very uniquely choked shotgun, one so built that every single pellet would leave the muzzle in a pattern aimed straight at one point on the target. (If this

Figure: 2

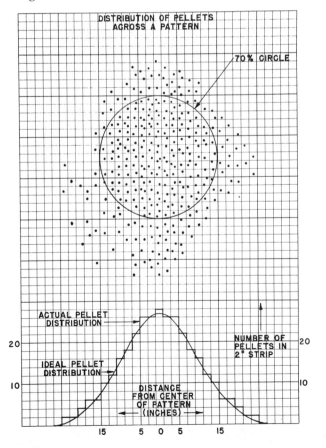

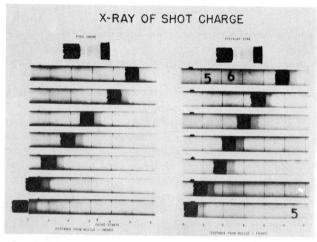

Figure: 3

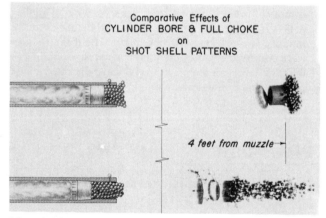

Figure: 4

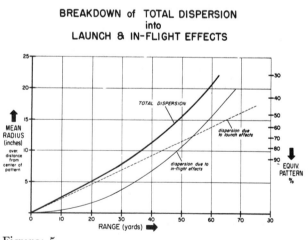

Figure: 5

deflections of air resistance, as described previously. Pattern size in this case would not be proportional to the range since the pellets are deflected continually in their paths. Hence, at 40 yards the dispersion is *more* than twice the dispersion at 20 yards since additional dispersion takes place in the flight from 20 to 40 yards.

Thus, there are two principal sources of dispersion: one due to in-flight effects, graphically described with the aid of Figures 1 and 2, and muzzle effects. These muzzle effects are caused essentially by the unique action of the shotgun choke. Some early experimental work on the choke action was assisted by flash X-ray pictures of the shot-shell loads at different positions in the barrel for both cylinder and full-choke barrels. Figure 3 shows a collection of pictures representing various distances of shot travel. The principal results of this work were to show the compression effects in both cylinder and full-choke barrels. (Note that in this explanation the extreme cases are compared; namely, full choke versus cylinder. The intermediary degrees of choking naturally will give intermediate effects.) The result can be listed as the following:

1. In both cylinder and full choke barrels the load is compressed about 27 percent while 6″ from the muzzle.
2. Passing through the choke, the length of the shot column is increased about 20 percent, the diameter of the column decreases by about 4 percent, while the net volume seems to increase from 7 to 10 percent.
3. The constriction of the choke causes a velocity differential of almost 60 ft./sec. between the front and rear pellets. (This checks with measurements of the resultant shot-string lengths at various distances from the muzzle.)

In general, the X-ray technique was felt to be somewhat deficient as a tool to study choke effects. However, it did seem to prove that the choke "squirted" the shot and it did demonstrate that the load of pellets, in this case, acted as a semicompressible fluid.

Figure 4 now illustrates the comparative action which takes place at the choke. In the cylinder-bore gun, the pellets are being accelerated by the wad, which in turn is being accelerated by the gases, until the pellets are free of the muzzle. At the point of emergence, the inertia of the front pellets pushes back on the rest of the load while the wad is pushing forward with the result that many of the pellets will be pushed laterally. This lateral acceleration, or push, causes some of the pellets to begin moving laterally which results in the spreading out of the load. (For purposes of illustration, this effect was slightly exaggerated in the upper-left drawing.) In a full-choke barrel, the pellets are given an inward component of velocity. The choke also tends to "squirt" the load; that is, it must necessarily be longer after passing through the choke than before. (Since the same mass is included in a cylinder of smaller diameter, the length of the cylinder of shot must increase.) This lengthening of the shot column means that the front pellets travel a greater distance than the back pellets in the interval of time that it takes the load to go through the choke. Consequently the front pellets will move faster than the rear ones and so the shot will string out slightly. This stringing

unique choke were to be fired on the moon, for example, the shot column would arrive at the target in the same condition that it left the barrel; namely, all in a nice, tight little clump.) Thus the only factor causing dispersion of pellets on the target, in this case, is due to the random

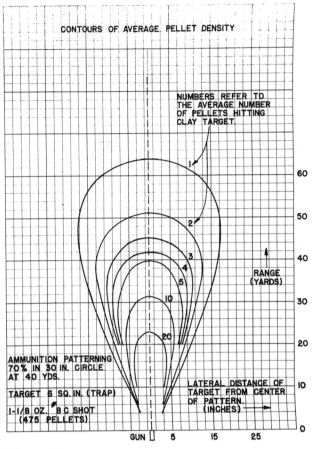

Figure: 6

CONSEQUENCES OF DISPERSION

The nature of dispersion and its causes have no more than academic interest unless tied in to the direct consequences to the shooter. The practical consequences of any given combination of target, shooter skill, and pellet dispersion are actually directly determinable from the solution to our "shotgun problem." Before proceeding directly to its solution, however, it will be informative to cover some interesting consequences of the manner in which dispersion varies with range.

Figure 6, for example, shows the *average* number of pellets which will hit a clay target at varying ranges and with different aim errors. For purposes of this illustration it has been assumed that the average projected or "profile" area of a clay target is 6 square inches. Moreover, for this particular example, it was assumed that we are using a trap load containing 1⅛ oz. of No. 8 shot which patterns 70 percent in a 30″ circle at 40 yards. The way in which dispersion varies with range is as shown in Figure 5.

Figure 6 shows, for example (by reference to the various contours and to the scale at the right) that a shooter who has no aim error, i.e., who always hits the target with the center of his pattern, will hit the clay bird with an *average* of one pellet at 64 yards, two pellets at 51 yards, and 20 pellets at 23 yards. If, however, he misses the target by 10 inches, it

Figure: 7

out of the shot also means that the wad is not able to push on any pellets (at the muzzle) except the rear ones. Hence, to a large degree the disruptive effect of the wad is eliminated.

An experimental program was undertaken in which patterns were fired simultaneously at various ranges. This was done by simply hanging target sheets at many ranges and then firing simultaneously through all the sheets. By proper analytical techniques, it was then possible to break down the relative contribution of in-flight effects and choke or muzzle effects to a variety of gun-ammunition combinations. This is exemplified in Figure 5, which shows the relative contribution of muzzle effects and of the in-flight characteristics of the pellets fired from the full-choke gun which gave an average pattern percentage of 75 percent at 40 yards. By reference to this scale to the right, and to the heavier curve, it is apparent that at 50 yards, for example, this combination gave 50 percent of the pellets in the 30″ circle. Reference to the lighter curve shows that had there been no muzzle effects (that is, if fired from a perfect choke) a 50 percent pattern would have been obtained at 60 yards. If, on the other hand, this same combination would have been fired on the surface of the moon, the pattern at 60 yards would have given 60 percent of the pellets in a 30″ circle, as shown by the broken line.

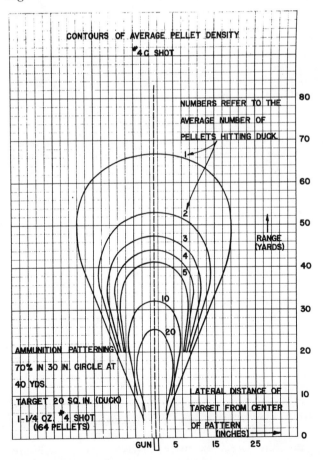

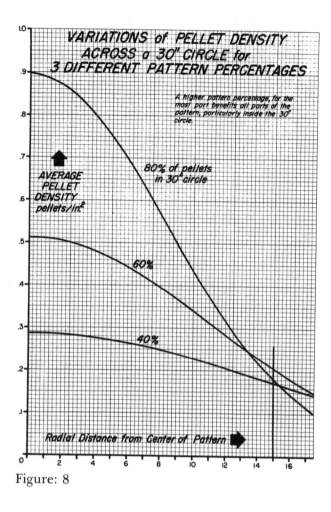

Figure: 8

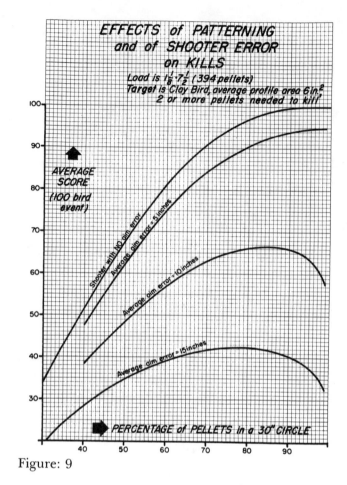

Figure: 9

can be seen (with the help of the bottom scale) that he will hit the target with an average of one pellet at 61 yards, and two pellets at 46 yards, and three pellets at 38 yards. Of course, for this latter case, three is the *average* number of pellets, which means that sometimes he will hit the target with four or more pellets and sometimes he will hit it with only two, or only one, and in a few instances, with no pellet at all. Such variation about the average number is more easily visualized by reference again to the black box shown in Figure 1. In Figure 1, for example, the channel numbered 36 should get an average of three balls when a total of 600 are dropped and aimed at the center white line. Yet, in this particular case, five balls fell in this particular channel. This helps illustrate the unavoidable statistical variation which results.

Figure 7 shows a similar case for duck shooting, where again for purposes of illustration, it was assumed that 1¼ oz. of No. 4 shot is patterning 70 percent in a 30″ circle. Assuming, also, a vital projected (to the shooter's line of vision) vulnerable area of 20 square inches, a shooter with no aim error will hit the duck at 67 yards with an average of one pellet.

Figures 6 and 7, however, have only shown the consequences of one level of pattern dispersion; i.e., 70 percent in a 30″ circle at 40 yards. A more graphic representation as to the consequences of various degrees of pattern tightness on the pattern itself is shown in Figure 8. This shows con-

centration of pellet in a trap load across the pattern sheet for various tightnesses of pattern. One interesting fact that is clearly revealed is that between 40 and 80 percent levels, an increase in pattern percentage for the most part benefits *all* parts of the pattern within the 30″ circle. As the pattern becomes tighter, however, there will be a loss of concentration of pellets at the edges of the 30″ pattern circle.

One answer to the "shotgun problem," however, is graphically shown in Figure 9. For this particular figure it has been assumed that we are using a 1⅛ oz. load of No. 7½ shot (394 pellets) and are firing at a clay target whose average profile area is assumed to be 6 square inches. It is further assumed for this illustration that two or more pellets are needed to break this target. The four curves represent shooters with different levels of skill. The top one, of course, represents the experienced trap shooter whose aim is always correct when he pulls the trigger. The next curve shows the shooter who is sometimes dead on and sometimes misses the target by varying amounts such that his average missing distance is 5 inches. The other two curves then show the same situation for progressively worse shooters. The scale across the bottom of this figure shows the tightness of pattern, as exemplified by the percentage of pellets in the 30″ circle, *at the range at which the shooter takes his target.* For example, the experienced shooter, standing at the 16-yard line while shooting trap, connects with his bird when it has only traveled some 14 yards or so and thus the distance from gun to target is about 30 yards. Reference to Figure 5, however, shows that at this range, with a good trap load, the percentage of pellets in the 30″ circle is more than 90 percent. And thus the curve tells us that this man will run 100 straight. On the other hand, the shooter with a larger aim error, or the one who shoots with no aim error but waits for the target to get out too far, gets a lower chance of breaking his target. For example, the shooter who waits until he is dead on, but whose bird is 50 yards away by the time this happens (from Figure 5) will hit his but accurate shooters, according to the chart, will only average about 68 kills in a string of 100.

It should be emphasized that these curves apply to trap shooting only. In other cases, where different numbers of pellets are required and a different load is used, the curve will show maximum points at different pattern degrees. Figure 9, for example, shows that this man whose average aim error is 15 inches for this particular game ought to have 78 percent of the pellets in his 30″ circle at the range at which he kills the target. This means that for this target and for this level of shooter skill the optimum dispersion is given by a 78 percent pattern. The important conclusion that can be drawn from this particular case is that in shooting trap, all shooters, except the rather poor ones, will benefit by tighter patterns. This can be made clear by simply picking any point on any one of the top curves and moving up the pattern percentage scale. In all cases, the scores would improve.

REVIEW OF TECHNICAL CONCLUSIONS

Up to this time, several basic factors relating to shot-shell development have been thoroughly discussed. Since these factors, which were derived from the Winchester-Western fundamental pattern study, are extremely pertinent to the balance of this discussion, they should be briefly repeated. These specific factors previously discussed are as follows:

1. The nature of pellet distribution.

2. Causes of pellet distribution or how it comes about.

   a. In-flight effect.

   b. Muzzle or launch effect.

3. The relationship between shooter error and pellet dispersion. This has shown that:

   a. A less experienced shooter compensates for his error through the use of a choke which is less restricted than a full choke. This situation may be true for all shooters where pointing time is extremely limited. Control of pellets in this direction is almost unlimited since no great problem is involved in obtaining more open patterns.

   b. Conversely, there are conditions of shooting where the range is longer and tighter patterns are needed. Under these conditions, such as would be encountered in handicap trap shooting, duck shooting, etc., the control of pellet dispersion is definitely limited. In other words, the limit is imposed by the degree that can be obtained through the use of a full choke.

The fundamental study therefore concluded that there is a requirement for tighter patterns in certain types of shooting.

THE SHOT COLLAR

Winchester-Western has for some time been aware of this problem or requirement and as a first step in finding a solution, two factors were oriented as being those most responsible for pellet dispersion. As previously mentioned, these factors were proven to be the in-flight effect and the launch or muzzle effect.

The in-flight effect is largely controlled by the pellet deformation which occurs in the forcing cone, as the pellets are pushed through the bore, and in the choke. It therefore follows that elimination or reduction of pellet deformation would assist in the control of pellet distribution. This conclusion was actually proven long ago through the use of Winchester-Western copper-plated or Lubaloy shot. . . . The Lubaloy or copper plating over the lead shot hardens the shot surface and minimizes distortion. This action results in higher pattern percentages. Unfortunately, the .0015″ thickness of copper plating must be applied by electroplating, which is a time-consuming and expensive operation. A more economical solution was desired.

The launch or muzzle effect upon pellet dispersion is the sum of all causes which induce dispersion in the muzzle by causing pellets to be launched in diverse directions. It is affected by choke constriction, the way in which the wad pushes into the shot column, and by other factors such as crimp, gas leakage, etc. The problem, in short, is how to get the shot out of the barrel without imparting radial movements to the outermost pellets. . . .

This solution to the problem revolves around a tiny strip of polyethylene which we have come to call the "collar" or "liner." Although this solution is deceptively simple, it has resulted in very greatly improved shot-shell performance. The collar is inserted around the shot column, insulating it from the side wall of the shot-shell tube. Upon firing, the powder gases push against the wad column which in turn pushes against the shot column. Inertia of the shot plus the force required to open the crimp cause the shot to exert a radial force against the polyethylene liner. The shot actually imbed themselves in the polyethylene and as the expanding powder gases force the wad and shot out of the shot-shell tube, the liner goes along. The liner insulates the shot from much of the pellet distortion normally received from the forcing cone. As the column of shot proceeds down the barrel, the liner goes right along, protecting the actual pellets from the abrasive action of the barrel wall. When the shot column reaches the choke and constriction begins, the same collar is still there protecting and insulating the pellets from the major pellet deformation which occurs in conventional shot shells.

Not only has this rather simple but unobvious technique greatly reduced pellet deformation, but is has also reduced the launch or muzzle effect. As the shot column emerges from the muzzle, so does the polyethylene collar. This collar actually holds the pellets together during launch and prevents radial dispersion of large numbers of shot as is customary in conventional loads. As soon as the entire shot column emerges from the muzzle, the collar, which is slit down one side, conveniently falls away. In thousands of rounds fired, no evidence of a low individual pattern result-

NEW WINCHESTER-WESTERN MARK 5
SHOT SHELL LOAD

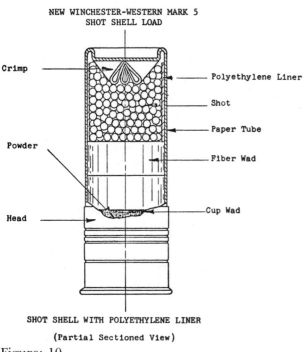

SHOT SHELL WITH POLYETHYLENE LINER
(Partial Sectioned View)

Figure: 10

NEW WINCHESTER-WESTERN MARK 5 TRAP LOAD
FULL CHOKE BARREL

NEW MARK 5 LOAD WITH PROTECTIVE COLLAR

CONVENTIONAL LOAD WITHOUT PROTECTIVE COLLAR

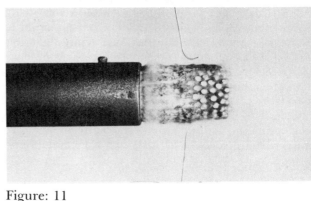

Figure: 11

NEW WINCHESTER-WESTERN MARK 5 LOAD
1 1/4 oz.-BB FULL CHOKE BARREL

NEW MARK 5 LOAD WITH PROTECTIVE COLLAR

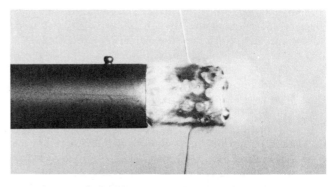

CONVENTIONAL LOAD WITHOUT PROTECTIVE COLLAR

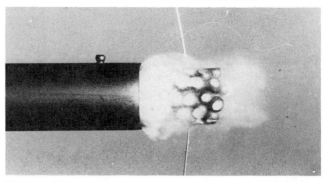

Figure: 12

ing from interference of the collar with the shot column has ever been found.

It is of interest, in passing, to describe some of the many materials and collar designs which were evaluated during this research program. Papers of all types, paper-plastic laminates, paper-plastic-metallic foil sandwiches, cloth, and a variety of plastic materials were evaluated. Designs include multipiece collars, pleated collars, varifold collars, closed-in collars, rimmed collars, etc.,—all were tried. All types of designs that reached from the ridiculous to the sublime were evaluated before the simplest possible design was accepted.

PERFORMANCE TESTS WITH SHOT COLLAR

As soon as the laboratory tests were extensive enough to conclusively prove that the two major factors affecting pattern dispersion had been successfully controlled, the gestation period of the new Super-X and Xpert Mark 5 began.... [More than] 150,000 rounds in 12, 16, and 20 gauges [were loaded] with a variety of shot sizes. . . . Scores of topnotch and average shooters carried out one of the most intensive evaluations ever. . . .

A review of the following figures clearly demonstrates the construction and performance characteristics of the shot shell. Figure 10 is a schematic drawing of a shot shell which shows the location of the polyethylene collar. Figure 11 compares a Mark 5 with a conventional 12-gauge 1⅛-oz. 7½ load fired in a full-choke barrel and shows the effect of the polyethylene collar in reducing pellet distortion. This high-speed photograph, taken with an exposure time of ¼ millionth of a second, actually shows the shot column as it emerges from the muzzle. An identical photograph showing this same comparison with BB shot in a full-choke barrel is shown in Figure 12.

NEW WINCHESTER-WESTERN MARK 5 TRAP LOAD
FULL CHOKE BARREL

NEW MARK 5 LOAD WITH PROTECTIVE COLLAR		CONVENTIONAL LOAD WITHOUT PROTECTIVE COLLAR

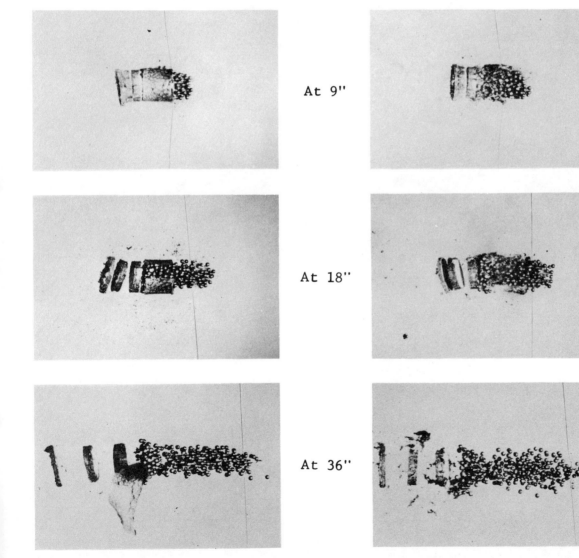

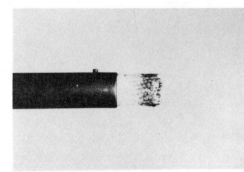

MUZZLE

At 9"

At 18"

At 36"

Figure: 14

NEW WINCHESTER-WESTERN MARK 5 TRAP LOAD
FULL CHOKE BARREL AT 36"

NEW MARK 5 LOAD
WITH PROTECTIVE COLLAR

CONVENTIONAL LOAD
WITHOUT PROTECTIVE COLLAR

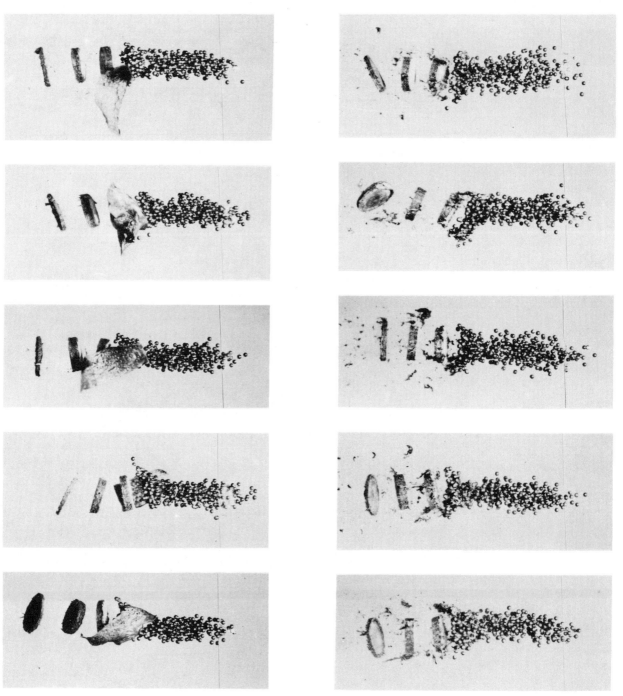

Figure: 15

NEW WINCHESTER-WESTERN MARK 5 LOAD
1 1/8 OZ. #7 1/2   CYLINDER BORE BARREL

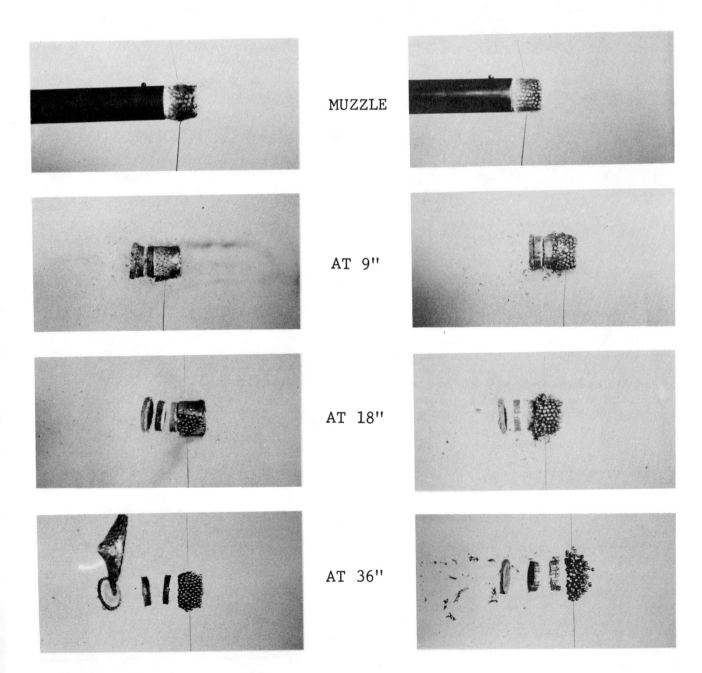

NEW MARK 5 LOAD
WITH PROTECTIVE COLLAR

CONVENTIONAL LOAD
WITHOUT PROTECTIVE COLLAR

MUZZLE

AT 9"

AT 18"

AT 36"

Figure: 16

NEW WINCHESTER-WESTERN MARK 5 TRAP LOAD
PELLETS FIRED FROM FULL CHOKE BARREL

NEW WINCHESTER-WESTERN MARK 5 LOAD
1 1/8 OZ. #7 1/2   CYLINDER BORE BARREL

NEW MARK 5 LOAD WITH PROTECTIVE COLLAR

LOAD WITH PROTECTIVE COLLAR

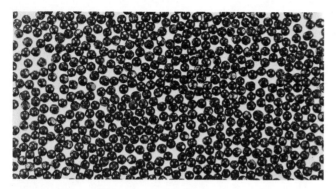

CONVENTIONAL LOAD WITHOUT PROTECTIVE COLLAR

LOAD WITHOUT PROTECTIVE COLLAR

Figure: 13

Figure: 17

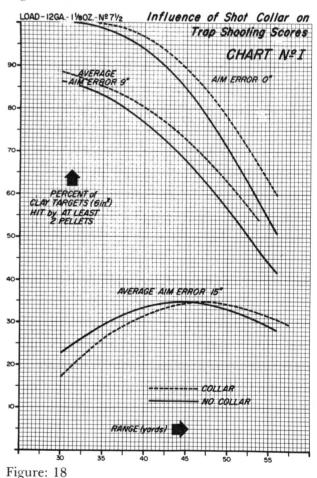

Figure: 18

Figure 13 compares No. 7½ pellets recovered after being fired through a full-choke barrel. It is clearly indicated that pellets from the Mark 5 load have a much lesser amount of deformation than pellets recovered from a conventional load.

Figure 14 then shows 12 gauge 1⅛-oz. 7½ loads, both Xpert Mark 5 and conventional, indicating the effects when fired through a full-choke barrel. These photographs were taken at the muzzle, at 9″ from the muzzle, at 18″ from the muzzle, and at 36″ from the muzzle. Of particular interest in this series of photographs is the action of the collar as it removes itself from the shot column. It is also of interest to notice the comparison at 36″ from the muzzle, together with the series of photographs which constitute Figure 15, because these photographs clearly demonstrate the reduction in muzzle or launch effect through use of the protective polyethylene collar. It should be noted that the diameter of the shot column with the Mark 5 loads is appreciably less than the diameter of the shot column of conventional loads without the collar.

In Figure 16 we find a comparison similar to that given by Figure 14, except that the firing here is carried out in a cylinder-bore barrel. Reduction in pellet deformation and reduction in lateral dispersion at the muzzle are clearly demonstrated. The photograph in Figure 17 compares the performance at the muzzle of 12 gauge 1⅛ oz. 7½ loads,

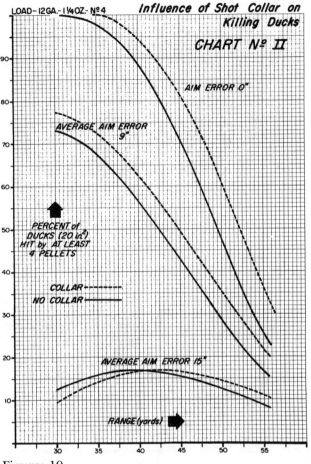

Figure: 19

generally benefits all parts of the 30″ circle. Figure 9 shows how the combination of shooter error and pellet dispersion affects scores on a 100-bird event.

The effect of Xpert Mark 5 on trap-shooting scores is shown on the chart identified as Figure 18. This chart is based on the assumption that a clay target presenting an effective target area of 6 square inches must be hit by at least two pellets to be considered broken. The load is 12-gauge 1⅛ oz. No. 7½ and the comparison is made between Xpert Mark 5 and the conventional load containing no collar. Three comparisons are made showing 0″ aim error, 9″ average aim error, and 15″ average aim error. This chart is based upon an average increase in pattern percentage of 5.5 percent for the Mark 5 over the conventional load. Reading vertically on the curves showing a 0″ aim error, for example, will indicate the effect of the Mark 5 load on the shooting score. Reading horizontally between these same two lines will indicate the benefit gained by the shooter in increasing his effective range. On the average, this increase in score will vary from 2 percent to 8 percent and the increase in effective range is approximately 3 yards. For the less skilled shooter with an average aim error of 9″, the benefits are only slightly less than for the expert shooter. For the less experienced shooter, who has an average aim error of 15″, benefits from the collar are received only at ranges over 40 yards.

Figure 19 is a similar chart except that it shows the influence of the shot collar in the killing of ducks. The load here is 12 gauge 1¼ oz. No. 4 and comparisons between the Mark 5 and conventional loads are made with shooters having 0″, 9″, and 15″ average aim error. This chart is based upon the assumption that the vital area of a duck occupies 20 square inches and must be hit by four No. 4 pellets to kill the duck. This chart is also based upon the fact that an average increase of 5.5 percent in pattern percentage is accomplished through use of the Mark 5. Reading vertically between the lines comparing the Mark 5 and conventional loads (at any aim error) will show how the percentages of ducks hit through use of the Mark 5 load will increase. Reading horizontally between these same lines will indicate the increase in effective range over the conventional load enjoyed by the hunter using the Mark 5. The skilled or average shooter will increase his probability of killing a duck 5 percent to 10 percent, and his effective range 2 to 3 yards by using the new load. Again, the poor shooter benefits from the new load only at extreme ranges.

In summary, it has been shown that the Mark 5 quite effectively increases the odds for the shooter. Moreover, as was shown in Figures 18 and 19, its superior performance can also be described in terms of an increased effective range; meaning simply that Mark 5 loads can reach out just a little further to make a kill.

There is a further way of explaining the superiority of the Mark 5 over a conventional load. It is, of course, apparent that one other way of effecting a similar improvement is by simply adding more pellets to a load. To get an improvement equivalent to that shown at the top of Figure 19 (the shooter with "no aim error"), it would be necessary to add a full additional quarter ounce of shot. On the other hand, it

both Mark 5 and conventional. This photograph clearly demonstrates the reduction in pellet deformation through use of the polyethylene collar.

The data compiled from thousands of patterns, from thousands of rounds fired under normal hunting conditions and trap ground firing, conclusively prove that the Super-X and Xpert Mark 5 load in combination with a full choke will effectively increase pattern percentages up to 10 percent. Although high-speed photographs and recovered shot from modified and cylinder-bore barrels show a reduction of pellet deformation, pattern tests show no significant change in the pattern percentage. A definite advantage, however, appears in that the normal patchiness which occurs in open-bore guns is greatly reduced through the use of the polyethylene collar. We have therefore accomplished our purpose of achieving pattern improvement and increase in long-range effectiveness in full-choke guns without disturbing pattern performance in open-bore guns.

After having reviewed the basic factors influencing pellet dispersion, and after having discussed how they are controlled through use of a polyethylene collar to give the desired results, the question naturally arises as to what are the practical consequences of this development to the shooter. In answering these questions it is suggested that Figures 8 and 9, previously discussed, be briefly reviewed. Figure 8 indicates that any increase in pattern performance

VELOCITY, NO. 6 SHOT*
(Winchester-Western)

Cartridge	Oz. Shot	3 ft.	20 yds.	40 yds.	60 yds.	Time of flight to 60 yds. (sec.)
12 Ga-3″ Mag.	1⅝	1280	884	667	525	.2351
12 Ga-2¾″	1⅛	1255	872	660	520	.2379
16 Ga-2¾″	1⅛	1295	891	671	528	.2334
20 Ga-3″ Mag.	1¼	1185	838	640	504	.2466
20 Ga-2¾″	1	1220	855	650	512	.2421
28 Ga-2¾″	¾	1285	891	671	528	.2334
.410-2½	½	1135	812	625	492	.2536

* Feet per second, cylinder bore. Full choke slightly higher.

would take an eighth of an ounce over the conventional load, to give an improvement similar to that shown in the middle curve; i.e., the shooter with a 9″ average aim error. It is unfortunate, however, that the only thing that can help the shooter with a 15″ aim error (bottom curve) is much more practice.

CONCLUSIONS

In addition to increasing the hit or kill probability and in lengthening the effective range, the new Super-X and Xpert Mark 5 shot shell have additional advantages. Barrel leading has been reduced to the vanishing point, in fact can be effectively forgotten. This is easily appreciated since the collar acts as a very efficient barrier between the shot and the barrel during travel of the entire shot column down the bore. This is obtained in open-bore as well as full-choke barrels.

That material from Winchester-Western Research is an example of the many problems involved with the flight of a charge of shot. We tend to think of a shotgun as a simple instrument when in reality it is vastly more complicated than the rifle. Furthermore, we are limited by a law of physics that tells us that we can't drive a round ball very fast; in fact the faster we drive it, the faster it slows down until it reaches the point where, at normal shooting ranges, it's not going any faster than the pellet that was started out at conventional speed! (With a round ball, air resistance varies with the square of the velocity. That means if you double the velocity, air resistance increases four times. Treble it and resistance is nine times, and so on.) You can drive shot faster at the muzzle, to be sure, simply by boosting the powder charge, but the result won't help in faster speeds a few yards downrange. As a matter of fact, the velocity difference between a 3-

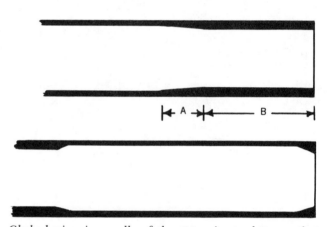

Choke boring is usually of the approximate shape as that shown in the top sketch—a parallel section forward of a taper. The sketch is not to scale and not all chokes follow the same contour; in most production guns, choke is formed by squeezing the barrel's outside to provide the approximate contour shown here. In better guns the choke is bored. The lower sketch shows what is commonly called recess choke, or jug choking. It is most commonly seen in a gun that has been rechoked.

inch 12-gauge Magnum and the tiny .410 gauge with the same size shot is almost identical. The following chart will prove illuminating:

The chart is useful in proving that, regardless of gauge and apparent size of the shotgun cartridge, velocity is approximately the same given the same size shot pellets. You can drive larger shot faster than smaller, and it will sustain its velocity better than smaller shot. With more area exposed to air resistance you might suspect that larger shot would be slowed faster, but that's not true because weight has a greater influence than surface area. A larger pellet retains its velocity better and that's why larger shot is a better performer at long range than smaller shot. However—and it's a big however—there are fewer of the larger pellets, so the pattern is more dispersed.

The preceding information from Winchester-Western Research gave information about choke and how it controls pattern. The usual comparison, given earlier, is that of a garden-hose nozzle, which can give you a small stream that travels a long way or a fine fog that's wide and doesn't go very far. Shotgun choke is roughly similar in that it changes the cone described by the shot charge. There are various degrees of choke from full choke, which is maximum constriction and which will put 70 to 75 percent of its pellets in a 30-inch circle at 40 yards (which is the standard definition), through modified, which gives you 50 percent, and improved cylinder, about 40 percent. There are other degrees of choke but these are the most common ones found in American guns of present manufacture. You can control the choke on any single-barreled gun by having one of the adjustable choke devices installed. Among these are the Poly-Choke, Cutts Compensator, and others. These devices change the constriction at the muzzle and therefore give you a choice of choke.

Controlling pattern is a tricky thing and a careful study of the previous Winchester-Western Research data will begin to explain why. You must deal with averages in a shotgun's performance. One shot at the patterning board tells you nothing. You have to fire many, many shots and average them. And I can tell you that it's a boring, monotonous job to shoot a pattern and then count the holes in the 30-inch circle, then shoot more of them to get an average.

When an Englishman builds a gun to order and the specifications call for a 55-percent pattern from one barrel and 65-percent pattern from the second, that's exactly what he gets. But the gunmaker has to experiment until the choke is precisely right to produce those results for his customer. Nothing like that is done with production guns. Chokes are made to a certain dimension, which may or may not produce what the barrel says it does. The only way you can tell is to pattern the gun yourself and, should it fail to deliver what you want, experiment with different loads, because you may find one that

does. Or you can install one of the adjustable devices. Or you can buy another gun and hope for the best. Those are your options.

NO CHOKE?

Ever since choke boring was first invented in the 1870s, most shooters have seemed to lean to tighter and tighter choke. Just about the crowning climax of this attempt has been the recent development of loads using protective shot collars *and* a buffering compound mixed in with the shot. Such loads produce exceptionally tight patterns and are excellent for long-range waterfowl hunting.

But how much shooting is done at waterfowl compared with upland gunning? Not very much. Duck and goose hunting is the smallest area of interest to American hunters by a wide margin. So why does everyone want a full-choke gun? The question isn't easy to answer, especially when you realize that most upland game is shot at distances varying from around 15 to 30 yards. Use a full-choke pattern here and your chances are excellent of either hitting the bird dead center, in which case he will be ruined, or missing him entirely because your pattern is too small. That's why there's been a move lately by knowing shooters to bores with far less choke. In fact, I think the best gun to use for such game as grouse, quail, doves, pheasants, and anything else taken at ranges less than 40 yards is a cylinder bore. No choke at all.

You can read all you like about the excellence of choking, and it certainly has its advantages, but they are largely for certain types of shooting, such as trap shooting or pass shooting at waterfowl. The average gunner simply doesn't know that much about range; birds seen against the sky are difficult to estimate, but when you consider that many trees average less than 25 yards in height, you'll see what I mean. When you are working with a good pointing dog, and a quail or pheasant explodes almost from beneath your feet, at what range do you think you'll be shooting? If it's more than 10 yards I'll be surprised, and if you're shooting anything tighter than a cylinder you'll either miss or bloody him to hell.

A long time ago I had an excellent gun that was bored very tight. One of the first times I used it was on opening-day pheasants in the Amish country of Pennsylvania. I just had two shots that day and killed both birds but I was fortunate; by some fluke I held far enough ahead of both of them to blow their heads off. The shots were no farther than 10 yards, maybe less. After considerable soul-searching I cut those barrels back just enough to remove all the choke. Now anybody will volunteer that that's a stupid thing to do. That it would absolutely destroy the shooting qualities of a fine gun. The late Major Sir Gerald Burrard, probably the leading authority on the modern shotgun, writing in 1931, clearly said that a barrel needed *some* choke. But things were different then. The shot was softer than today's, wad columns were far less efficient, and smokeless powder was still pretty new (in fact, many shooters still preferred black-powder loads in those days).

I didn't ruin my gun. It shoots superb patterns at close range and is an efficient gun to use on any bird within reasonable range. And that includes just about all upland shooting.

The promotion of too much choke is, I fear, a by-product of the waterfowler and we have already seen he is of very small numbers. (Every five years the Fish & Wildlife Service of the U.S. Dept. of the Interior makes a national survey of fishing and hunting. This survey is widely regarded as the most authoritative on the subject in existence and closely parallels most surveys made by the industry, certain magazines, and other interested parties. In the latest survey available, the number of persons who hunted small game was 11,671,000 and those who hunted waterfowl 2,894,000—a 4 to 1 ratio. These ratios do not change much from survey to survey. There simply are four upland hunters to every duck hunter.)

It does seem, in retrospect, that it's pretty silly to cater to the duck hunter in this manner but it's done all the time. The upland gunner does not need full-choke bores and he does not need Magnum loads. Indeed, he's far better off with a cylinder-bored gun shooting 1 ounce or 1⅛ ounces of shot in 12 gauge than anything more. Fact is, even most duck hunters would kill more birds if they used cylinder-bored guns, too, since decoyed ducks are rarely shot at, or should not be, at ranges beyond 40 yards.

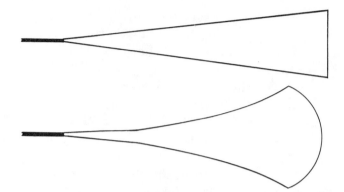

The usual impression of choke performance is indicated by the top sketch, which is representative of the drawings that accompany most explanations of choke. The example is totally false. A shotgun's shot cluster more nearly approximates the lower sketch, because there are numerous deformed pellets that do not fly true and that fly less true the farther they go. This does not imply that such patterns are not useful, because the spread is helpful for close targets. The point of this illustration is to show that a shotgun charge does not perform as you have probably been led to believe.

CYLINDER BORE

The cylinder bore is a gun with no choke at all. There are very few guns made this way because some very slight constriction is more desirable. However, I own a true cylinder-bore gun that I value very highly and it performs splendidly within its limits.

Before the modern fold or pie crimp replaced the over-shot wad and roll crimp, there is no question that a cylinder-bore gun was at a disadvantage, because that over-shot wad went out in front of the shot and tended to scatter the cluster. This simply doesn't happen with today's ammunition. Another important consideration is that a cylinder-bore gun works best with light loads. I have no hesitation whatever in recommending a cylinder bore at ranges up to 30 yards so long as light field loads are used. If you try the heavy Magnum loads you'll find that performance suffers.

Nearly all the sketches that get published depicting the differences in degree of choke always show the spread in the form of a perfect cone. With straight sides to the circle of appropriate size. This simply isn't the way a shot cluster flies. As mentioned earlier, there are many deformed shot in the cluster that do not fly true. Their flight lies in a parabolic curve, which becomes more curved as the range increases. Moreover, these sketches are always presented from above, which does not consider the force of gravity—and gravity has an important role as range increases because we now have another parabolic curve as the pellets rapidly lose their velocity beyond a certain range (that distance depending on the shot size, since larger pellets retain their velocity better than small ones). There is simply nothing very orderly about the flight of a shot cluster and attempts to sketch a "typical" charge in flight can be very misleading.

CONTINENTAL CHOKE MARKINGS

The countries belonging to the International Proof Convention use a standard marking to indicate the degree of choke of all barrels proved in their proof houses. The Japanese also follow the same system; some makers also use the words while some only stamp the appropriate number of stars, as shown below. It is important to note that the markings are determined by the actual constriction—that is, the measurement of the choke—and not on its actual performance. This means the boring may or may not actually deliver what is marked and you should make pattern tests to determine exactly what you have with the loads you will use.

*	Full choke
**	Improved modified
***	Modified
****	Improved cylinder
CL	True cylinder

Sometimes the gunmaker adds a guarantee that his gun does, indeed, deliver the choke specified, in which event this means the testing was done with cartridges produced in that country. It can mean that there is a slight difference in the testing circle, which is measured in centimeters rather than inches. The result will be approximate—but not exact.

LENGTH OF THE SHOT PATTERN

The length, as opposed to the spread, of the shot pattern is often misunderstood. It is most often

referred to as the shot "string." If you pattern your gun against a sheet of paper at the standard distance of 40 yards, for instance, this will indicate the spread, but it will *not* indicate when each of the individual pellets arrived at the paper. It becomes obvious, then, that those pellets that are outside the pattern are those that left the muzzle in a deformed shape. And that they, because they offered more air resistance, probably arrived later than the rest of the shot. It also becomes obvious that these deformed pellets may appear at any place in the pattern, simply because their flight is erratic.

All of this boils down to the fact that your gun may appear to pattern perfectly as shown by the pattern sheet, but because the shot may be strung out over some distance, you may have holes in the pattern through which a bird may fly unmolested. Such things can be tested, but the testing is a lot more complicated than is readily apparent. You can, for example, track the flight of an individual rifle bullet by the simple expedient of placing pieces of paper at intervals over the range say every 10 feet over 100 yards or whatever. That can tell you the exact flight of a bullet, whether it is tipping or not tipping and, if so, where. But you can't do the same with a charge of shot. Shot stringing can be tested by a movable piece of pattern board, moving at a predetermined speed. The results are complicated to analyze and such a test cannot be made with any degree of accuracy by the average person. Moreover, as with any patterning, you must fire quite a number of shots and take averages, because the variations from shot to shot are too great to place any emphasis upon a single shot. Or even a small number of shots.

This is a really complicated subject and there are no simple answers. Indeed, the major ammunition-loading companies have not placed a great deal of emphasis on it, nor have they conducted a great deal of research. Consequently, the subject itself is relatively unknown. The important thing to keep in mind is that your shot spread has depth as well as width. And there's really no way you will ever know exactly how much depth exists in your pattern. I believe (this is an unscientific opinion) that the fewer deformed pellets you have, the shorter will be your shot string. But I haven't proved it. I also believe

These six photos show a charge of shot, using the Remington Power Piston, leaving a full-choke 12-gauge gun. Note that, in the fifth photo, the shot charge has already begun to string out due to the squirting effect of the choke. Note, too, that the Power Piston is still compressed and still pushing the rearmost pellets. (Unretouched photos courtesy Remington Arms Co., Inc.)

today's ammo, with its protective collars that reduce shot deformity, will produce shorter shot strings than older ammo. But there is also deformity from shot pellets pushing against other shot pellets and there is no way to control this.

A long shot column raises pressures—and provides different patterns than a shorter one. For example, a 1-ounce load in a 20-gauge gun provides a longer shot column than in a 12-gauge gun and it also requires higher pressure to develop the same velocity. The same 20 gauge will also produce a longer shot string given the same load as a 12 gauge.

There is no question that small-bore guns provide excellent patterns at short ranges. In fact, some .410-bore and 28-gauge guns deliver 15- and 20-yard patterns as good as or better than some bigger guns and hence are sometimes actually better for *some* bird shooting. But when you consider averages—and you must—it's pretty basic that the best all-around bore is the 12 gauge, which you can load lightly with an open choke for grouse and quail or heavily with a full choke for waterfowl. It is at the extremes of range that the bigger bore really asserts itself

and I have no hesitation whatever in suggesting that if your shooting is entirely at smaller birds at relatively close range you are as well off with a 20-gauge gun as with a 12. But if you do some shooting at distances as far as 40 or 50 yards, then you would be well advised to choose the 12 because it will deliver an equal or better pattern of heavier shot, thus more killing power, than any smaller gauge.

In rather exhaustive tests undertaken by Bob Brister, and reported in detail in his book *Shotgunning* (Winchester Press), he pretty firmly proves that the solution to shot stringing is to deliver an *adequate* number of round shot to the target. This opposes the old theory of getting as many shot airborne as possible. The way to get this charge of shot airborne, according to the Brister tests, is to use as hard shot as possible, to use a buffering compound to help prevent shot from squeezing themselves in their ride down the bore, and to use as large a gauge as possible.

Hard shot is available both in factory-loaded ammunition and to the reloader. (The best known hard shot is Winchester-Western's copper-plated Lubaloy, not to be confused with

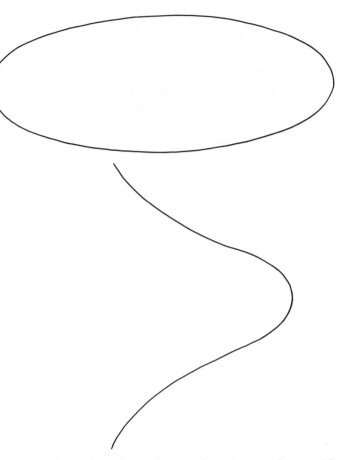

The shot string, whether long or short, is most often considered in these terms, all the pellets in a straight line heading for the target. This impression is totally false. The shot column more nearly follows this example. The heart of the cluster moves in the direction of the target, but numerous "flyers," from deformed shot and shot, are sent in the wrong direction as they leave the muzzle. An actual pattern comes closer to resembling an opening umbrella than a simple, elongated column moving straight and true.

lesser-quality copper-washed shot.) A buffering compound is currently used in a few Magnum and buckshot loadings, but it is not otherwise available to my knowledge at this time. The reloader also may not buy it, but he can substitute other materials (such as Cream of Wheat, for example). Using as large a gauge as possible, other things being equal, will deliver the charge with fewer deformed pellets. This means 1¼ ounces of shot from a 2¾-inch 12 gauge will normally produce better patterns than the same load from a 3-inch 20 gauge.

While there were early tests involving shot-stringing, as already mentioned, those shooters

used softer shot than is readily available today. (Shot is hardened by alloying the lead with antimony as well as by plating.) One of the earliest shooters to realize the importance of the short shot string, and at the same time to be in position to do something about it, was John Olin who at that time was the head of Western Cartridge Company. Olin applied for a patent on a progressive-burning powder in 1923, and in 1926 copper-plated lead shot. In 1930, Western announced the first shot cartridge with a short shot string—the Western Super-X.

Shot stringing is also caused by variations in pellet size. Since pellets are graded by sieving, it is inevitable that, in a charge of #6 shot for example, there will be some individual pellets that are closer to #5½ than 6 and some closer to #6½ than 6. The result is that the larger pellets will outrun the smaller ones due to their greater weight. This may seem a small factor, but when added to the deformed pellets in the charge, a cluster of shot, when it reaches 40 yards and beyond, begins to string out significantly. You may conclude that not all the pellets in the shot cluster travel at the same speed and, as distance increases, the effect of this variation becomes more significant.

The methods used over the years to measure the stringing of a shot column have taken several directions. As early as the 1880s, one method employed was to rotate a huge paper wheel at a constant speed, in front of which was a sheet of ordinary pattern paper. The test was made by firing through the stationary paper after which the shot proceeded through the revolving paper wheel. The former was for control, to make sure the pattern was standard; the latter indicated the amount of stringing. Later test methods employ a large pattern sheet mounted on an automobile traveling at 40 miles per hour at 40 yards distance, the figure of 40 mph being considered a reasonable average speed for birds most commonly shot at. Surprisingly, both these methods give similar results, another indication that shotgun performance has not changed much in the past 100 years.

It may, however, be concluded that shot stringing is of far less practical importance than you may think. If you assume that approximately 50 yards is roughly the limit of a 12-

gauge gun's usefulnesss (and that would be a sensible rule to follow), then shot stringing is of no relative importance whatsoever. One reason is that birds rarely are shot at when flying at precisely 90° to the gun, and most computations are based on that. If an angle of 30° is accepted as a more practical angle, then the relative speed is reduced by half. A bird that might conceivably get through a strung-out pattern at 90° when flying at 60 mph (which is fast for a bird) would probably be hit when that angle is reduced to 30°.

For most upland shooting, where shots are taken at ranges from 10 to 30 yards and bores are pretty wide open, shot stringing is virtually nonexistent. The only situation where shot stringing becomes important is in long-range shooting at waterfowl, doves, or in live-pigeon shooting.

PANCAKE PATTERNS

The term was often used in the past to describe the ideal pattern's dimensions. It means patterns should be flat, like a pancake, and it's another

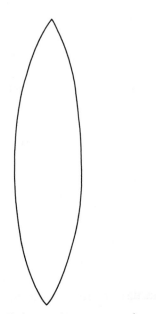

This is what the so-called pancake pattern ought to look like. It's claimed such a pattern is almost ideal and will produce the best effects. This is not necessarily true (and a perfect pancake pattern is impossible anyway) because some stringing is desirable and necessary to accomodate errors in aiming.

way of saying the short shot string is ideal. The cluster of shot should spread evenly to the degree desired but it should have almost no front-to-rear dimension.

The theory behind the flat pattern is evidenced by the British when they reasoned long ago that it was better to deliver a light charge from a larger bore than to go to a smaller-bore gun for a lighter load. The result was their 2-inch 12-gauge loads, which enabled them to build guns of extraordinary lightness because the loads used lighter charges. Interestingly, a 1-ounce charge of shot in 12 bore occupies about 9/16 inch front to back in the cartridge, while the same charge in a 20-bore cartridge occupies about 7/8 inch, nearly 3/8 inch longer. This should explain the reasoning behind the move to a 2-inch 12-gauge load.

The usual load employed in these cartridges was 7/8 ounce of either #6 or #7½ shot from England; at one time, Remington loaded some 2-inch cartridges with 3/4 ounce of shot on special order. For some reason they were never popular in this country, even though attempts were made to introduce Americans to the advantages shortly after World War II. Yet the 2-inch 12-bore cartridge is all that is needed for upland game and for decoyed ducks at 40 to 45 yards. The charge may be lighter, but it is higher in its percentage of *efficient* pellets and much more nearly approximates that desirable goal of a pancake pattern.

Should you be lucky enough to find a nice 12-bore English double (a few were also imported from the Continent years ago) you'll have to cut cases to the right length and get or make special loading tools. But I'd guess you'll be pleased with the result and will enjoy some fine shooting. One word of caution though: Don't let anyone deepen the chambers of one of these guns. They were made light for the purposes intended; use of heavier loads will certainly damage and probably destroy the gun.

The advantages of the 2-inch 12-bore, then, are that the gun is lighter, the load superior out of the larger bore than out of a 20 or 28 bore, and it has higher velocity combined with a shorter shot string. It all adds up to a very bright picture and it's too bad the market doesn't realize it.

If you apply this logic to other questions you will quickly note that the 3-inch 20 gauge is no bargain. It may handle the same 1¼-ounce charge as the 2¾-inch 12 bore, but the latter burps the charge out of the muzzle in a shorter shot cluster, much closer to that desirable pancake pattern than the same amount of shot from the smaller 20 bore. Logic tells us therefore that it is wiser to lower the power of a 12-bore gun than to reduce bore size if we want both a lighter gun and lighter recoil. Unfortunately, the American hunter will never buy this concept.

It has been claimed that high velocity decreases the effect of choke; the reason being that the pellets are jostled harder and thus deformed more. There are other reasons why added velocity beyond the optimum is of no value but this is one more. If you add 100 foot-pounds to your muzzle velocity, you should move up to a tighter choke constriction or else you'll lose whatever else you might think you've gained.

SPREADER LOADS

Sometimes called scatter loads, these are loaded to scatter the shot and provide cylinder or improved-cylinder performance from full-choked barrels. The standard way of accomplishing this is by placing cardboard inserts in the shot charge; when fired, these inserts absorb the pressure of the pellets when the charge passes through the choke, then rebound and spread the pellets. Patterns often rival those from a skeet-bored gun.

HIGH VELOCITY VS REGULAR OR FIELD LOADS

As we have already noted, velocities are virtually the same, assuming the same size shot from a shotgun regardless of gauge. The same is true whether it's a Magnum or a field load. The only advantage to any shotgun Magnum load is that it packs more pellets. (It also delivers more recoil, requires a heavier gun, and makes more noise.) More pellets mean a denser pattern, or they add a little bit to the range at which a killing pattern can be delivered. But they add far less range than most gunners think they do. I guarantee that you can kill just as many geese with a 12-gauge field load of #4 shot as the guy with a 10-gauge Magnum, so long as you know when to shoot and so long as you can handle your gun.

Just as a matter of interest, from an old Winchester catalog dated 1921, some loads for 8-gauge cartridges are given, the heaviest loads being in smokeless powders for 1¾ ounces of shot. That's less than the 3-inch 12-gauge Magnum today. So you needn't look at those old-timers with quite the awe they might otherwise inspire. (On an earlier page, Winchester listed a black-powder load for the 8 gauge with 2 ounces of shot driven by 7 drams of black powder. That's a potent load!).

KILLING POWER

It is generally assumed that it takes from 4 to 5 pellets to down a bird, assuming the proper size shot for the game and/or situation in which you're gunning. Thus you'd be better off using #4 shot for pass shooting at the same ducks you'd use #6s on if they were coming in to decoys. By the same reasoning you'd use 7½ (or as they say "sevens and a half") on early season ringnecks while you'd switch to 6s later in the season when the birds flushed a bit wilder.

Just as with rifle-bullet performance, you measure pellet energy. The energy of each individual pellet is small, but the combined energy of many pellets will be sufficient to bring down the bird. Don't forget that some birds, especially in winter plumage, have quite a bit of armor with their feathers. Take a 50-yard shot at a goose with #2 shot; each pellet delivers 5.5 foot-pounds of energy at 50 yards. A 5-hit shot will then deliver 27.5 foot-pounds of energy and that's enough (actually 15 foot-pounds is enough to drop a goose if a vital hit is made). So shotgun killing power has to combine pattern with energy. A look at the following table will give you some idea of individual pellet performance:

SHOT ENERGY FIGURES

Shot Size	Shot per Ounce	40-Yard Pellet Energy (foot-pounds)
2	88	7.98
4	135	4.77
6	225	2.22
7½	350	1.28

In production of shot, the molten lead is poured through a perforated pan about 190 feet above a vat of water (which explains the tower). As the lead falls toward the water, it forms into spheres. After the shot are dried and polished with graphite, they are culled in various operations to eliminate misshaped pellets.

You must also consider that the shot size used must be large enough to penetrate the vital area of the game you're hunting. With a hit on a goose at 40 yards with a handful of #7½ shot your chances of bringing him down are remote (you'd have to score a number of pellets in the head) because each #7½ pellet has insufficient energy to get through the mass of feathers.

MAXIMUM RANGE

The maximum range of a charge of shot will vary among the different sizes; the larger, such as BB or #2, will travel much farther than #9, for example. As we have already seen, round pellets lose velocity very quickly due to air resistance. Maximum range is achieved with the gun held at an angle of approximately 30°. A shot charge will have a maximum range of about 250 yards on an average, although the larger sizes

can go as far as around 300 yards while an ordinary charge of #6 or #7½ shot won't do much better than about 200 yards.

If a charge of shot is fired at a precise vertical angle each pellet will fly straight up and stop before it begins to fall again (assuming each pellet is perfectly round). Therefore the only force bringing it back to earth would be gravity, which exerts a constant force, and freely falling bodies attain a certain maximum velocity because air resistance increases as velocity increases. Under this circumstance the maximum velocity reached by a dropping #6 pellet would be 30 foot-pounds.

DROP

Drop, the falling of a shot pellet from the horizontal, is usually of little or no consequence with most bird shooting, which is generally at such short range that a drop of a few inches is within the confines of the pattern anyway. But at longer ranges with large shot it can be an interesting factor. For example, a BB-size pellet takes about .6 second (six tenths of a second) to travel 100 yards. And it drops about 11½ feet!

You might add that bit of information to your calculation the next time you're tempted to take a shot at a goose when he's 80, 90, or maybe 100 yards out.

RANGE

Despite the Magnum rage, and the beefing up of many high-velocity loads over the past years, the principal manufacturers of both guns and ammunition are not deluded. According to Ithaca, "a 40-yard shot is a long shot, a 50-yard shot is a very long shot and a 60-yard shot is a whale of a long shot." Most companies would subscribe to this.

From where, then, does the opinion spring among hunters that they can bag waterfowl at ranges as far as 100 yards? This is hard to say. There are unscrupulous writers who often brag about some pretty unbelievable shots, but not that many hunters read magazines in the first place. There are some advertisements that can easily leave the reader with the impression that this or that gun or cartridge will bag birds at longer ranges than normal. While this sort of advertising is somewhat misleading, again, not that many hunters read the ads. Most of the sky-busting, most of the violating—indeed, most of the slob hunting—is done by those who don't read magazines or books. So who knows where these impressions and practices come from!

SHOT HARDNESS

The truth is that most shot is softer than is implied. But it's also true that this is often an advantage, not a disadvantage. Let's explain this a bit.

The type of shooting that demands hard shot is only that kind of shooting that demands tight

One of the seives through which molten lead is poured at the top of the shot tower. Shot size is controlled by the size of the holes. Finished shot is seived again for final grading.

The test for shot roundness is quite simple. Shot is rolled down a slanted tray, such as this one, which has a gap at the bottom. Round pellets roll fast enough to jump the gap; those which are out of round do not. They fall through the gap and are sent back to the top of the tower for remelting.

Large shot, such as the buckshot in the left hand, is formed by cutting lead wire into units of the proper length, as shown in the right hand, then cold forming them in dies.

patterns at long ranges. Typical types are trap, especially handicap trap, where the target must be smoked at 50 to 60 yards, pass shooting at ducks, geese, or doves, live-pigeon competition shooting, and on very rare occasions, upland-bird shooting when the birds are flushing wild at great distances. Otherwise the hunter —and the skeet shooter—is better off with softer shot.

Lead shot is hardened by the addition of antimony. Very hard shot—extra hard if you prefer—is only loaded in trap loads because it's so expensive to make, and there is considerable rivalry between Winchester, Remington, and Federal for the prestige of supplying competitive ammunition for these events. Another way to harden shot is copperplate it, as Winchester does with its Lubaloy shot. This is not to be confused with some shot that has a copper color but really amounts to what the trade calls a "copper wash," not truly a plating. The latter is a far different and much more costly process. Many European shooters use nickel-plated shot and this is also available in the U.S. from American sources,

although they don't tell you in their catalogs that it is available.

Hard shot for trap shooting and live-pigeon shooting is used because it deforms less in the ride down the barrel. Therefore, it tends to proceed in a straight line much better than any shot that has been either pushed out of shape, or that has been abraded by scraping along the barrel.

Now, there are certain kinds of shooting where deformed shot provides a distinct advantage. This may be defined as any shooting at close range and would include skeet and close-flushing birds such as quail, grouse, some pheasants, and the like. For any target under 20 to 25 yards, you're better off with all the deformed shot you can get! In fact, there is square shot available in Europe just for the purpose of opening patterns.

Shot is deformed in several ways. The power necessary to propel a charge of shot out of the gun barrel is considerable and, while it is developed progressively, it is still a force to be reckoned with. If you have ever shot a game of pool, you have racked up the 15 balls in the neat triangle provided and then slammed them with the cue ball. No matter how often you do this you cannot do it the same way twice, because there are so many spherical contacts that a difference of a tenth of a thousandth of an inch will result in the corner balls' flight being different each time. And that's only with 15 balls. Apply the same reasoning to a charge of 1¼ ounces of #7½ shot—approximately 438 individual pellets, some of which are resting directly on the wad, others along the side, still others in the center. All of them are affected to some degree by the push from behind and all of them are affected by the shove from the sides as the charge goes through the forcing cone, the bore, and then the choke.

The softer the shot, the more each pellet will be somewhat deformed, even if it rests in the center of the charge. While a perfect sphere will travel a fairly straight path to the target, one that has any deformity whatever will fly in some degree of dipsy-doodle erratic flight. Nearly every American male has some idea of what happens when a baseball pitcher throws the spitball —a ball sufficiently moistened to upset its balance. The same basic thing happens to each tiny pellet in the shot charge.

Usually, pellets that ride the barrel's surface are scraped so that one side is flattened, although this has been minimized substantially by the modern plastic shot collar. Pellets at the base of the charge are also flattened to a degree because of pressure, while other pellets are more apt to become dimpled by being shoved against one another under high pressure. Once the charge reaches the choke you have a situation similar to squeezing a marshmallow into a piggy bank—a cluster of pellets being driven up a large hole must now be driven through a smaller hole and the result is more deformation, more abrasion, and slightly increased velocity from the squeezing or squirting effect.

It is important to realize what makes a tight pattern: the combination of barrel and its boring, the right load, and the right shot. And it's equally important to know when such tight patterns are really needed, because there are more times you're better off with an open pattern than a tight one. Center a close-flushing pheasant with a tight-pattern, hard-shot trap load and you'll have nothing left but a handful of bloody feathers. A far better combination for such shooting would be an open-bored gun with soft shot, which would spread the pattern enough to 1) increase the chances of hitting and 2) disperse it enough to leave the bird fit to eat.

Another factor affecting the pattern can be the continuing pressure, from behind, of the wad. When the shot charge enters the choke and is reduced in its outer diameter, there is a slight slowing of the whole group, which means that the wad is pushing harder than before. The leading shot are sort of squirted out at slightly increased velocity but the wad continues to shove from the rear and has the effect of interfering with some pellets at the rear of the charge. This is why a case can be made for the roughened bore, because that will slow the wad while the shot is allowed to run through the constriction unmolested. Other, and more scientific, tests to accomplish the same thing have given sufficient proof to validate the point.

To further prove that deformed pellets give broader patterns, more desirable for certain kinds of shooting, some factory loads are now

available without the protective shot collar that was so highly touted a few years back. The collars have a purpose and are a decided advantage under some situations, but they are by no means the answer to every maiden's prayers.

Despite the rush to plastic for both cases and components this is not necessarily the answer to all the shotgun's mysteries and I think you'll see more changes in the near future. A case in point is the Winchester-Western Double, introduced in 1976, a Special Skeet Load that employs the same basic wad design as before but without the shot-protecting collar. The net result of this development is that they are now saying "wait a minute boys, you don't really want that collar we've been promoting for nearly 20 years because it makes patterns too tight." And the same thing is true with the return to paper cases for target trap loads. (Remington and Federal also offer similar loads so the whole industry is still in the learning process.)

WADS

Not too many years ago wads were made of cork, cork composition, or felt. Cork made an excellent wad but, being a natural product, it varied from batch to batch so the next step was to go to a composition made of ground-up cork

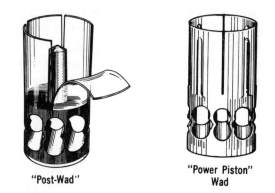

"Post-Wad"   "Power Piston" Wad

Here are two popular Remington plastic wads. The Power Piston is used in conventional loads and serves to help tighten patterns by protecting the shot as it rides down the barrel. The Post-Wad is one of a number of methods on the market for opening as opposed to tightening patterns. The post acts to absorb the shot as the charge goes through the choke, then pushes it out again once the charge leaves the muzzle. The effect is to provide open-choke patterns with choke bores.

held together by an adhesive. Felt was also regarded as an excellent wad material and was widely used for years. These wads were manufactured in varying thicknesses because the load required these variations depending on the power of the cartridge. Wads also were lightly greased on their sides to lubricate the bore slightly. And, when seated over the powder, the wads were always seated to a predetermined pressure to obtain the necessary resistance to the gases.

But along came the age of plastic and all that changed, for the better I believe. For one thing, the plastic wad can be used with almost any load because it can be crushed to accommodate wide variations in loads. And it is sufficiently resilient to cushion the sharp blow when ignition occurs. It also has a little skirt on its rear end that flares out and seals the bore nicely. Better than felt or cork ever could.

There are literally dozens of different wads on the market, all slightly different, all with different copyrighted names, but all doing just about the same thing. In addition to those found in factory-loaded ammunition, there are others made by companies specializing in reloading materials. And although they do similar things, and even though cases are similar, they are not alike. And that's the reason shotgun-reloading handbooks are so much more extensive than those for rifles or pistols.

For example, I've recently been doing a lot of target shooting with what are termed low-pressure loads. To explain: The ordinary factory-loaded trap load shoots a charge of 1⅛ ounces of shot and develops about 10,000 lup (lead units of pressure). DuPont has provided, with certain of its powders, loads using only 1 ounce of shot that develop only about 5,000 lup, but which achieve the same velocity as those loads with twice the pressure. My experience has been that, so long as I do my part, these loads powder targets just as well as any other and they produce less recoil and, evidently, less wear on the gun. They are pleasant to shoot in my Perazzi Comp I trap gun. How can this happen? It's done with progressive powder and there are two DuPont numbers that provide such loads in the area of 4,500 to 7,000 lup, with the appropriate cases and wads and primers. You must precisely du-

plicate the loads as listed in DuPont's manual. My point in mentioning all this is to help prove the unbelievable complexity of shotgun ammunition and its performance.

These low-pressure loads also require a slightly different shooting technique. Because the barrel time is very slightly longer, it takes more time for the shot to reach the muzzle even though it does achieve the same velocity and, once airborne, there's no difference at all. You can also load 1⅛-ounce loads with the same powders (DuPont SR 7625 and PB) at pressure levels around 7,000 lup with the same sort of results but I have found that 1 ounce of shot works very well.

LIGHT LOADS

The subject of light shotgun loads has always appealed to me, Not because I don't like to shoot heavy loads (Magnum rifles do not bother me) but because I have found that light loads usually will do all that can be expected of a shotgun.

For example, Sir Gerald Burrard reported that, during World War I, shooters were limited to loads of 1 ounce due to wartime shortages. The common load at the time was 1⅛ ounce, but the British found that the light load was perfectly adequate and effective and much more pleasant besides. They were not anxious to resume the old standard. It might be of interest that the three major ammunition makers, Winchester, Remington, and Federal, all supply 1-ounce shotgun ammunition in 12 gauge. Try them. Use your gun properly and I think you'll find the same thing happening to you.

These loads, moreover, are generally loaded with softer shot than trap target loads, which means wider patterns due to more deformed pellets at the short ranges over which you'll be shooting birds.

THE EFFECT OF SWING

It is sometimes assumed that the shot string can be influenced as it exits the muzzle much as water out of a hose is moved from side to side by the swinging effect of the gun. No chance. It can't happen. The reason is that the shot charge is, at the most, about an inch long and its velocity is around 1,200-1,300 fps depending on the load. The time it takes this charge to clear the muzzle has been computed to be around .00006 to .00007 second!

It has not been computed just how fast the gun would have to be moving in order for the swinging to have any effect, but you can assume there is no way in which any man could possibly swing his gun fast enough to produce the hose effect.

BALLING

It happens rarely today, but there used to be a phenomenon known as shot balling, which meant that several, sometimes more than several, pellets became stuck together in their ride up the barrel and often flew an unusual distance. There were two common causes of balling. One was known as welding, meaning that pellets were whacked together and stuck in a lump from too high breech pressure. The other cause was fusion, which occurred when gas slipped past the wads and melted some pellets enough for them to join. Welding was often the cause of a too-steep forcing cone or an overload of powder or both. Fusion was due to poor wads.

Every once in a while someone thinks he could make a great long-range combination by cutting a shotgun cartridge through near the bottom of the charge of shot so that part of the case would fly out right along with the shot charge. The practice is dangerous as well as stupid. It's dangerous because the diameter of the case is larger than bore diameter let alone the choke constriction and will raise pressures. Another danger is that there is always an excellent chance the tube might stick in the barrel while the shot clears and the next shot would burst the barrel. Yet even though it is dangerous and cannot possibly have any significant, or consistent, effect on any target whatever, you'd be surprised how many times it is done.

FORWARD ALLOWANCE

Forward allowance is the term generally given for the amount you must lead a target, the spot at which you must aim in order for bird and shot pattern to coincide in their separate flights.

This allowance varies with many things of course, some of those factors being: speed of your gun's swing, speed of the target, distance of the target, direction of the target, and speed of your reflexes. And all of these things are factors you must compute mechanically, without thought, if you expect to hit. The best way to become a good shot is to practice and a skeet field is the place to start. Depending on your swing, you'll find you have to lead a bird at station 4 by 3 to 4 feet. And the clay target is only 21 yards away!

If you start your swing behind the bird and overtake him, you'll fire at a lesser forward allowance than if you held the gun stationary and let the bird fly into your sight picture. That's because your gun is moving. Speed, distance, and direction of the target are obvious. It's always very difficult to guess the range at which you're shooting, especially with a bird rapidly moving away from you. But consider this next time you have a shot at some distance: Your shot velocity has slowed substantially, so much that it takes as long for a charge of shot to travel from 50 to 60 yards as it does from the muzzle to 20 yards.

An additional factor involved with forward allowance is your reaction time and this cannot be computed. How long it takes for your mind to say "shoot" and then for your finger to press the trigger is something nobody can predict. While it is measured in milliseconds, there also is the time required for the sear to release the hammer, to hit the firing pin, to strike the primer, to ignite the powder, to drive the shot out of the barrel.

Forward allowance, or lead, is thus a complicated subject and one in which much conjecture and subjectivity are involved. Moreover, except when shooting clay targets, you're dealing with a live bird flying at an unknown speed and in an unknown direction. You can't write rules for that.

BUCKSHOT

There are certain states—usually those with flat terrain—and sections of other states that require you to use a shotgun with buckshot for deer hunting. I have never liked this idea but that's beside the point. (I especially don't like to hunt

An original Brenneke shotgun slug, one of the first and most famous of such projectiles. The slug is designed with its weight well forward for stability in flight. The grooves are meant to impart rotation from the air, much as an arrow spins from its feathers, which are angled. It is debatable that much rotation is derived from these grooves, however.

RIFLED SLUGS

The rifled slug is a single projectile used in shotguns where legal for deer or other large-game shooting. At very close range, where accuracy is not paramount, the slug packs a hell of a wallop and is deadly. At any appreciable distance it loses accuracy fast and is of questionable performance.

I believe the first slug to be noteworthy in modern times was the Brenneke, a slug that is still on the market, imported by Interarms. Most of the American manufacturers also make rifled slugs. Before using, check your local laws because some states and areas allow buckshot only, while others allow either one so long as the gun employed is a shotgun and not a rifle.

The rifled slug has slanted raised ridges on its sides that are supposed to cause twisting of the projectile similar to that of a rifle bullet. Perhaps a more accurate comparison would be the way the feathers on an arrow are placed to impart some rotation. Part of the theory is that the slug will keep flying point-on if it is stabilized. Whether or not these ridges actually do anything is questionable. A slug does fly point-on but the reason is that it's so forward-heavy that it can't tumble. The distances over which a slug can be used effectively are so short that it's impossible to believe the spinning, if indeed any exists, is functional.

Quite a few deer hunters who live in slug areas do one of two things: They buy an extra slug barrel for their pump or auto gun and equip it with rifle sights and sometimes a scope. This makes much sense, for you can't sight close enough with an ordinary shotgun barrel to hit a deer consistently even at 50 yards. Others buy one of the cheap bolt-action shotguns, put decent iron sights on or mount a scope and use that gun for slug shooting only. These can often be fairly accurate although the slug is a short-range proposition at best.

At one time, the Williams Gun Sight people tried to market a small muzzle attachment that fitted on the front of a shotgun barrel and was shallowly rifled. A good idea, it gave far superior accuracy when tried. But alas, those stupid bureaucrats in most states who have charge of such matters said "no"; it now consituted a rifle and

in any area where hunters are loose in the woods with buckshot because they have 9 pellets — 12 gauge 00 buck — and thus a better chance to cause an accident than if they had a rifle.)

Buckshot is effective on a deer at close range; some guns do better with buckshot than others and you should pattern your gun to see what is actually happening. Today's buckshot loads are often loaded with a granulated filler mixed in with the shot to help reduce deformation and this works very well.

The flight of a buckshot pellet is subject to the same laws of physics as a charge of bird shot but, there being fewer pellets, deformation is more critical. Buckshot, no matter how you consider it, is a short-range proposition.

Standard Shot Chart—Diameter in inches

No. 12	11	10	9	8½	8	7½ *	6*	5*	4*	2*	BB	No. 4 Buck	No. 3 Buck	No. 1 Buck	No. 0 Buck	No. 00
.05	.06	.07	.08	.085	.09	.095	.11	.12	.13	.15	.18	.24	.25	.30	.32	.33
APPROXIMATE NUMBER OF PELLETS TO THE OUNCE												APPROXIMATE NUMBER TO THE POUND				
2385	1380	870	585	485	410	350	225	170	135	90	50	340	300	175	145	130

These are the loads on the market today with the exception of steel-shot loads and other special premium loads such as copper- and nickel-plated shot loads used for trap shooting.

was therefore illegal. A gunsmith of my acquaintance, now dead, in upstate New York used to shallowly rifle 20-gauge barrels for slug use. They shot like a dream and western New York State is slug-country farmland where the deer grow fat and heavy. But this, too, was illegal and it didn't pay to get caught.

SHOTGUN SLUG BALLISTICS

Gauge	Velocity (fps)		Energy (ft/lbs)	
	Muzzle	100 yds.	Muzzle	100 yds.
12	1,600	960	2,480	895
16	1,600	1,010	2,170	870
20	1,600	940	1,560	535
.410	1,630	890	650	155

SELECTION OF GUN AND LOAD

The choice of a gun and load is a matter of personal concern but there are so many factors to be considered that it might pay to dwell briefly on the subject.

There was a time, not too long ago, when there was a clear choice between the major gauges; 12, 16, and 20. Today the 16 is virtually gone, and the 20 overlaps the 12. Other things being the same, you are better off with the larger bore, because the shot cluster will occupy less space fore and aft and should be delivered to the air in more compact form. On the other hand, a 20-gauge gun can deliver, with light loads and in a light gun, just as effective patterns as one ever needs. In my opinion, for any field shooting and for decoyed ducks, a 20-gauge gun with field loads is ample.

All the same, I have a wonderful 12-gauge side-by-side Merkel that's bored improved and modified that fits me like a glove and is light and smooth as silk. It's a real pleasure to use this gun and it often gets taken out of the rack for use just because it's what it is. A similar thing happens with an older Merkel over/under 16-gauge gun that I have. It still gets a lot of use just for sentimental reasons.

In case you haven't guessed, I am a double-gun man. Always have been and always will be. The double has many advantages, but it lacks the flexibility of single-barrel types where you can have a half dozen barrels for varying purposes. That's up to you. But you ought to observe one rule: If you have a very light gun you should use light loads. Always. In the first place, assuming it's a double, it was made light for light loads and won't be safe with overloads. In the second place, the recoil with a too-heavy load in a light gun will be severe. And, last but not least, if you can shoot your gun you don't need a Magnum load.

ADJUSTABLE CHOKES FOR DOUBLE GUNS

If you buy a double-barrel gun, you get a fixed choke in each barrel, in most cases. There is at least one exception to that rule and, while it applies to a very specialized gun, it might well be a development that others will adapt.

The Italian firm of Perazzi, whose products are imported by Ithaca, has recently perfected a removable-choke system for a skeet model and a trap model. In this system, individual chrome-plated choke tubes that screw in place are furnished with the gun and, when screwed home, make a perfect fit just as if they were a part of the barrel itself. At this writing, this is the only adaptation of such a device for any double-barreled gun that I know about, although something similar has been employed by Winchester on its pump Model 1200 and auto Model 1400 for several years. Called Winchoke, the Winchester system lets you change your gun from full to modified to improved cylinder just by changing the choke tubes that come with the gun. This is a slick device indeed.

Whether or not this system can be applied to a game gun is another question. I'm not about to say it can or cannot. A game gun is lighter, which means much thinner barrel walls especially at the muzzle, and there simply might not be enough metal there to cut the necessary threads without dangerously weakening the tubes at this point. This is not a problem with either a trap or skeet gun, because these guns are always heavier than a game gun to 1) soak up some of the recoil and 2) provide steadier shooting. The require-

ments for target and game guns are different. The average trap gun, for example, uses a full-choke barrel 30, 32, or 34 inches long and the gun weighs 8 to 8½ pounds. A 12-gauge game gun, on the other hand, ought to weigh closer to 6½ pounds, which is exactly the weight of my Merkel side-by-side 12-gauge game gun.

The science of shotgun ballistics, despite the fact it has changed hardly at all for more than 200 years, retains as much mystery as it did in the beginning. Indeed, there is some reason to suspect it may be considered more complicated today than it was years ago. We have scratched the surface but we haven't done much more than that and a great many answers are still to be found.

The following charts, all from Federal Cartridge Corporation, may be of interest:

SHOT-SHELL VELOCITIES

	Type	Dram Equiv.	Oz. Shot	Shot Sizes	Muzzle Velocity
12 GAUGE	3″ Magnum	4	1⅞	BB,2,4	1,210
Red	3″ Magnum	4	1⅝	2,4,6	1,280
	2¾″ Magnum	3¾	1½	2,4,5,6	1,260
	Hi-Power	3¾	1¼	BB,2,4,5,6,7½,9	1,330
	Field Load	3¼	1¼	7½,8,9	1,220
	Field Load	3¼	1⅛	4,5,6,7½,8,9	1,255
	Field or Game	3¼	1	6,8	1,300
	Target	2¾	1⅛	7½,8,9	1,145
	Target	3	1⅛	7½,8,9	1,200
	Slug	3¾	⅞	Rifled Slug	1,600
16 GAUGE	2¾″ Magnum	3¼	1¼	2,4,6	1,260
Purple	Hi-Power	3¼	1⅛	4,5,6,7½,9	1,295
	Field Load	2¾	1⅛	4,5,6,7½,8,9	1,185
	Field or Game	2½	1	6,8	1,165
	Target	2¾	1⅛	7½,8,9	1,185
	Slug	3	⅘	Rifled Slug	1,570
20 GAUGE	3″ Magnum	3	1¼	4,6,7½	1,185
Yellow	2¾″ Magnum	2¾	1⅛	4,6,7½	1,175
	Hi-Power	2¾	1	4,5,6,7½,9	1,220
	Field Load	2½	1	4,5,6,7½,8,9	1,165
	Field or Game	2½	⅞	6,8	1,210
	Target	2½	⅞	8,9	1,200
	Slug	2¾	⅝	Rifled Slug	1,570
28 GAUGE	Hi-Power	2¼	⅞	6,7½,8	1,250
Red	Hi-Power	2	¾	9	1,200
.410 3″	Hi-Power	Max.	¹¹⁄₁₆	4,5,6,7½,9	1,135
Red 2½″	Hi-Power	Max.	½	6,7½,9	1,200
	Slug	Max.	⅕	Rifled Slug	1,830

SHOTSHELL VELOCITY vs. BARREL LENGTH
Bird-Shot Loads*

Gauge	Load	Range of Barrel Lengths to Which Data Applies (Inches)	Loss in Velocity for Each 2" Shorter Barrel (ft/sec)
10	Heavy & Magnum	32-22	10
12	Light	32-22	10
	Heavy & Magnum	"	15
16	Light	30-20	15
	Heavy & Magnum	"	20
20	Light	30-20	15
	Heavy & Magnum	"	20
28	Heavy & Magnum	28-20	25
.410	Heavy	28-20	25

*Note — Data applies to both 2¾" & 3" shells. (2⅞" and 3½" shells for 10 gauge; 2½" and 3" shells for .410 bore)

SHOTSHELL VELOCITY vs. BARREL LENGTH
BUCKSHOT AND RIFLED SLUG LOADS*

Ga.	Load	Range of Barrel Lengths to Which Data Applies (Inches)	Loss in Velocity for each 2" Shorter Barrel (ft/sec)
10	Heavy	32-22	15
12	"	32-22	15
16	"	30-20	15
20	"	30-20	15
28	"	28-20	15
.410	"	28-20	25

*Note — Data applies to both 2¾" and 3" shells.

CHAPTER SEVENTEEN

HANDLOADS

Shotgun-cartridge reloading is a vastly more complicated game than rifle reloading; most old rifle reloaders who take a look at the shotgun end of handloading are amazed at the numbers of loads available. Many reloading handbooks, such as the DuPont book, contain dozens of pages of shotgun loads while only a half dozen suffice for rifles. In this instance there are a couple of reasons: DuPont lists only a relatively few rifle loads with a very few of the available bullet weights while they go all out with respect to shotgun loads. They may figure the shotgun reloader needs more advice and, if this is their reasoning, I'm inclined to agree.

Most rifle reloaders are pretty savvy about what they're doing. Moreover, they have a number of excellent references from the bullet producers that are hard to improve upon. Besides, rifle reloaders tend to load for specific reasons— chiefly to improve accuracy or to employ certain bullets that are not available in over-the-counter ammunition.

With few exceptions the same thing is not true in shotgun reloading. The shotgun handloader loads to save money. Shoot a few rounds of trap or skeet and you'll soon learn that handloading will let you do a lot more shooting than would be the case if you had to buy your ammo in factory boxes. I seriously question that very many hunters reload their shotgun cases although a very few do and perhaps more should.

It should be said at the outset that it's hard to

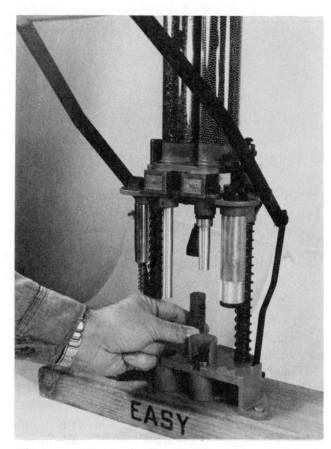

The Lyman "Easy" reloading press for shotguns is a simple press. The old primer is expelled at left, a new one seated with the long bar second from left, a charge of powder is dropped through this bar (it's really a tube), then the wad is seated where the cartridge is being positioned in the photo and a charge of pellets loaded from that tube. Crimping, final closure and resizing are accomplished by forcing the loaded case in the right-hand die. There are different inserts available for the drop tubes to load pre-established charges of the correct powder and shot as determined from tables.

Typical of a progressive loader, this tool performs all the operations noted for the Easy press except it does the work faster by handling several cases at once. Shotgun reloaders reload primarily to save money, and considerable savings can be realized. They also reload to create loads that are not available in factory-loaded ammunition.

match the perfection of most factory ammunition. But it can be done and, in a few cases, these loads can be bettered. A fellow named Tom Roster writes the reloading column for a monthly magazine called *The American Shotgunner* and Tom is doing some very interesting things with reloads. In fact, some of his work is being noticed by the major factory loaders to the point where he may well be ahead of them in load performance. The serious shotgun reloader would be well advised to subscribe to this publication and learn from Mr. Roster.

One of the reasons shotgun loading is so complicated is the amazing number of different cases around. Changes in these cases have come about so fast over the past several years that there are many boxes of dozens of different kinds of ammunition still on dealers', shooters', and hunters' shelves and who knows where else. Since it is absolutely vital that each case have its own combination of components, which must not be varied, it follows that this alone offers many combinations. Then there also exist a wide variety of primers, a wider variety of wads, and a vast number of different powders. Add the consideration that you may want to use any load (in 12 gauge) from 1 ounce to 1⁷⁄₈ ounces and you wind up with many pages of loads. Lyman's new

Shotshell Handbook, for example, has nearly 200 pages, size 8½ × 11, of nothing but loads. And even that doesn't have them all!

The major producers of powders for reloading are Alcan, DuPont, Hercules, Hodgdon, and Winchester-Western. Those who produce wads include Alcan, Federal, Pacific, Remington, Winchester, CIL (Canadian Industries Ltd.), Hodgdon, and Omark-CCI.

Aside from saving money, which appeals to my nature, there are things you can do with shotgun reloading that you can't with factory ammo. Among these loadings are very light loads with slow-burning powders, such as DuPont's PB and SR-7625, which, when loaded with only 1 ounce of shot in 12 gauge, produce significantly lower breech pressures and attain the same velocity as heavier powder charges. The result is very pleasant shooting and, I've found, perfectly adequate results. You can do similar things in other gauges.

Another thing you can do with reloading is to use some of the older guns for which ammunition is no longer available. Among these would be guns chambered for 2⁹/₁₆-, 2-, and 2½-inch cartridges and so on. Simply trim longer cases back to the correct length and load these cases lightly, letting the wad column absorb the smaller space available (not applicable to ultrashort cases).

It is not my intention to advise anyone how to reload in this book. There are a number of reloading books on the market that do an admirable job of that. Just don't get too bewildered by all the loads. Take an inventory of your fired cases, see which you have in the greatest quantity, and then choose a load from one of the tables and start from there.

One of the most innovative developments to come along recently is a shotgun cartridge reloader made almost entirely of plastic, which sells for the low price of $29.95 (in 1977). Called the Lee Loader, it's available in 12, 16, or 20 gauge, and the unit comes complete with almost any bushing you might want for powder or shot charges. If necessary, you could fiddle with one of the bushings to increase powder (by carving a bit of plastic out with a knife) or to reduce (by using rubber tape). But Lee has supplied a table of load varieties that are simple and quite adequate for almost every use.

The tool won't do for the dedicated trap or skeet shooter with a lot of reloading to do, but it should be the answer if you only do a little loading and time is not at a premium. Maybe you shoot 12 gauge at trap or skeet and use a 20-gauge gun occasionally for hunting. All you need with the Lee outfit is the expenditure of $30 plus a bag of wads and you're in business. This is quite a bargain.

CHAPTER EIGHTEEN

WHIMS, ENGRAVING, CRAFTSMAN- SHIP

Two of these subjects are pretty delicate. The things one likes or dislikes in guns are purely personal, and yet some discussion of them can be useful. Any appraisal of craftsmanship, on the other hand, is a pretty grimly serious business. In the first place it isn't within the purpose of this book to list which guns are good and which are not. It is, rather, the purpose of this effort to give some background that will allow such decisions to be made based on sound knowledge.

A long time ago, the late Captain Crossman, who wrote for *Outdoor Life* for many years, had a pat answer to a question that always amused me. People often said to him that a pretty gun (meaning a fine, nicely engraved gun) never shot any better or any harder than a plain one. Crossman's reply to that was "a necktie doesn't keep you warm either."

Guns are many things to many people. Some are the tool of their owners; and I would include the shotgun a farmer keeps near the henhouse, the .22 a trapper carries on his trapline, and other such routine, functional uses. These are purely tools; no romance, no soul. Just a bang and another fox won't raid a henhouse, another trapped animal is ready for the stretching board. This doesn't necessarily mean that the people who use some guns as a tool don't also own fine guns which they respect and admire. Indeed, many do. Many owners of fine guns also have guns for "loaning," for rainy days, and for other such uses that come up when you don't want to risk one of your favorite guns.

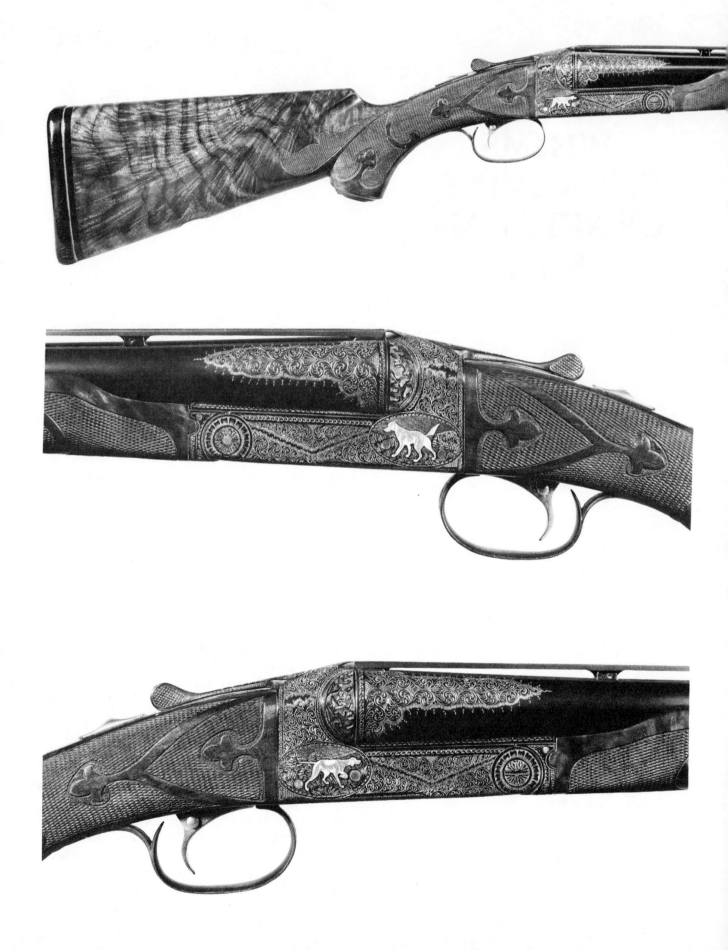

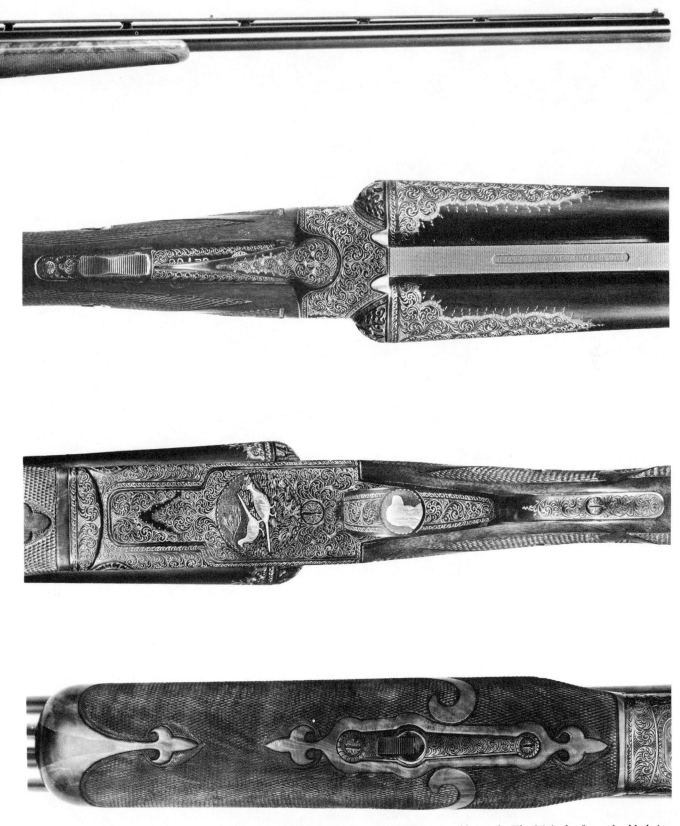

A Winchester Model 21 Grand American Grade double gun viewed from every possible angle. The 21 is the finest double being made in America today; cost of manufacture is so high on these guns that they are made to special order and only in highly ornamented grades.

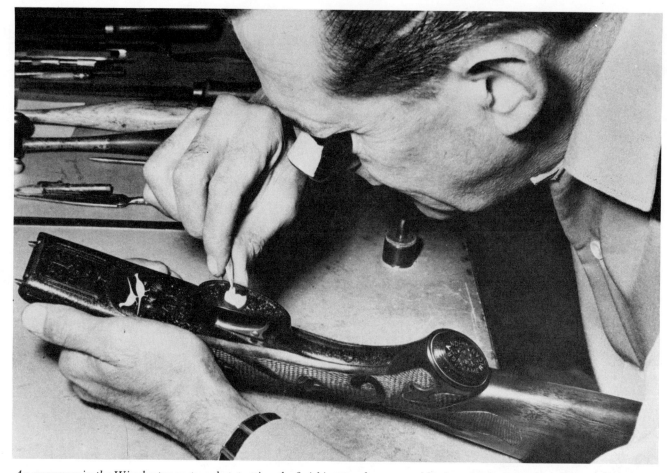

An engraver in the Winchester custom shop putting the finishing touches on a gold inlay of a dog's head in a trigger guard. The gun is a Model 21 double, Grand American grade. Engraving is a painstaking talent requiring true artistry plus the ability to finely cut tough gun steel.

I've always felt that the reasoning that you "can't afford" a fine gun was stupid. Elsewhere in this book I mentioned that I've had many opportunities to buy fine guns but didn't have the money. So I've been stupid. I've blown enough money in other ways that would have gotten me a gun collection worth a fortune today. All you have to do is look at the stock market situation from about 1960 through 1976 and you'll get an idea of what I mean. So if you truly like fine guns, invest in them. They're well worth buying. Then take care of them properly. That means you should use your guns, just give them the proper care and respect to which they're entitled. That reminds me of a fine old Woodward 20-gauge over/under I saw one day in Abercrombie & Fitch's gun department. It was used. Well used. But you could tell that its owner had

taken care of it and had handled it fondly. As a result, it was in superb shape and commanded a superb price.

Using a gun doesn't hurt it, so long as that use is loving and respectful. So long as you protect it as much as you can and clean it properly at the end of a day's use. Nobody objects to seeing a fine old gun that has its finish slightly worn from the hand by carrying in the field. In a way, this adds to the enchantment, because you know that old gun has seen many fine campaigns and you wish it could speak.

There are guns around that either do not have makers' names, or are out-and-out fakes. You'll see many guns offered for sale that are private branded, which means that they may bear the name of a wholesaler. This was a common practice in years gone by when a manufacturer

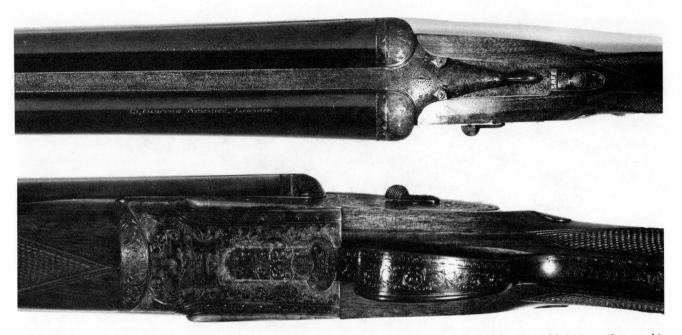

Top and bottom views of a Holland & Holland Royal Grade gun. In 1965 this gun retailed for about $3,000 at Abercrombie & Fitch. In 1976 the same gun would bring about $15,000 . . . and a several year wait for delivery. There are people who will claim other guns are as good but nobody can make a legitimate claim to make a finer gun in the world. This particular model is the top of the line and has the self-opening feature (meaning that you just push the top lever over and the gun virtually opens itself) and hand-detachable sidelocks evidenced by the thumb lock on the left side of the gun. Note that the trigger guard is broad on its right side . . . for more comfort to the right-handed shooter.

would brand guns for many dozens of hardware wholesalers. It's still being done, but not to the extent it was done 50 or 75 years ago. Most of these oldtimers are double guns and ought to be viewed with skepticism. The moral of all this is that you should buy only from a dealer who knows his product and who stands behind it. There are so many different names on these older models that it's virtually impossible for anyone to know them all unless he's in the business.

I believe the *shape* of a stock is important. It is just as easy to manufacture a stock that's shaped like a stock should be as to make a monstrosity. The same amount of work is involved. Yet some factories turn out stocks that are supremely ugly. Whether it's because they don't know any better, whether their designers are purely mechanical engineers, whether their machinery has limitations or just what, I don't know. But since some companies can make a decent stock, it follows that the job can be done in volume production and there's no excuse for

ugliness. As I've said before, you spend a great deal more time looking at your gun than you do shooting it. You may as well have something nice to look at.

I realize everyone doesn't like what I like, and this can have a lot to do with what I'm saying here. But then, you can apply exactly what I'm saying to the other guns if you don't agree with me. Nevertheless, there are some basics that shouldn't be broken, but that are broken every day.

You don't really *need* a "best" gun. There are a lot of guns around that will shoot as well and last as long. But it's still not the same. I remember a long time ago while talking to the late Lucian Cary (an excellent writer who wrote about guns for *True* magazine when that magazine was in its heyday) and we were talking about the niceties of a well-made, well-finished gun. The point came up that it really didn't matter what the insides of a gun looked like and Lucian, who violently disagreed with that point, said "*you know what it's like.*" And that's really the crux of

Closeup of a Midas-Grade Browning Superposed showing the intricate engraving pattern. Those ducks, and the lines surrounding them, are gold inlays. Such work doesn't make a gun shoot any better, but it certainly adds to the owner's enjoyment. Furthermore, a good gun will never lose value.

Browning's Superposed over/under gun was available in six grades with engraving as shown. This model has now been taken off the market and replaced with a "Presentation" grade series. The new models are the same basic gun, but with different types of engraving and with American walnut stocks. As a result, the older Superposed models are now worth considerably more money.

the whole thing. *You* know what your gun is like inside and if you can't get any joy out of looking at the insides of a well-made, top-grade gun, you have no "gun soul." And if you have no gun soul you wouldn't be reading this book and you wouldn't give a damn anyway; you'd buy a mail-order gun and be just as happy.

The fit of a gunstock is another whim of mine. It goes hand in glove with stock shape. A shotgun ought to fit if you expect to be a good wingshot. If all you care about is ground-raking (shooting birds on the ground) it doesn't matter what you use. There are only a few experienced gunfitters in the United States today and only a few try-guns. And only a few fitters can properly use a try-gun. The only way to get a shotgun to fit you is by this route.

Shotgun stocks turned out by all the production factories are made to fit Mr. Average Man. You may or may not be him. Chances are you're

Bottom view of a Merkel side-by-side gun showing a reasonable amount of good engraving. This gun is well made, nicely ornamented, but is not the equal of a fine English best gun. However, it only costs a quarter to a sixth as much, too.

Remington Arms Co., Inc. is America's oldest gunmaker, having begun operation in 1816. This is their ten-millionth gun, made in 1956 and presented to M. Hartley Dodge in 1957. Mr. Dodge served the company as chief executive officer for many years. The gun is a Model 58 "Sportsman" which has been replaced by the present Model 1100.

not, but just the same, these stocks don't do a bad job of fitting a lot of people better than they can shoot anyway. They are what is known as a good compromise.

I hate to see the glossy, shiny finishes that most stocks come with today. They can be seen a couple of miles away on a sunny day, and that is ridiculous. Did you know that they are the result of market testing? Makers put them on the racks in gun stores side by side with nice, dull, oil-finished stocks and consumers picked up the flossy stuff and that's what they bought. That's why most stocks are so glossy today. It's a mistake, but the market demanded it. Of course, if they'd never made the experiments in the first place who knows what might have happened.

That reminds me of another market test in which it was learned that people picked up guns with longer barrels quicker than they did those of conventional length. Place several guns in a store rack, one of them a couple of inches longer than the rest, and that's the gun that'll be picked up. Marlin for some years has sold a 12-gauge

bolt-action shotgun with a 36-inch barrel. They call it the Goose Gun and it sells like mad. Inspired by those sales records, when that company brought out a pump-action shotgun they included a 40-inch barrel in the line of interchangeable barrels. A 40-inch barrel! And, yes, it's selling. It has also provoked a number of jokes, like where can you find a station wagon long enough to carry it? But people buy these things.

ENGRAVING AND OTHER DECORATIONS

There's no question that engraving adds class to a gun, and that it adds value as well. It ought to add value—good engraving is expensive. There was a time, in the late 1800s and early 1900s, when a number of fine engravers plied their trade in the New Haven area. One of these was the great Rudolph Kornbrath, still spoken of as "the immortal Kornbrath." Kornbrath worked for Winchester; some say he moonlighted for

Marlin on occasion and it's quite possible he did. Then there was the Ullrich family—a whole family of engravers of whom, it has been claimed, August Ullrich was the best. The Ullrichs also worked for Winchester and it is known that some of them also worked for and moonlighted for Marlin as well. Some of the guns of the period, both Winchester and Marlin, are engraved with the true master's touch. And make no mistake about it, an engraver is an artist of the highest order.

There are more engraved guns coming out of Europe and Japan today than are being made here. Not too many Americans have picked up the art, the prime reason being money. Engraving is very costly and the wage scale here is still higher than in some other parts of the world. You can get picky, though, about the animal forms you see on some examples of imported engraving. My own favorite engraving is the small English scroll with no dogs, no birds, no game of any sort. Just scrolls; to my eyes this adds up to sheer delight. Many engravers add gold, silver, and ivory inlays, which are then carved in relief. The inlays can take the form of animals, or initials, or whatever you want.

I've shown some of the work of two of this country's best engravers practicing today: Alvin White and John Warren. This is not meant to slight others, because there are other excellent men practicing the art. It's to give an idea of what is being done here today. I've also shown some closeup views of fine engraving done on Merkel shotguns today. Merkels are made in Suhl, East Germany, and are among the top guns produced anywhere. Also shown are some jobs turned out by some of our major factories, all high-class stuff indeed. And a great adjunct to a fine firearm. Even if you can't afford to have a good engraver do the whole job for you, it's a touch of class to have the gunsmith's name and the caliber engraved rather than stamped in the steel.

Engraving *is* expensive. Good engraving is even more expensive and its cost is something you'll have to evaluate for yourself. It takes an estimated 25 to 30 years for a man to become a "master engraver"; depending upon the amount and intricacy of the engraving to be done, the work itself can take from several hours (for initials for example) to a hundred hours or so. Convert those hours into dollars and you will quickly run up a big bill. The reader who has more than a casual interest in engraving should read a book by E. C. Prudhomme, himself an engraver, entitled *Gun Engraving Review*, published by Gun Engraving Review Publishing Company, Ward Building, Shreveport, Louisiana, in 1961. The book contains many pictures, some in color, by many of the world's best engravers of today and yesterday and is well worth studying. It will give you an appreciation of the art and it should help you to select good engraving from bad.

Another form of decorative work on guns is etching, a process where the work is covered with wax, then the design is traced into the wax down to the bare steel. Acid is then applied and eats the design into the steel. Etching can be attractive when correctly done. In fact, the etching process can produce an interesting finish not unlike fine sandblasting when acid is evenly applied to whole surfaces. Like engraving, it calls for careful work; the result is considerably different but to some eyes it can be most attractive.

AN APPRAISAL OF CRAFTSMANSHIP

I hate to have to say this, but it's true and it must be said; many, but by no means all, of the guns turned out today are not as well made as they were a few years ago. The same thing may be said of cars (where a certain "planned obsolescence" philosophy has long been part of the business) and many other products as well. My object in telling you this is simply to signal this fact. In no way will I tell you what guns I think are not up to snuff; the chief reason for avoiding any such finger pointing is that things change. What's well done today may be poorly done tomorrow, and vice versa.

The external appearance of any gun can be misleading. Some perfectly decent-looking guns are positively rotten when you view the inside. And there a number of imports that are fairly handsome outside but terrible underneath. It's been an old European custom for years to slap some pretty shoddy merchandise together, polish it neatly on the outside, add a few lines of engraving (by an apprentice) and ship it to the States for some rich American to be fooled. Dur-

An Ithaca Model 37 pump gun receiver and Ithaca single barrel trap gun, both engraved by the company's master engraver, the late Bill McGraw. During his long career, McGraw engraved guns that were sold to Presidents Teddy Roosevelt and Dwight Eisenhower, to General George Marshall, Annie Oakley, and even Al Capone! McGraw engraved guns for Ithaca for 62 years.

An engraver at Remington working on a Model 1100 Premier grade gun. Engravers work with hand tools as shown and with chisels and hammers. The engraver's vise is swiveled and can be moved to any angle in any direction. Most of the major gun makers maintain their own staff of highly skilled engravers.

ing the 20s and 30s this was a common German practice. All sorts of "sporting" guns were made up from battlefield pickup Mausers and sold here, in Africa, and other parts of the world, that were pure junk. But as in the past, there are a few good guns coming from Germany and other countries on the Continent and there is some really excellent production coming from Japan. Some of the latter is, on the average, better than many of the guns being made here.

As I said earlier, the looks and appearance of a gun are largely a matter of personal preference and you alone must be the judge of what you like or don't like. Now, having picked up a gun that appeals to you, study it carefully. First, if it is a well-known American brand, or an import made for a well-known American company, you know that you have recourse to the maker—although that sometimes takes a bit of doing to get satisfaction. But it's better than getting stuck with something unknown made by an unfamiliar name.

Study the outside carefully; a fine external finish usually means careful attention to detail inside as well as out. Work the action. It's usually a little stiff in a new gun, but note how it works and look at the parts while you're working the mechanism. In today's production there are many stamped parts, many plastic parts—perfectly all right if the gun is priced accordingly. But you may not want to see plastic used in an expensive gun. That's something you'll have to judge for yourself.

I have discussed the matter of today's gun production with a lot of people in many phases of the industry. Most of us are old enough to remember what gun production was like before World War II. We admit and respect the fact that guns cannot be made today as they were in the 30s. Nobody could pay for them. Moreover, the advances in machine tools and other manufacturing techniques have been enormous. These new machines can produce better parts faster and therefore at less cost than could ever be done before the War. They also can produce more accurate parts with better machining. And the advent of precision casting, usually called "investment casting," is an excellent development that produces parts to very exacting tolerances requiring very little in the way of finishing.

I feel that, because of these advances, many of today's guns can and should be made better than they are.

But I think one of the reasons they are not is that the public has become brainwashed. They are told, by advertising, by many of the writers, and by reading catalogs, that this is what guns should be like. How does a young fellow who's just getting an interest in guns, who has no one to turn to for an opinion, know what a gun ought to be? How does he define quality? He reads the Spritz catalog. That's how he learns, and he likes the looks of the Spritz Model 100. He believes what the copy tells him. Next he visits a gun store where he's confronted by a clerk who doesn't know a Spritz from a Winchester from a Remington from a Simson Mauser. He takes the Model 100 Spritz in his hands and he thinks it's great—because he's been led to believe it's all the catalog says it is. If you multiply this lad by all those in his position you begin to get a picture of hundreds of thousands of new gun buyers who just plain don't know what a gun ought to be. So the crap sells and keeps selling.

In many cases you've got to look deeper than the exterior, something you can't do very well in the gun store. There can be some terrible things under the exterior of some fancy-name guns at pretty fancy prices. On the other hand, there are also some excellent guns for the price on the American market today. Some of these are absolutely top-quality guns at absolutely top dollar. They're well worth the money and if you can swing it you'll get a good buy. There are also some excellent-quality guns available at quite low cost. These represent an excellent buy because the combination of price and quality is right. (You can't expect to get a Rolls-Royce for the price of a Ford Pinto but should expect to get your money's worth from either one.)

Did you know that the nice figure on many imported stocks (especially the Japanese shotguns) is actually painted on? Clever workmen, the Japanese can take a plain piece of English walnut and make it look like one of the handsomest stocks you've ever seen. The practice is legitimate; just don't try to refinish one of these stocks, though, because you'll soon be down to plain, bare wood. It can be a bit startling to see a large number of such guns in one of the better

If you own a fine double gun you should not snap the firing pins without there being something in the chamber. When the blow is unsupported, it causes the pin to become crystalized and break. Pacific has recently begun producing "snap caps," shown here in a 12-gauge Merkel gun, one in the left barrel and the other standing in front of the gun. The little nylon cap is spring supported and cushions the blow. The neoprene ring surrounding the snap cap is to prevent ejection when the gun is opened. Every owner of a good double ought to have a set of these for his gun.

gun stores where all the stocks look very similar — and very handsome — but that's how it's done. I wouldn't call this practice the equal of a finely figured stock, not by a long shot. But I do think it is legitimate, for it provides a good-looking gun that, with care, will last.

"CUSTOM" WORK

By all odds some of the very best, and some of the very worst, examples of gun work are turned out by shops calling themselves custom gun shops. There are today a few examples of very small shops — some are one-man shops, some house a handful of dedicated craftsmen — that are turning out absolutely superb examples of gun work. I would just as soon not name these because it would be unfair to list only a few. I'd miss some others.

I think the most absurd word in all gundom is "custom." It ought to mean a firearm that is produced to order exactly as the customer wants it and/or what is decided by the maker and his customer (the maker should add input because he's the expert). And in many cases that is pre-

cisely what it does mean. In other cases, "custom" is applied to any product that isn't turned out by a major arms factory; such output ranges from hideous to dangerous. This also is the area in which most of the other abuses occur, such as failing to stamp the caliber on the barrel, reboring and rechambering without changing the original maker's identification, and similar shenanigans.

Bad as the metal aspects of these guns are, however, it must be said that the stocking is even worse. If you order a custom gun — or a custom stock — you should insist that it be what you ordered. And you should not tolerate any violations of the agreed-upon specifications or workmanship. The inletting of this stock should be such that you should not be able to insert a piece of ordinary writing paper — not anywhere. When you dismount the metal from the stock (and you should make this inspection) the inside should be neat, clean, and tidy and an exact mirror image of the metal parts (with proper allowance for movement). There simply is no excuse for any other kind of work and you should not accept it. This doesn't mean that you shouldn't allow the gunmaker some leeway in his own ideas. But these things should be discussed and agreed upon in advance.

Another thing to look for is that the stock's pores be filled. Wood is porous, and part of the finishing operation is to fill these pores. This is done in many ways, but a brief description of one of the old, tried-and-true methods will serve to explain it. I've always used GB Linseed oil, a carefully nurtured secret formula put up by a man named George Brothers who has now sold the product and process to Harrington & Richardson. You simply apply a coat of GB, preferably right after the final sanding of the stock with the finest finishing paper you can buy and while the sanded dust is still on the stock. This will mix with the finish and fill the pores. Let it dry thoroughly and then sand again right down to the bare wood. Some say you can do this with a single application but it's always taken me several. What you're doing here is filling the pores with finish and the result will be perfectly smooth. Every stock should be perfectly smooth with every pore perfectly filled.

Some other things I would regard as whims

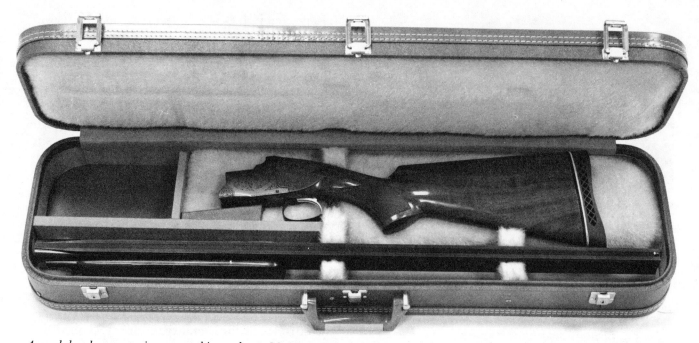

A good, hard gun case is a smart thing to have. Many guns, such as this trap gun, come with a case as standard equipment. It's the best way to transport any gun.

would include such items as a straight or pistol grip on a double gun, which is a matter of personal preference. A beavertail forearm that is considerably wider than that on a game gun is usually associated with target guns; its purpose is to keep your fingers away from hot barrels. If you're ordering a custom double, you can specify a buttplate or simply have the bare wood finished and checkered, which looks very elegant.

A selective or nonselective single trigger (when offered as an option) is also an item of personal preference. I see no real reason to have a selective trigger, but that's up to you as the buyer. A target gun ought to have a recoil pad but a game gun does not, unless you expect the game gun to be used for dove shooting or some other sport where a great amount of shooting will be done.

Fancy wood? By all means, if you can afford it. But buy from a reliable maker and note very carefully just what really fancy wood is. It has become my cynical opinion that sometimes the word "selected" wood means the blank is taken

out of the rack with the eyes closed. I've seen some wood passed off on high-priced guns that would make nice floor boards in a log cabin. Good wood is scarce today and you'll have to pay dearly for a good, fancy stock but it won't depreciate in value.

An awful lot of guns today are being produced with such adornments as white line spacers between buttplate and stock, grip cap and stock. And with some sort of Mickey Mouse decoration in the grip cap. The purpose of the latter is to draw attention to the gun when it stands in the dealer's rack, but these things don't belong on a good gun. And there's an unfortunate trend today to use Phillips head screws to fasten buttplates, I think these screws ought to be banned from the market. They don't belong on a gun in the first place and it's too easy to have the screwdriver back out of them.

A bit of class that's often found on higher-grade guns is the initial plate; whether or not you have it engraved it looks nice when well done. This is placed in the bottom line of the stock, about 3 inches forward of the butt.

CHAPTER NINETEEN

ACCURACY

The accuracy of a shotgun? Yes, there is such a thing, although the term may seem a little strange.

A shotgun's purpose is to deliver a killing pattern of shot pellets where it will intersect the flight path of a bird in order to kill the bird. While the chief requirement of achieving this is the excellence of the pattern, it is also necessary that the pattern be on target. It may surprise you to know that not all guns do that.

You should shoot your gun at a target to learn where the center of that pattern is shooting. And you must remember that, like a rifle bullet, shotgun pellets are also subject to the law of gravity and do not pursue a straight flight. The pattern drops as it goes and small pellets fall faster than larger ones. A pattern that is on target at 20 yards can be several inches lower at 50 yards.

Moreover, some guns shoot high, which means that you must hold below the bird, while others are "right on" and it's best to swing and blot out the bird before you shoot. Generally speaking, there is nothing you can do about shotgun accuracy—except to hold where you will compensate for whatever differences exist with your particular gun. Remember, if you shoot a gun with interchangeable barrels, each barrel may well shoot to a different point of impact, so every barrel ought to be checked out. For example, I shoot trap on occasion with a fellow named Lou Trinque, an excellent shot by the way. Lou can take one shot with any gun you

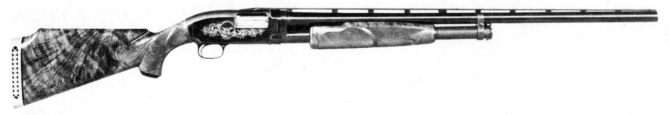

Shotgun accuracy is vital to the trap shooter. Shown is a Model 12 Winchester Pigeon Grade Trap gun which must deliver its patterns tight and way out to break clay targets consistently as far as 50 to 60 yards.

A Winchester Super-X Model 1 Skeet gun, where accuracy is also important. In skeet, as opposed to trap, targets are only about 21 yards away and accuracy is more a matter of gun fit and correct pattern.

hand him, spot where the shot charge goes in relation to the target, and powder the next target every time.

Not too many shooters have this ability; certainly the average hunter does not and that's why he must target the gun carefully. Targeting a gun should be done by taking a large sheet of paper and pasting an aiming point in its center. Then carefully sight the gun and shoot. The test should be made about at 40 yards. It would be best to make this test with a steady rest such as a benchrest like the rifle shooters use; the results from an offhand (standing) shot would be suspect.

Of course accuracy also comes into focus when you think about shotgun slug use. But this is more closely allied with rifle shooting than the usual use of a shotgun. In the first place, you should only use a gun with "slug barrel," if at all possible, and these barrels come with rifle-type open sights and are sighted in just like a rifle. They also are bored to obtain the best accuracy from a slug (which must pass through the tightest choke barrel for obvious reasons). Slug accuracy at best is not up to that of a rifle, but is usually adequate to bust a deer at ranges up to 50 yards. (The other alternative is the bolt-action gun, which can be purchased pretty inexpen-

sively; mount a low-power scope and use the gun exclusively for slugs.) There really is no such thing as slug accuracy with any other sort of sights because regular shotgun beads are not capable of close enough sighting. Under no circumstances should you try slugs in a side-by-side double gun. It won't deliver any kind of accuracy.

There are guns on the market, mostly of Continental origin, that offer the choice of rifle or shotgun. The most common type is called a "drilling" and consists of a double shotgun with a rifle barrel underneath. The drilling comes with a little open rear sight that can be made to stand up by moving a small button. Other types of this sort of firearm are an over/under gun with rifle barrel alongside; some have the rifle barrel on top and others have four barrels. Some pretty fancy combinations are seen on occasion. Presumably the need for such a gun arose in Europe where a man out hunting birds might run into a stag or boar where the rifle load would come in handy. Some Americans have picked these guns up and use them similarly where, for example, both grouse and deer seasons are open.

An interesting American gun along similar lines is the Savage over/under offering with a 12-gauge barrel on top and a .308 Winchester barrel below. That's a pretty potent combination indeed, suitable for most North American game. The same gun, which is made by Valmet in Sweden, also can be had with a .222 barrel below. Savage also makes, in its own plant, other combination guns in a pretty wide variety of chamberings from .22 Long Rifle to .30/30 Winchester and with a 20-gauge shotgun barrel on the bottom.

Savage has had guns of this kind in their line for many years and they have always been popular. This is especially so since populations of wild turkeys have been expanding, because one rarely knows whether turkeys are a shotgun or rifle proposition. At one time Marlin made a similar combination gun but the market really isn't big enough for more than one offering of this type.

RECOIL EFFECT ON ACCURACY

The effect of recoil tends to make a shotgun shoot high or low, or sometimes to the right or left, particularly with a side-by-side double gun. This is because the gun begins to move in recoil before the shot charge leaves the muzzle, and the direction in which it moves determines where it shoots. This is often accommodated by the stock.

For example, the right barrel of a double gun will tend to move the gun to the right, because it's off the center line. (That's why a gun for a right-handed shooter should fire its right barrel first; it's easier to get back on target for a second shot.) This is often partially taken care of by employing some cast-off in the stock, meaning the center of the butt is set off to the right so as to give a straighter line in recoil. But the same amount of cast-off will accentuate the off-center recoiling of the left barrel (which isn't important because that's the last shot). Single-barrel guns and over/unders recoil straight back, and cast-off is less of a factor in such guns although it is used in some custom stocks for better fit. (Cast-on, for left-handed shooters, is the same thing in the opposite direction.)

Guns also shoot high or low and the remedy—control would be a better word—is a combination of drop and pitch. Drop, if excessive, tends to lower the center around which the gun pivots and will produce high shooting. Pitch, the angle of the butt, can make a gun shoot high or low

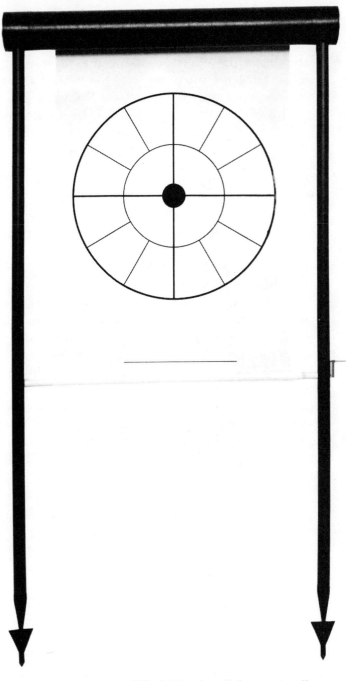

Shotgun patterning is a difficult job primarily because it calls for large sheets of paper at 40 yards. Large sheets of paper call for a large frame and, you hope, a windless day. Shotgun Pattern Works of Janesville, Wisconsin has a package that makes it much easier. The unit is shoved into the ground and the sheets are rolled from top to bottom like a window shade. It comes with instructions than can be followed easily and will make the job simpler, more professional, and more accurate.

because it affects the position of butt on the shoulder.

There are other factors that can make a gun shoot off the mark. One of them is the attaching of an adjustable choke device. These gadgets are larger than the barrel diameter, which means they have the effect or raising the front sight. This translates into depressing the muzzle and a low-shooting gun is the result. Knowing gunsmiths who fit these devices usually bend the barrel enough to make it shoot higher and thus compensate for the higher front sight.

THE ALL-AROUND GUN

Is there any such thing as the mythical all-around gun? Riflemen have been talking about such a thing for years and have never come up with anything like a satisfactory answer. Nor can the shotgun shooter.

When you consider the ramifications of the wide uses to which a shotgun may be put you will quickly see that there is no real solution to this question. The demands for a gun for skeet; trap; upland birds; decoyed ducks; pass shooting at ducks, geese, and doves; and the vastly different requirements for a satisfactory gun for grouse and woodcock in New England opposed to one for pheasants in South Dakota serve to illustrate the point. If you're a double-gun man you can, at great expense, order a gun with several sets of barrels. These can be had in different gauges as well. To be most satisfactory the barrels should be of the same length and weight. But this doesn't consider the stocks and it would be wise to have different stocks for some of the different uses too.

Of course there is hardly anybody who seriously shoots both trap and skeet; it's usually one or the other. And the guy who hunts grouse and woodcock in the New England woods rarely hunts much else so much of this discussion is academic. But if there is to be an answer, it probably lies either in a pump or autoloading gun with their great range of interchangeable barrels—and stocks in many cases. This is the most practical and one of the least costly ways to get around such a problem. Another is to use an adjustable choke device, which will provide sufficient variation for many gunners.

Still, there really is not any one single gun that will serve for all types of shooting. I would suggest that, eliminating any formal target shooting and strictly considering a game gun, you are best off with a double gun in 12 gauge which should be bored Improved Cylinder and Modified. Learn to use the gun within its limits and you should be able to fill your bag so long as you are offered decent shots. This won't be everybody's answer but it would be mine.

INDEX